Wilderness Is Where You Find It

BOB SIMPSON

Algonquin Books

of Chapel Hill

1988

Wilderness

Is

Where

You

Find

It

with twenty-four color photographs

by Bob and Mary Simpson

In memory of my brother Jim

Published by

Algonquin Books of Chapel Hill

Post Office Box 2225

Chapel Hill, North Carolina 27515-2225

in association with

Taylor Publishing Company

1550 West Mockingbird Lane

Dallas, Texas 75235

Design by Molly Renda and Bonnie Campbell.

LIBRARY OF CONGRESS CATALOGING-IN-PUBLICATION DATA

Simpson, Bob, 1925–

Wilderness is where you find it.

1. Outdoor life—United States. 2. Wilderness

areas—United States. 3. Hunting—United States.

4. United States—Description and travel—1981–

I. Title.

GV191.4.S56   1988   796.5'0973   88-6199

ISBN 0-912697-89-X

FIRST EDITION

Contents

Illustrations

Preface

We had been writing of our experiences on the wanderlust express over the previous thirty-odd years when Louis Rubin, our friend and publisher (we are fortunate that he is both), suggested a book relating several of our expeditions in and out of the wilderness. My traveling companion and bed warmer agreed; it was such a good idea that I should begin immediately. Surely it would be a snap for me to recall a dozen or so mini-adventures and put them down on paper. No one asked my opinion—that to compile something of interest to anyone but myself would be a monumental task. However, with both Louis and my wife pressuring me, I had no choice.

To select outdoor adventures and misadventures of interest has been a matter of throwing out most of what I recall best, for example: the occasion when I lived on canned salmon, tomato juice, and grapefruit juice when my plane developed engine trouble and I had to spend a few days on a tropical island; or the morning, before I knew as much about boats as I do now, when I took my wife and brothers for a sleigh ride on an ocean swell while trying to make it through an inlet—how was I to know a hurricane was offshore? Or the summer when Mary and I took jobs as caretakers of a tropical island, a paradise so infested with palm trees that coconuts frequently threatened to cave in our heads and mosquitoes were so thick that they formed drifts like snow on the window sills. There was a cave in Arizona that we explored until the lantern went out; there was the hurricane we rode out on our boat while watching houses wash by.

One of my hopes is to make readers more aware of the short time allotted us all: by my reckoning the average man has only about fifty hunting seasons available in his lifetime, and these come on top of the many other pleasurable things that should be enjoyed. I'd like others to know something of the adventures waiting all about them, for the taking if they are willing to pay the price, though not necessarily in dollars. But they must not wait, for time is like a handful of live eels—mighty hard to hang on to.

To be sure, adventuring cannot be done without a good base camp. My wife Mary has supplied this, besides having a tendency to get me off my duff by suggesting such unlikely projects as a quick wilderness trip to Alaska, or "Let's take the boat to Florida." I never know where she might lead me; sometimes it's arctic, sometimes tropic. Home has always been wherever she hangs my hat. It may be on a boat in the Keys, in a tent in the Rockies, or in a fisherman's shanty on the Carolina coast.

Roaming produces friends like the Tingles and the Loesches, who taught us much of the little we know of ranch folk. There cannot be enough praise of the women who provide the base camps. Marion Tingle has forgotten more about horses than I will ever know; Bette Brunson's fortitude and cooking skills earn her a medal of merit.

Of other outdoorsmen, Franc White, who taught me how to start a fire Boy Scout style with a Dixie-cup of gasoline, has a streak of selflessness a yard wide; he paddled me all around Ontario for a solid week in hopes that he could catch me a moose.

And then there's John Gaskill: somehow John could always be expected to come up with an impossible adventure, no matter the odds. And of course Royal Brunson: his mind is an encyclopedia of wit and outdoor information. I can always count on his identifying a green gentian, knowing the breeding habits of a meadowlark, the habitat of a wolverine, the flight plan of a goose, or where to find a whitetail or a golden trout. We have discussed geology and snails while photographing mountain goats.

While dealing credits, I cannot overemphasize the encouragement and patience of Louis Rubin, author, publisher, teacher, editor, and friend. Nor can I forget the on-the-job training while writing free-lance columns for diverse publications, especially the Raleigh, North Carolina, *News and Observer.*

BOB SIMPSON
Peltier Creek
Morehead City, North Carolina
December 1, 1987

1.

What in the World Am I Doing Here?

Earlier that afternoon, there in a muddy spot alongside the trail, we had seen the largest bear track I could recall. The claw prints were clear, sharp, and long. The fresh indentation had not been made by a black bear. This was grizzly country.

Elk and moose tracks were all about and a golden eagle was skimming the face of the sheer canyon wall on the other side of the creek. Though a mere ribbon of shining water, the little stream skipped and splashed among the polished rocks. A mink poised on a log over the stream and watched us pass.

We still had a few miles of thick country before the trail led up to the meadow where we figured on making camp that night, and the blazes were faint. The brightness of mountain valleys had been subdued by long shadows, and before we had the horses unpacked, fed, and picketed for the night, what was left of the sun was coating the distant peaks of the Pintlars of western Montana with a muddle of golds and reds. With camp set up, supper and chores finished, Mary and I put down our bedrolls a short distance from the tents of our companions, just far enough from the campfire to avoid any errant sparks. After another cup of coffee and a few minutes of fire-side socializing, we turned in.

The Belt of Orion stood out brilliantly in a blue-black autumn sky. Settled comfortably in our sleeping bags, we were determined to do some serious stargazing, but I must have fallen almost imme-diately into deep sleep. It was some time later that an alarm bell in the back of my brain told me to ease my eyes open. An enormous dark form loomed over me, completely blocking the heavens. I felt warm, moist breath in my face.

I slid my hand alongside me to my .45 pistol. Even a .45 is weak medicine against a grizzly, but I was hoping at least to keep Mary out of harm's way. The cold metallic bulk of the pistol felt only slightly reassuring as I pulled it free.

Abruptly there was a snort, followed by the crash of metal, the clatter of falling wood, and the breaking of branches. All of a sudden, the whole camp was awake. Flashlight beams shot wildly around in the moonless night. The camp stove was upset and with it a cast iron skillet and other pots. Silhouetted against the midnight sky was a bulky form. The culprit was Pokey, Mary's horse and the camp pet.

Working my way back into the warmth of my sleeping bag, I asked myself a question I had asked before: "What in the world am I doing here?"

The answer came, in part, in a recollection: it came back to me how the big thrill of a Dakota winter was the rabbit hunt. As I remembered it, the first full moon after the first good snowfall was when Dad always took us rabbit hunting. On the western plains there are two types of rabbits, big ones and little ones, that is, jacks and cottontails. Our family was partial to cottontails. After supper we'd pull on overshoes and mittens, wrap scarves over our faces, struggle into winter coats and extra trousers, and head up into the hills. And it was cold! Great clouds of steam hung in the air after every breath, instant shards of ice glittering in the moonlight. Stars were so brilliant that they looked like beacons despite the glare of an icy moon bathing the white-shrouded hills and valleys in a cold blue light. We never used a flashlight; we hadn't the slightest need, even if it would function in such intense cold.

The snow squeaked and its icy crust shattered like glass as we trudged along. Sometimes we used crude, homemade skis or snowshoes, but most often not. We just slogged through, single file, resting frequently. The most dangerous thing that we could do was to overexert. Lungs frostbitten from gasping $-30°$ to $-40°$ air was an early lesson never forgotten, and sweat could suck out the body heat as a tornado sucks the contents from a house. "Wind chill factor" was not in our vocabulary, but we were fully aware of its effect. The harsh beauty of the plains in winter makes the mind reel—the blacks and whites, the air so clear that the kerosene lights of a ranch house could be seen ten miles away. The lights are electric now, but it is still a fierce land.

Our favorite hunting area was along the railroad tracks of the Soo Line, long gone now, that circled from our little town up into the hills. The coulees and draws were dotted with wild plum thickets, box elders, and cottonwoods, all buried under the snow. There was a reason for hunting at night—moonlit nights brought the rabbits out to play. They'd trample great circles in the snow, with intricately connected lanes. Sometimes as many as two dozen rabbits would appear suddenly, cavorting and frolicking in a frenzy for fifteen minutes or more. Then, even if not interrupted by coyote or man, all would, as abruptly, disappear. It reminded me of a square dance. Dad said that these antics had a purpose: to confuse pursuing predators, particularly weasels.

As the youngest one in the family, it was my job to retrieve. Our English setter wasn't allowed to participate, for fear of spoiling his bird-hunting skills. After Dad had shot two or three rabbits with the open-sight .22 rifle, I'd plunge down the embankment, floundering, crawling, swimming through the dry snow to fetch, with Dad guiding me from above. More than once I'd disappear into the soft snow, wallowing around in the powdery, suffocating mass until someone could pull me out, while from his vantage point as director of operations Dad discussed my bear-cub clumsiness.

The north side of the house served as our deep freezer. Rabbits, ducks, pheasants, and an occasional prairie chicken hung from the eaves in their fur or feathers, frozen solid until it was time to cook them. Both cottontails and jacks were delicious, though the meat from the jacks tended to be tough. Still, a five- to fifteen-pound jackrabbit was a lot of food for a hard-up family of six in the Dakotas during those Depression years.

Long-rifle hollow points were for jacks, .22 shorts for cottontails. The latter—short, fat butterballs—could be roasted, stewed with gravy, or even baked in a pie—you couldn't go wrong. And the fur— we boys worked the rabbit skins, tanning them Indian fashion, then cutting them into long strips to weave into blankets or sleeping robes. They were warm enough for the coldest winter night. Fur-lined mittens, even rabbitskin socks, were mighty comfortable.

Living on a Sioux reservation, among the Wahpetons and Sisse-
tons, we picked up many Indian concepts, despite a strong tendency
in the community to discredit any and all Indian ways. I was introduced to a different philosophy, not to be found in the textbooks of
the time. From Indian companions and especially from their elders,
many of whom had been circulating at the time the Seventh Cavalry
ended its career on the Little Big Horn, came the attitude that the
earth is bigger than man. The human animal is just another temporary resident, completely dependent upon the land. As custodian, he
has a great responsibility on his shoulders. The Indians considered
the white man to be ignorant of the ways of the earth. I drifted back
to sleep thinking of what had seemed so obvious to them and how
much they understood about things.

Coming up in the dust-bowl era of the Depression, as the third
son of a prairie newspaperman, it was my good fortune, although I
didn't recognize it fully at the time, to have a father who loved the
outdoors. Despite the hardships that he and my mother faced in
raising a family, they taught us that we did not need lots of toys or
fancy clothes to enjoy living. Their idea was that with good books
and an understanding of the natural world, there was no limit to
the adventures available. Following a stint of flying with the Marine
Corps in World War II, and finding my military skills no longer
needed, I linked up with an adventuresome wife-companion, also
Marine Corps surplus. After discovering that it really does cost more
to feed two than one, we took to free-lance outdoor writing as an
acceptable way to keep on enjoying what we wanted to do anyway.

Though we live in coastal North Carolina and like it, the West
has always seemed a natural place for Mary and me to be. Our fathers
had spent some time there, Mary's father in Wyoming, and my father
homesteading on the Yellowstone River in Absaroka County, Montana,
before he married Mother. He lived the rest of his life in the Dakotas,
where I was born on an Indian reservation and raised on the back
end of a flatbed printing press. A long time later Mary and I met,
courted in Colorado, and lived in South Dakota and Florida. Now
we divide our time between North Carolina and Montana, for the
West has remained in our bloodstreams.

It must have been a quarter-century ago that I made my first
western big game hunt. At the time I was just getting a good start

writing magazine articles and was selling outdoor columns to several newspapers. It was mid-September, and John Gaskill had invited me to join him and Vance Harrington on a trip to faraway Montana. John had a friend there who would guide us. Besides, Vance had an airplane and this way we could pool our resources and share the costs. This sort of expedition seemed a good way to broaden my horizons.

The Carolina coast on the day we were scheduled to leave was wrapped in a blanket of pea-soup fog so thick that even the gulls were walking. The gray mists had moved in during the night and shut down all activities. Admittedly I was already nervous. By this time I had flown through another war, still without having learned to trust anyone fully with a flying machine. Nor had I ever flown or hunted with Vance before; but it was his plane and he was a sober chap. It was well past noon before the fog began to lift. Hurriedly we finished loading our gear and took off.

The weather improved rapidly as the land rose towards the Appalachians. Green-clad ridges lifted over the horizon, and craggy rocks seemed softened by forests interspersed with innumerable streams that had banded together to make rivers as they pressed relentlessly towards the southeastern coast and then beyond the watershed towards the far-off Mississippi. We made the first stop in Tennessee. By this time it had become apparent to me that Vance knew his business, and long before we landed the following evening, with the setting sun gleaming off the Mississippi River at St. Louis, the flight had turned into pure pleasure.

Cross-country travel by light plane is as different from the standard commercial flight as home-baked bread is from the store-bought stuff. First of all, you are flying with almost unlimited visibility all around you, instead of trying to get a glimpse of the ground from the fourth seat over through a dinky eight-inch porthole. Next, in a small plane you are winging along at a sedate 100 to 125 miles per hour instead of ripping over the clouds at 600 miles per hour or more. This leisurely speed gave us enough time to watch panoramas unfold fully before they were lost in the haze of autumnal skies. Skimming along three or four thousand feet above fields and farms, where you can look into backyards and villages and watch the clouds reflected off lakes and rivers, gives an appreciation for a nation made up of many individuals, rather than of indistinguishable gray masses. Grain fields, harvested now but still golden, pastures still green, prairies and plains seeming to reach forever, ribbons of highways and waterways, all merged into the oneness of a vast, unbeatable, and thriving land.

By the time we left high and arid Cheyenne, the flattened prairies of the Midwest were behind us, and we were on our way to another world. The sun was high before we flew over Montana's Sapphire Mountains in the western part of this treasure state. They looked dense and rugged as we circled, hoping to spot the E Lazy H Ranch as we made our approach to the Hamilton Airfield nearby. Upon receiving our phone call, Gene Tingle, a tall, well-built man with a warm smile, came immediately to the airport, where we loaded our gear into his car and set off for the ranch. The hospitality of Gene and his wife Marion, themselves former North Carolinians, has remained ever since a part of the attraction that this high country of tall trees and rushing streams holds for us.

Our guide, Val Loesch, had already gone into the hills to set up camp. As soon as we arrived, Rae Bradley, who also lived on the ranch, asked me to step out to the corral while she caught her horse; she needed someone to hold the animal while she replaced a shoe. Although it was late afternoon, Rae stuffed a sandwich into a bag and, wearing only a light jacket, rode off into mountains already covered with snow. I shivered in the frosty air. After spending the night by the trail with a campfire for company, Rae located and brought Val out the next morning so that we wouldn't lose any time in our hunt.

The four of us—John, Vance, Val, and I—spent nearly two weeks hunting, riding, and exploring from our camp on one of the upper drainages of the Bitterroot River. The hunting was good, but eventually we began running low on food. With a foot of snow already on the ground and what looked like another storm in the offing, we decided to call it quits and leave the next morning. It was pitch dark and close to 4:00 A.M. when we rolled out of warm sleeping bags, built up the campfire, and got the coffee boiling and bacon frying while Val rounded up and hayed the horses. The wall tent was stiff with ice and snow. Almost everything else was hard and unyielding, too, when we began to pack, so it was nearly mid-morning before camp was fully struck, gear mantied and packed, horses saddled and all ready to move out. The final mix of grounds and coffee poured into icy cups would have to hold us till we got to where the stock truck waited several miles below. The pot was hung on a pack saddle, and Vance and John took the lead in case any game should appear along the trail. Val and I followed, each leading a string of duffle-laden pack horses.

By early afternoon we reached the truck that Val had left at the end of a logging road. We loaded the pack stock and most of the gear, but because there wasn't enough room for all the animals in a single trip, we elected to have John and Vance drive while Val and I took the saddle stock. We would meet at the ranch later.

It was cold. A bone-numbing breeze groaning through trees heavily burdened with snow sent small clouds of ice particles swirling all around us. The sun was an icy blue blur through gray-white clouds. All the world was white except for the black shadows of the lodgepole forest. Steam from the horses' breaths and ours whipped away in frosty crystals as we wound our way down steep slopes through the forest, following blazes indicating that a trail lay some-where beneath the snow.

By now the lack of lunch and the scantiness of breakfast gave me the sensation of belly scraping backbone, and the cold was sinking deeper and deeper. Val set the pace. No stranger to this life, he had spent a good many years as cowhand and sheepherder in these mountains. The horses were good and knew the way, but by the time darkness was setting in we were scarcely halfway down and the cold was intensifying. Every fifteen minutes Val insisted that we get off and walk. By then, I was sure that I was frozen into the saddle. Stiff and clumsy, I'd manage to slide off, clinging to the horn and horse for support, my legs seeming too brittle and numb to hold me up. I wanted to ride, but common sense told me that feet and legs would be frozen if I didn't keep the circulation going. By my hanging onto the horse and letting it support me, enough circulation was gradually restored to permit me to walk on my own. Then we would ride for another fifteen minutes or so. Whenever Val slid out of the saddle and started to walk again, I followed suit.

Despite the cold, it was impossible to keep from being over-whelmed by the mountains, the wintry snow gleaming and sparkling as the final light of day, a feeble golden glow, broke through a rent in the horizon. Ice particles seemed to float in the air in a frozen haze of spangled frost. Little icicles hung from the horses' faces, and Val's whiskers were a wreath of white. I suppose that I looked the same.

It was nine or ten o'clock before we reached the old Forest Service road that led to civilization. "We've made it, the rest should be easy," so went my benumbed thinking. But how could I think with all my bones rattling? The darkness was nearly complete; the overcast skies were of no help.

The horses stopped abruptly. Examination, by leaning from the saddle and groping with numbed fingers, revealed a wire gate stretched across the road. It hadn't been there two weeks before.

Val dismounted to open it and as he was feeling for the opening, he let out a string of blue curses that warmed the air. Normally, he is a very soft-spoken guy, easy to get along with, but the words were spoken with feeling: "That ——— so-and-so put a padlock on the ——— gate! ——— his ——— soul!"

I slid off to see what I could do. "It's another fifteen miles around! This isn't his road—it was built with public money!" By now Val was fumbling with the pack in the darkness, uncovering the double-bitted axe and sliding it from its sheath. I held the horses while he cut down the gate. He named the rancher who owned the property adjoining the National Forest lands. "He's pulled this before. He thinks this forest is his private preserve. Normally I close any gate I open, but the bastard has pulled this once too often. I 'spect I'll see the sheriff about it tomorrow."

We rode past the tangle of wire. The skies were clearing and the cold was getting even more intense, ice and snow crunching and creaking underfoot. The stars were beginning to appear. The time was nearing midnight before we saw the welcome lights of the ranch giving off a soft glow, like distant candles in the darkened valley below. The pace of the horses quickened as we approached. They, too, were ready for warmth and food.

When we finally reached the gates that divided the ranch pastures we were welcomed first by the barking of the dog and the nickering of horses. Then the door of the long, rambling, log ranch house swung open, spilling yellow light onto the snow. Gene Tingle was shrugging into a coat and coming out to help us. We pulled up

and slid stiffly off the horses. My legs seemed scarcely able to hold
me as I led my mount into the steamy animal warmth of the log barn.
With uncooperative fingers I fumbled at cinch and bridle and put a
big scoop of oats into a nosebag. Gene helped us with the saddles,
telling us that Frances had supper waiting. "Go ahead, get some hot
coffee. I'll finish up."

Frances Burow, mother of Rae, whose horse I had held while she
was shoeing it preparatory to our expedition, lived in a small house
just below the main ranch house. She and her husband had sold the
E Lazy H to Marion and Gene, but she had continued to live there.
Val and I headed for the door of her little house where Frances stood
silhouetted, wiping her hands on her apron while great clouds of
steam escaped into the night air. "C'mon in!" The table was heaped
with food. The oven door of the woodburning range was propped
shut with a stick, while pots and kettles simmered on the top, puffing
steam. While she was thrusting mugs of boiling hot coffee into our
numb hands the most delightful aromas imaginable tantalized our
nostrils: a great pan of piping-hot cinnamon rolls, rich and dripping
with butter, cinnamon, and brown sugar; a huge, succulent roast
waiting in a puddle of red-brown juice. Already partly sliced, it was
accompanied by heaps of mashed potatoes, vats of gravy, all sorts of
vegetables, and two or three ranch-sized apple pies. "I kinda figured
you boys'd be hungry."

To know Frances is to know the West of old. She had been, vari-
ously, a Hollywood stunt rider, a rodeo pickup rider, a wilderness
cook and guide. She could still sit a horse with the best. If you have
ever seen any of the old Western movies, with the heroine riding
over a cliff aboard a runaway rig or the like, you have undoubtedly
met Frances. Her first recollection, she told me, was of somewhere in
Arizona. Her mother was leading a pack string of mules and carrying
the baby. Frances, her brothers and sisters, and the family sewing
machine were stuffed into the packs, and they were on their way
to join their prospector father.

If there is a heaven for gastronomes, Frances must be the keeper
of the portals. We had just been admitted. Gene came in shortly,
sweeping off the snow and joining us for coffee and pie. He told us
that she had predicted when we would be in, having been long accus-
tomed to the habits of wranglers, cowhands, hunters, and the like.

I've always figured that heaven has a place of honor for women such as Frances. I claim to be an expert judge of pies and other types of first-class cooking, and everyone in the Bitterroot knows that she was the best baker of apple pies in the valley. And that says it all.

Soon afterward we departed for the east coast, where my wife, dog, and boat waited. More than a year passed before I learned how the locked gate issue was settled. Mary and I were returning to North Carolina from having spent most of the winter camping in Florida, on the Gulf Coast, across the desert Southwest, and up the Pacific Coast. When we reached the Bitterroot, Mary said, "I want to see the place where you fell in love with a cook." There I learned of another gate encounter: this time Val, returning alone with a string of horses, was confronted by a couple of men with rifles. Challenged for trespass, he bluffed them, saying that, first, he was being followed by the rest of his party. Further, they were watching from above and had the armed men covered. He advised them not to try anything foolish. He added that at one time there was a one-room public school on the road and that the road had been used and maintained by the state and the Forest Service. They weren't sure that they wanted more trouble, especially when Val now insisted that they either remove the lock or get a warrant for his arrest.

Westerners, with good reason, value their privacy highly. They consider trespass a serious threat to their life-style and will not hesitate to do almost anything to enforce their rights. On the other hand, a lot of public land has been converted to private use purely by bluff. If certain ranchers had succeeded in closing this road to public use, in effect they would have converted all the National Forest lying behind the fence to their private hunting preserve. Val visited the sheriff soon thereafter, and the upper regions of this particular section of national forest still remain open to the public.

2.

On Tracking and Backtracking

One day the following summer, while I was photographing sports-fishing catches on the waterfront in Morehead City, North Carolina, Cap'n Arthur Lewis brought the boat *Wahoo* into port with two blue marlin aboard. The angler was Dr. Royal Brunson. He was taking a day off from his research at the Duke University Marine Laboratory nearby. A professor of zoology at the University of Montana in Missoula, he was engaged in postdoctoral studies of marine gastrotrichs, for which he is well known in scientific circles. Until he informed me differently, I had surmised gastrotrichs to be some kind of stomach worm. To this day I'm not sure what gastrotrichs are, even though I've seen them—they do look like miniature worms —but while Royal was working in coastal Carolina that summer I was able to guide him to a few out-of-the-way water holes for collecting specimens. Not only was it the beginning of a long and close friendship, but his knowledge of wildlife and skills in hunting have helped me learn much about the natural world. Royal was to introduce me to more western hunting, guiding me when I took my first mule deer, and acquainting me with the antelope of the Great Plains.

The mere mention of antelope aggravates one of my pet peeves, which is that the average American school has failed to tell its students enough about native American fauna. Above the sofa in our cottage on the North Carolina coast is the mounted head of an antelope buck. He stares across the room at the buffalo skull, which seems not to stare back except when my brother helps decorate for Christmas. Then the former resident of the National Bison Range sports glowing red and green (port and starboard) Christmas balls for eyes. I have noticed visitors sitting around the fireplace, furtively studying both heads with considerable curiosity. Sooner or later it comes out that almost no one recognizes either animal. They would have recognized elephant, zebra, giraffe, and rhinoceros, but not badger, musk-ox, and certainly not the all-American jackalope. Our educational system does a fine job on distance, but seems to be a laggard in our own backyard.

The American pronghorn antelope is the fastest animal of the North American plains. Once it was near extinction. During my childhood in the Dakotas, the heart of their native habitat, I never saw one alive; I saw only their pictures and moth-eaten mounted heads. I first became aware of this omission when a small band of them flashed across a road near Marathon, Texas, a few months after my wife and I took up vagabonding. Since then, state fish and game departments have reintroduced antelope into the Dakotas so successfully that where I was raised they are today a relatively common sight, abundant enough to be a legal game animal and sometimes even a problem to local wheat farmers.

One autumn day when we were sitting around in Royal's office at the University of Montana, he asked if I'd like to hunt antelope. I didn't have to be coaxed.

"When do we start?"

"Let's leave Thursday afternoon."

Royal and two of his graduate students, Randy Miller and Jay Cross, piled into my Volkswagen bus with sleeping bags, guns, and warm clothing immediately after the last class that Thursday, and we set out for the plains of eastern Montana, in the neighborhood of North Dakota. By driving in two-hour shifts, two of us attempting to sleep in the back while another drove and the fourth kept the driver awake, we rolled on through the night. It's a long way across Montana, but by mid-morning we were near a former student's ranch where we had permission to hunt. We parked on a high ridge overlooking unending miles of honey-colored grasslands that spread from horizon to horizon. Here we began spying out the country.

Some years before, a hunter had told me of going after antelope in Wyoming. His technique was to get into a Jeep, drive about till he spotted a band, and proceed to race the animals. He was ecstatic about the thrill of driving fifty or sixty miles an hour across roadless plains, jumping washes and skirting coulees while shooting at the fleeing animals. He and his friends wrecked vehicles at various times, but only once did they fail to get game. That was when they all ended up in the hospital at the beginning of the hunt, after the driver had failed to see a coulee in time to dodge. I was relieved that Royal hunted in a different fashion.

Antelope are credited with vision equal to or exceeding ours with eight- to ten-power binoculars. They have a cruising speed close to forty miles per hour, and according to some sources can exceed sixty, so a certain degree of finesse is required in hunting them. When not pressed heavily, they will often allow people to get within a mile before fleeing, as long as they see no evidence of a stalk.

It was my first trip with Randy and Jay, and I was considered the eastern dude. Both of them had done a good bit of western-style hunting and were eager to demonstrate the proper procedures. But Royal was our guide, and his technique was simple. Spot a herd that is at least a mile away. Keep well concealed while studying the terrain and the moving tendencies of the herd. Locate the biggest and best buck, then move back over the brow of the hill, sometimes even driving well out of sight. Leave the car, and return along the draws and creek bottoms to begin the stalk. Evening was near before we had a chance to try his method, but we soon sighted several bands of a dozen animals or more. One group looked to be vulnerable to our approach.

Circling from the back side of a ridge, we split up, two of us to circle east, thence north, following behind a hill. The other two would follow a dry creek bottom west till we could crest out while still keeping behind the abundant sagebrush. Just before we separated Jay cautioned me that it is easy to be fooled by distances out here—the clear air, you know—and things can be much farther away than a casual estimate would indicate. At that time he was training to qualify for the Olympic shooting team, so I paid attention.

Royal's approach procedure worked to easy perfection. Jay and Randy had got to the northeast and we were to the southwest of the resting band. When all were in place, Royal signaled the final approach. I slithered belly down in a draw and eased up the back of the hillside, keeping a cluster of rocks and sage between the animals and me. At what I considered the right moment, with as much stealth as I could muster, I rose to a shooting position. Directly in front of me a large black-chinned buck with proud horns was looking at me and starting to rise, too, in curiosity more than alarm. I looked at him through the crosshairs and recalled Jay's warning about judging range. Uncertainty rattled around, and I raised and lowered the sights while trying to decide whether he was actually within the 300 yards at which I'd sighted the rifle. A chorus of shots rang out and the hillside was covered with the dust of fleeing animals. It was too late. The buck was gone. Randy had got a fine young buck, Jay had wounded one and it took a second shot. Royal hadn't had a chance. I paced off the distance from my buck—an easy 120 yards. Angry with myself for lacking confidence, I said nothing.

Next morning, we split up again. Jay and Randy had an ambush planned from atop a haystack. Royal and I searched the countryside till afternoon, when we rejoined the others. By late afternoon the odds seemed against us even when we located another band, well up on a hillside but with no way for an easy approach. Together we worked along as close as we could, but the distance looked out of practical shooting range to me.

Jay and Randy argued, "Not over 300, maybe 350 at the very most."

"An easy shot for that rifle of yours."

I looked again. It seemed a long way to me, but I had been fooled before. They kept urging, so I assumed the prone position, tightened the sling around my arm, and worked myself into a competitive shooting position. Having shot on various rifle teams, I considered myself at least fair as a rifleman. I then eased around till the crosshairs didn't waver. There was no wind. It should be an easy shot. But it still looked like a long distance.

The buck was lying directly in line, his head up. If I sighted on the chest any drop would be along the spine. Unable to get the notion of great distance out of my head, I raised the rifle till the crosshairs fell on the head, which would allow for as much as a four-foot drop. Still not satisfied, I set the crosshairs on the tips of the horns, while my companions kept urging me to hurry. At the last moment, thinking it could be 500 yards, I lifted the aiming point another six inches above the tips of the black horns. I squeezed the trigger. Rolling under the recoil, I saw the bullet strike about eight feet below the animal, now in full flight. Twelve feet of drop, I calculated mentally, then set off to pace 710 yards to where he had been.

I gave up listening to others' estimates of distance, and the next day got a nice buck, after stalking with Royal's assistance to within seventy-five yards. Estimated cost of that antelope, including mileage, licenses and all the rest: sixty dollars a pound by the time I got it back to North Carolina. Even with the meat beginning to approximate the price of caviar, I considered the hunt worth every cent, especially when my wife's maiden aunt, who would never knowingly have eaten wild meat, asked for seconds. My estimate of costs did not include taxidermy, which was another lesson. The buck came back from a cut-rate taxidermist looking like a squashed mouse caught eating an unripe persimmon. This was my own fault. I was trying to save shipping costs, so I had chosen a taxidermist within fifty miles of my home in North Carolina who, having no idea what an antelope looked like, tried to make it as close to a whitetail deer as possible. The whole experience was an education.

But I had been bitten by the bug. The hunt was the thing — the wide-open country, the limitless vistas of that near-virgin land, the sounds of coyotes, the sight of defiant badgers digging in the rocks, the bellying along through cactus and finding an arrowhead, an agate, or the fused remnants of a meteorite, the pungence of freshly-crushed sage. It was sitting by an open campfire shivering as the sun set, but soon falling asleep, warm in a down bag, while trying to watch the passing of the stars; then, in no time at all, the welcome of dawn breaking red on open plains. These are unknowns to those who do not follow the ways of the hunter. The antelope that watches the buffalo in my library reminds me daily that such experiences were sacred to the Indian and should be to the white men who have hunted this native of our plains. And never again will I need to tally the costs of a hunt.

By now the West had become a habit. Almost every year, as soon as the absolutely essential summer work was completed, we hit the trail west, eventually ending up in the high country, usually of western Montana, which inevitably included our friends the Tingles. Their E Lazy H Ranch, where we had based my first hunt, was in the foothills of the Sapphire Mountains which make up the east wall of the Bitterroot Valley. Most often the season culminated in a pack trip. It was Marion and Gene who taught us most of the basics and pleasures of packing.

Pack trips are a return to the primitive preautomobile era, when man's best friend wasn't his credit card but his horse. It is a traditional American method of travel, developed with the expansion of the West, remaining today largely a strenuous form of recreation perpetuating pioneering skills. Its closest kin is canoe camping. Neither packing nor canoeing is as common in other parts of the world; though copied elsewhere, they reached a form of perfection in the New World. There are far more efficient methods of wilderness travel, the easiest and fastest probably being by helicopter, but this is missing the point. The pleasures of being in a wilderness cannot be measured by the speed or the ease with which one travels.

Packing is hard work, but I have found no better way to experience and enjoy wilderness than to travel with saddle and pack horse. A horse or a mule, depending upon terrain and conditions, can carry up to a quarter-ton of cargo for short distances, but, like a man with a pack, there are practical limits. Besides, a pack trip is not a test of strength, but a combination of the pleasures of hard physical work with the most comfort you can create with the least amount of gear. Around two hundred pounds is the optimum load for the average horse or mule if you intend to make reasonable distance without abusing the animal.

This leads to the theory of the lighter the better. The Back Country Horsemen organization, a strong advocate of saving our wilderness, has cooperated with the Forest Service in developing a practical pocket guide to lightweight packing as an aid in the maintenance and management of the wilderness. I have wrestled with large, heavy canvas-walled tents, cases of canned goods, untold tons of personal gear from cast-iron pots to battery packs, and have discovered the virtues of using lightweight gear instead of a dozen horses, half of them carrying just horse food. The worst case I can remember is packing in case after case of soft drinks for an elk-hunting party to a camp where it froze every night and there was a beautiful clean spring nearby, generously gushing gallons of purest water.

The logistics of packing into the wilderness for even as little as a week are impressive. For example, how much hay, grain, and range pellets (concentrated horse feed) will it take for how many horses to carry four riders and their food, cooking equipment, tents, sleeping bags and mattresses, night shirts and raincoats plus cameras, fishing tackle, rifles, axes and spare clothing, and horse supplies? And if the party does succeed in getting game, how will it be packed out?

Pack boxes and panniers come in pairs. They are filled with the nonperishables. Breakables are wrapped or inserted in padding. For example, if fresh eggs go along, they can be placed, whole, in the pancake mix or flour; they may even be carried in the horses' oats. Glass jars are the biggest challenge, for a broken jar of pickles can do wonders for the biscuit mix, and not just in flavor. Unless you have seen a reluctant horse stand on its ear, apparently with the sole intent of premixing the coffee and powdered cream with everything else, or get into a kicking match, or slam into a very solid tree along the trail, it's hard to imagine how difficult it is to guarantee that a cargo is breakproof.

All the rest of the gear is wrapped in manties, large squares of canvas that protect the cargo from shifting and keep it in a compact mass. It is very important to pack and balance each load for weight and mass. A usual load would be two sixty-pound bales of hay man-tied on each side, slung high and secured with a packer or diamond hitch. This makes about 120 pounds on each side, a substantial load. Any other gear must be very light, such as a lantern or sleeping bag packed on top and amidships. A good packer won't let the load vary more than a couple of pounds between sides. The load must also be very secure: a shift or a part of the cargo coming loose will often send an otherwise docile horse into an uncontrollable fright.

One time, on Weasel Creek in the Sapphires, we were watching a buckskin mare in another outfit when she decided that she didn't like the load. There were chocolate cookies mixed with mayonnaise and marmalade and scrambled eggs on display for a half-mile down the trail. We once had a mare so sure to perform that her cargo was always baled hay and grain. Even then, she usually unloaded it first thing. Yet once under way she was all right, unless we made too long a stop, such as when we had to clear a trail of fallen timber.

Funny things can happen around horses and mules, although at the time they may not seem so funny. Val Loesch and I had a pack string on the Burnt Fork when we found the trail blocked by downed timber. Val, in the lead, unsheathed his axe and set to work while I minded the string. After a bit he had the trail opened and we got under way. A few hundred yards farther along we found another tree down and the process had to be repeated. At this point, we noticed that the rifle was missing from its scabbard on the right front side of his saddle. We were perplexed, knowing that it had been there at the start. Riding drag, I offered to go back and search for it while he cleared the latest obstruction. At the site of the previous blockage, I found along the trail a strange looking hole in the snow, and therein was the missing rifle. I returned it to Val, and he put it back in the scabbard. We set out again.

Within a mile or so was another log jam, and clearing had to be done again. We got under way only to discover once more that the rifle was missing. Dutifully, I went back to where we had been detained and found the rifle by the side of the trail. I caught up with Val and the string. Now more suspicious than puzzled, I kept an eye on his rifle when we paused for another fallen tree. As soon as Val took his attention from his horse, it turned its head, reached back, and with its teeth carefully pulled the rifle from the scabbard and dropped it off to the side of the trail. After that, Val slung his rifle aft on the saddle, out of reach of a horse that had apparently become a gun-control advocate.

Pack trips are outdoor expeditions in style. They can occur for any of a dozen reasons. Ours have been mainly three: to hunt, to fish, to look at the mountains, or a combination of these. Involving so much preparation, a pack trip can be rather expensive if you must rent the horses and all the equipment needed. If you are lucky and have friends with horses, equipment, and expertise—well, it can make a world of difference. Today most of us are limited to professional outfitters who make a living taking people into National Parks, a wilderness, or near-wilderness. This type of trip usually includes guides, cooks, and wranglers who cater to the client, and it is a wonderful way to go, if for some reason you can't do it yourself. A friend of ours, Garrett Sutherland, went on such an outing years ago and reported that, to her amazement, not only did they have wine along, but scented toilet tissue as well. They were met at the end of every ride with mess and sleeping tents set up and a hot meal waiting.

Further, they had padded saddles, which often proves comforting to the backside. She added that, despite such niceties, the outfitting lacked certain common necessities, and she was forced to use Band-Aids and shoelaces for small repairs.

If you should consider hiring a packer or guide, nothing will tell you more about him than the way he handles stock. If his animals are stove up, gaunt—"ganted up," Westerners say—and bearing scars or sores from ill-fitting saddles or harness, he probably doesn't know what he is doing, or else he is a sadist. Avoid him. More times than we wish to remember we've encountered outfitters who were either clumsy, inexperienced, or didn't care. Hunting up the Lost Horse once with the Tingles, we came upon a corral full of starving horses, gaunt and ribs showing, no food or fresh water available. Obviously, they had been there for some time. They belonged to an out-of-state renegade outfitter who, we were told, made a practice of purchasing stock in California and bringing them immediately into the high country for a season of outfitting hunters. After he had worn out the stock, the outfitter disposed of them. Mary and Marion were so enraged that they reported him to the Forest Service, which is responsible for commercial packers' permits. We suspected that it may have been a waste of time, for the outfitter was still in business the following year.

Another year, before the season opened, we happened upon a string of mules, beautiful animals with good gear. They were being used to teach packing to students. An excellent concept; however, in this case, the instructor must have been out of town for a while, because every animal was galled, with raw, bloody patches showing from beneath the gear. It was a case of students not having learned to fit harness properly, and failing to see the need for checking often and closely for chafing. I suspect that the owner of the stock was mad as hell at seeing his animals in such wretched condition. Skilled packers are able to work horses and mules hard for months at a time and keep their stock in good shape; the other kind can ruin a poor beast in a day. To pack with animals that enjoy going into the hills as much as you do is a cooperative effort as rewarding as getting there. And when you go on such an expedition with the right people it is soul-satisfying. Such are the Tingles, Val Loesch, and many more.

*   *   *

One year, early in our wanderings, we found ourselves high on
the edge of the Selway-Bitterroot Wilderness. At that time, the lake
where we camped on the rim of the Rockies was seldom visited other
than by adventurous souls. It was a picture of mountain wilderness.
Its surface, reflecting sky and surrounding peaks, was dotted with
spreading circles from rising trout. On the shore opposite our camp,
an osprey stood tall in a storm-shattered pine, watching for any careless misfits of the finny world. Its duty was to keep the lake's stock
of trout strong, healthy, and wary. Anything failing to meet these
standards fell into the category of being fit only for eating. The bird
had done its job well, the inhabitants meeting all the desired requirements of true wild mountain fish. Few others knew that this lake
also contained some of the last remaining golden trout to be found
in America. We had been conducting a successful inspection tour to
test their fighting ability and flavor. But as in all endeavors there is a
time to fish and there is a time to lean back and savor the many other
things that make the fishing worthwhile.

The sounds of splashing had aroused my curiosity, so, rolling out
of the hammock where I had been resting from a hard day of fishing,
I picked up the camera and made my way down the steep bank to
where I could see what was making the noise. Just around a point,
where the lake shoaled a bit, three moose were feeding. A big bull
was obviously interested in a young cow, while ignoring a female of
more mature years. Setting the camera on a tripod, I attached a tele-
photo lens. The bull may have thought the privacy of his lechery
was being invaded, for when he lifted his head, antlers still festooned
with aquatic grasses, he eyeballed me and began to advance, slowly
at first, but picking up steam as my retreat increased in speed. My
brother Bill snapped an action photo of me stepping up the slope in
right good form, with the image of the bull, following not many feet
behind, nicely framed in the bend of my elbow. The bull must have
considered the threat removed, for he pursued me no further. The
rest of the day, on and off, we could observe the courting and cavorting, admiring from high on a bluff overlooking the lake, the ability
of these magnificent animals to walk the lake bottom, submerged,

coming up only occasionally for air. We have seen deer foraging lake bottoms, too, but not walking underwater.

Like most people who know the animal, I have a great deal of respect for this critter. Curious, unafraid, at times belligerent, and always unpredictable, the moose can appear like a ghost out of the blackness or fade just as imperceptibly. He can be quite formidable, too; for example, a few weeks before, we had heard a story going the rounds about this chap who was employed by the Forest Service to operate a bulldozer. He was busy carving a road when he happened upon a bull moose. Bored with the dirt-pushing, he thought he'd tease the animal a bit, just for the fun of it.

Now not many of us would deny that a bulldozer is one tough hunk of steel. By evening, so the story went, this man's buddies noted that he hadn't showed up at quitting time. They went up the mountain and found him cowering under the machine, waiting for the moose to leave, with several hundred dollars damage done to the bulldozer. It is said that never again did the dozer man challenge a moose. We weren't arguing with this family of moose either, contenting ourselves with watching the cows swim across the lake towards the Idaho border. The bull soon followed and they all disappeared into distant woods.

That evening, along about suppertime, the clouds started moving in and a fierce thunderstorm began to build. Lightning slashed and zipped among the peaks and a steady crashing of thunder echoed through the mountains, the storm gods quarreling among themselves and throwing fiery spears at one another while the Norse god Thor hammered on his anvil. We'd been sleeping in the open, or sometimes, if weather looked threatening, stringing up a tarp. This evening we had sought a little more protection from the rain and wind and had set up a small tent, a military type originally intended for mountain troops. It was just big enough for two with basic gear, and we'd erected it on a small level area a few yards from shore.

During the night the storm passed and Mary and I were sleeping soundly when something disturbed my repose: a measured sort of squish, squish, pause, squish, squish, that grew closer and closer. Suddenly it dawned that this was the sound of hooves in the mud. I froze. That bull moose was coming back. In fact, he was on us.

I could feel his presence above the tent, examining this strange thing in his territory. It was too late for us even to think of escape.

Seldom do I go into the wilds without a gun: usually a .45-caliber pistol, sometimes a shotgun or rifle. This time, because we were in bear country—one had wandered into camp earlier that evening— I had in the tent with us a 12-gauge automatic, loaded with double-ought buckshot. I snatched it and waited, scared, perplexed. I had nothing against Mr. Moose, I didn't want to shoot him if I could avoid it. Besides, if I had, he would probably have landed on top of us and flattened us rather effectively with his thousand or so pounds. On the other hand, if I waited he might very well pick up the tent and its contents and toss them around a bit before stomping—well, that alternative didn't suit me too well either.

There was a long, long interval of silence as the two of us, that is, the moose and I, considered our choices. Mary and I were virtually breathless, but we could hear the moose's soft exhalations and intakes of air. It seemed an eternity—then silently, but for the soft squish of mud, the giant beast turned and faded back into the lake. We peered out between the flaps. The moon was shining brightly between the ragged ribbons of clouds racing by. Its beams shimmered and danced on a lake surface mirroring its brilliance. All the world was black and silver, and far down the lake shore a tall and proud dark form moved silently into the night. The moon shone on his great spread of antlers, and I was happy to see him go.

There was another moose that I wasn't so happy to see go. It was one of the first big game hunts Mary and I had ever made. Mary was making sourdough hotcakes on a bluff overlooking a small lake in Ontario. On the shore below, beside our blue canoe, I was scanning the shoreline with binoculars, looking for the elusive moose. It seemed the practical thing to do while waiting for breakfast. Suddenly, what I saw made me scramble hastily up the bank, all the while trying to give the appearance of not moving. A large black animal had just sauntered out of the woods onto a spit of land.

I gulped, "There's a moose down there!"

Mary snatched the binoculars; she always has to verify that I know what I'm looking at. "It sure is! Let's go!"

In the time that it took Mary to turn off the stove I had picked up

the rifle. We hurried down to the canoe and shoved off. The animal
was foraging, unconcerned, at the edge of the shallows. We were well
into the lake when, still without seeming to notice us, it turned and
moved into the timber, only to reappear a short distance beyond as
if about to reenter the lake. Tall grasses lay conveniently between the
moose and us, and we concealed ourselves there, Mary steadying the
canoe as best she could while I took aim. I fired just as the beast
stepped down from the bank, hitting the big animal high on its
shoulder hump. It fell out of sight beneath some trees. We paddled
furiously, but saw it get up and fade into the woods while we were
still only halfway across the open water. Mary vaulted onto the beach,
so charged with adrenalin that she dragged the canoe ashore half its
length, with me still in it. She took off in the direction of the
wounded animal. All I could think of, as I dropped my paddle and
grabbed the rifle, was, "She's just like a beagle after a rabbit." In a
few minutes she stopped and pointed; she had found the place where
the moose had gone down, but it was not in sight.

Only after a couple of hard miles of close tracking did Mary slow
down a little bit—but she was on the scent, so to speak, and would
not be deterred. It was obvious that the wound was not serious, and
the moose would not be deterred either. We found no more signs of
bleeding, and the animal hadn't slowed a bit. It was as I suspected:
I had only creased its neck in the hump, stunning it, much as old
horse hunters did when they wanted to stun a horse without seriously
injuring it. Finally, we came upon fresh manure, and the spot where
it had paused to wallow and feed. There was no sign of blood. "Well,"
agreed Mary, "it got away, but it's going to be all right. You just
grazed it."

It was nearing sundown before we left off following the tracks of
this long-legged woods walker that had stridden unhurriedly across
mile afer mile of marsh and woodlands without pause. It dawned on
us that we were now a long way from both camp and canoe, and that
they lay in different directions. We became aware, too, of hunger,
after nearly six hours of hunting and tracking without breakfast. By
the time we got back to the lake to retrieve the canoe and returned to
camp, it was six o'clock and almost dark. On the hastily abandoned
griddle lay three pancakes, stiff and a little burnt. Those not charred

had been worked over by the whiskey jacks. I set to building a fire while Mary was refreshing the continuing pot of stew with more vegetables. She put the cover on, and I heard a big sigh. She was looking across the lake. Tears were running down her cheeks.

"Disappointed?" I asked.

"Not at a bit—this has been one of the greatest days of my life, that's all."

I never have been able to understand women.

Months later, Mary was reading to me from one of Jack O'Connor's books on big game hunting, in which he advised slow tracking. She looked at me accusingly, "Did you know that when I was tracking that moose?"

"Yes."

"Why didn't you stop me?"

"I couldn't have stopped you if I'd tried."

"I guess not."

"Did you know there were two moose that day?"

"Were there really?"

"Yes."

"Why didn't you tell me?"

"Would it have made any difference?"

"No."

"It was a great day, wasn't it?"

"Yep, the greatest."

3.

By Mule to the Bob Marshall

We were soon back on the east coast, engaged in our usual activities, which included participating in a celebration held in the small seaside town of Beaufort, North Carolina. It was known as the Spanish Invasion; and the event revealed to us some major changes in the American way of life. Bear with me while I explain how Mary and I became intensely interested in the decline of American mules, which were to become an important segment of our own future.

Surely everyone is aware that mules were the prime builders of the nation — they hauled the freight, worked the mines, and plowed the fields for the first two hundred years of our nation. But now it is evident that the United States has fallen into a state of serious decline, having been steamrollered into mediocrity by the monotonous uniformity of progress. The steady slippage of our way of life was first brought to my attention by the chief marshal of that now several-years-defunct, annual celebration in Beaufort, when Grayden Paul, the head honcho, couldn't find a mule to pull a mule cart.

The climax of the two-day event was a reenactment of an invasion by Spanish pirates that had occurred in the early 1700s. The celebration required local citizens to play the parts of both pirates and citizens. According to the program, the pirates sailed into the harbor firing their cannons and muskets, and the citizens came out of the bushes to meet them, toting their shotguns, fowling pieces, and other artillery. The participants built big bonfires, symbolizing the burning of a fortification, and there was much chasing of women, whooping, and screaming in a most enjoyable fashion. The alleged purpose was only to entertain the tourists.

Over the years the show kept getting better, more black powder was expended, more and more tourists showed up, and more and more participants and bystanders got caught up in the excitement, so that pretty soon the pirates had a hard time even getting into the harbor for all the boats and partying in the way, and half the pirate crew fell overboard in the melee. Fortunately no one ever drowned. Perhaps the final straw came when one of the volunteers set fire to the keg of gunpowder used by the shore battery. It was a spectacular event, again without casualties, but understandably officialdom began to lose courage and one could see more problems coming.

Back to Grayden Paul. The schedule called for the pirates to come ashore, chase and entertain women, and have a rowdy good time. Then the local guardians of home and family were to come out of the shrubbery, rescue the ladies, whether they wanted rescuing or not, and capture the pirates. Now, about the mules: it seems that no mule was available to pull the cart in which the heroic militia was to carry the captured Spanish pirates to the hoosegow in the grand finale. "In fact," said Mr. Paul, "there are no longer any mules in Beaufort, or anywhere else in Carteret County, to pull a simple two-wheel cart full of pirates." Horses were considered until someone remembered the first celebration, when a couple of local heroes came on horses. The cannon went off, and it took two days to find the riders. I'm not sure that the horses were ever found.

Because of this critical situation a group of concerned citizens formed the Protect-the-Mule Association (PTMA), hoping to correct a serious community loss. If you think it isn't serious, try to name a major city with a good supply of mules. I can think of a hundred without mules, including New York, Charlotte, Boston, Des Moines, New Orleans, and San Francisco. There used to be a good supply near Missoula, Montana, at the U.S. Forest Service remount station, but today the Forest Service seems to be phasing out mules. Only the town of Benson, North Carolina, recognizes them and holds an annual Mule Day. The last we heard, even there they had to award top place to an ass one year because of a mule shortage, although perhaps that was only a rumor. The only place I can think of that has a respectable equine population east of the Mississippi, aside from the Kentucky race tracks, might be on the other side of the river in St. Louis, and those aren't mules, they are mainly beery Clydesdales.

I'd be willing to wager there's not a good old-fashioned mule in St. Louis, though Missouri mules were once famous for their size and stubbornness.

Not many months after the PTMA organizational meeting, Mary and I were in a remote wilderness camp, where most of the pack and riding stock was mules. Our party was sitting around the fire one evening, with a buckskin mare's bell telling us where her mules were, and we got to extolling the virtues of this beast as compared with other forms of transportation.

Mules are good for riding, plowing, pulling, mowing, and cussing. They require no gasoline or oil, pay no road tax, and seldom rust out. They are good for at least twenty years of hard labor. They furnish fertilizer and will keep the lawn mowed, including the azaleas. I know folks who pay ten, fifteen, even twenty-five dollars a week to have someone come and mow their lawns. Yet for the price of a season of lawn mowing, they could not only get the grass cut, but the garden plowed as well.

At the risk of sounding snobbish, we should point out that the mule is known to science as *Equus asinus x caballus*, but of all the remarks I have heard addressed to a mule, I must confess I have never heard any man call one by that name. Besides having a scientific identity, this creature appears in our folklore. It is said that George Washington had the first mules on mainland North America and was very favorably impressed. They were gifts from the King of Spain. In the South a certain beverage is named for them, honoring their strength. It is known as "White Mule."

The mule is truly an outdoor animal. At least it is not often kept as a house pet. It is as American as apple pie. It is an easy rider, the Rocky Mountain Cadillac, we call it in the West, where its voice has also given it the name Rocky Mountain Canary. Actually, it is the burro that has first claim on these names, but both mule and burro are well known as easy riders with unique vocal cords. There is no prettier sight than a string of mules along a mountain trail, hooves clip-clopping in unison, bells jingling, leather squeaking.

Someone reasoned that the merits of mule power are best evaluated by comparison with today's pickup truck. The life expectancy of a hard-used pickup is seldom more than three to five years. While a mule gets off to a slower start, requiring around two years of patience for breaking in and tuning up, it is good for as long as thirty years. We are speaking of an initial investment of $75 to $400 for a mule, in contrast to the very few serviceable pickups, even used, that sell for less than four or five thousand. Maintenance, too, should be considered: tires—radial, snow, and sure grips—cannot be had for less than about fifty bucks each, not including balancing and alignment or relining brakes. Yet a farrier will come to the mule and put on a whole set of shoes, which act as tires and brake linings combined, for around $25. The only thing at all likely to need realignment is the farrier himself.

Now consider the cost of a valve job, rings, points, plugs, windshield-wiper blades, and antifreeze. While all this expense is adding up, a mule just goes on recycling oats and hay, without any problems whatever in meeting fuel emission standards. How so? you ask. Well, who ever heard of fertilizing a garden with burned gas and oil? Even the upholstery of a mule is self-renewing. More significantly, the mule is an integrated system, with automatic pilot and homing device, thus eliminating drunk-driving problems with its inertial guidance. It is an established fact that a mule will go farther on a pound of oats than a pickup will on a gallon of gasoline. Oats are cheaper, too.

And there is the trade-in value. One usually pays to have a dead pickup hauled away, but a mule's salvage value is at least thirty cents a pound, if done in time. An average-sized, 1,100-pound mule will feed a lot of pet dogs, even calculating with modern math. Noise pollution abatement controls are incorporated into the oats, but to call a mule a hay-burner indicates prejudice. A mule will still go, if only to the granary, when it has run out of food, but just try to coax an out-of-gas pickup to a filling station.

There are several standard colors to chose from, ranging from mouse grays or browns to some very exotic designs such as Appaloosa, known to some as spotted asses. Models may be standard, deluxe, long-legged, compact, or oversize, but all models are guaranteed four-wheel drive with self-locking brakes. A point-by-point comparison will reveal that about the only thing a pickup and a mule have in common is that they are both sterile, so both are nonrenewable resources. While vast industries are standing ever ready to propagate pickup trucks, the nation is forever faced with a deplorable mule shortage.

Back when I was the young caballero type, I too was among those who disdained the mule. I couldn't fancy myself looking proud and dashing on such a mount; and who could imagine a centaur being half man and half mule? But I have since found that there are pretty animals, and then there are those that get the job done. A sensible animal, the mule will not knowingly go where there is danger to it. This is one of the reasons that neither the cavalry nor the Indians chose mules, for a mule will not tackle anything that it doesn't feel it can handle. As my wife remarked after she and her mule met a grizzly bear on the trail, "All you have to do is stay aboard." Most normal confrontations are no problem to a mule; it can outwait, out-wit, outrun, or outkick anything that spells trouble.

I can sum up my own observations simply: don't get a horse when you need a mule. Many people still underestimate them. Mules are tough: it is said that the only time a mule ever gets sick is when it is about to die. On the famed Overland Stage Line that ran from St. Joseph, Missouri, to Sacramento, California, most of the teams were horses selected for their speed and strength. Yet there was one stretch of the trail in Colorado where the heavily loaded wagons and coaches had to be dragged through sixteen miles of soft sand, fetlock deep, with not a drop of water or shade available the entire length. Horses simply could not survive. Here a spike team, consisting of five mules, one in the lead and two spans following, took over, crossing and recrossing the sand routinely.

But don't think mules are slow. A team called the "Arkansaws" held the stage lines record of ten miles in forty minutes. Another team called the "Benham Mules" pulled their load, averaging about thirteen miles per hour, covering nearly fifteen miles in fifty-five minutes.

Probably I can only speak for myself, but I suspect that the feel-ings may run akin in many of us. I fell in love with wilderness many years ago. Any wilderness will do, but western mountains with pack animals have always held a special sort of meaning. This romance has stretched over a lifetime. It started when, as a kid, I first began wan-dering in the lonesome prairies and untamed hills of South Dakota near where I was raised. That feeling was rekindled when I began working with the Wildlife Federation as a field director, where my duties introduced me to the hunters, the fishermen, the wildlife clubs, and the wild places, particularly of North Carolina's back country. This was long before my first big-game hunt on the Burnt Fork, but I think that was where I became aware of my feelings, later enhanced when we were hiking the wildernesses of places like Glacier National Park with highly educated and intelligent people who loved and understood the wilderness long before I did. The memories of these expeditions I still cherish.

To wander the high country takes two things, time and finances. A lot of hard-bitten old coots, including some old-time prospectors, run dudes or pack mules or both in the back country. If you were to ask them if they like this sort of work they would tell you that it's the only thing they know how to do. And without doubt they also would be telling you a rock-rimmed, twenty-four-carat-gold-plated and salted lie. But by looking deep into those shifty eyes you will see the truth. Such a person is actually lovesick with the wild and unin-habited land, and wouldn't take all the city-slick civilization in the world for the privilege of roaming those ranges of pine-covered, snow-capped rocks and knowing the feeling of self-reliance that comes to those who suffer that peculiar type of lovesickness.

The simple excuse of working in wild mountains with horses and mules was at that time, and still is, sufficiently attractive to me that I have often been willing to forego all thoughts of profit and security just to be there.

One of the most memorable summers we have ever spent started in a well-plowed vegetable garden at the end of a private airstrip near Swan Lake in northwestern Montana. There we began working long hours with the mules that would take us on an extended summer pack trip deep into the Bob Marshall Wilderness, an isolated, primi-tive land of snow-spotted mountains, grizzly bears, and picture-book lakes tucked into deep valleys and fed by melting glaciers, snow-fields, and thundering waterfalls.

John Gaskill, who by then had moved from North Carolina's blue-green sounds and golden beaches to northwestern Montana's lake country, had asked us to film a packing-fishing-camping foray into this most remote wilderness in the Lower 48. He knew of my experience in filming various outdoor sports, such as marlin fishing, and as a free-lancer for network TV news. He concluded that we could make a team as soon as he convinced investors of the practicality of filming a movie in the prime wilderness of Big Sky country. John's long-range plans at the time were to spend winters criss-crossing the nation, showing a film that would depict the splendors of the high country. Between spring runoff and the onset of winter he hoped to use his time guiding dudes on fishing and hunting trips.

Everything had fallen into place. He'd already located a sufficient supply of mules in the Southeast, trucking them to his place near Big Fork, Montana. Mary and I agreed to give the idea a whirl. John would take care of supplying the stock and equipment, and our assignment would be to script and shoot a film of such quality that it could be shown to audiences nationwide.

That was when the first minor problem arose. During the excitement of buying the mules for the pack string, John somehow ran afoul of a draft-horse pulling contest in Kentucky. As I heard the story, while the teamster was egging on the heaving, snorting team, dust flying, animals grunting and straining, a sled loaded with several tons of concrete weights landed on John's foot. In and out of the hospital with a crushed foot, plus a severe infection that threatened amputation, John was forced to hobble about on crutches; it would fall to Bart Davis, the wrangler, and me to train the mules for packing and riding. John supervised while recuperating. The doctors forbade his involvement, but they didn't know his determination.

Getting set for a wilderness expedition takes weeks of preparation. First there is the stock, both riding and packing. And saddles, for both riding and pack, with all the attendant sundries, such as spare cinches, ropes, bridles, blankets and pads, and farrier supplies. Animals must be fed, so there are grain, hay, and salt. Trucks are usually required to transport the stock to the trailhead. All this adds up to quite a collection even before considering man's seemingly unlimited needs: food, cooking gear, tents, sleeping bags, lanterns, fuel, rafts, axes, first-aid kits for man and animal, and spare bootlaces. Our job would be to tend to the cameras, film, sound and lighting equipment, script, and secretarial work. But there was to be more to it than that: horses were not unfamiliar to us, but the pack train was to be made up of Kentucky mules, wild-eyed broncs that had yet to be converted into dependable pack and riding stock. It was impossible not to become involved in the education of the mules, and, through it, ourselves.

When Mary and I arrived on the scene, mules, outfitter, and

wrangler were already there. John, Bart, and I were to spend long, hot days convincing a dozen mules that it is better to be Indians than chiefs on a narrow trail. A buckskin bell mare established her position right at the start: with snapping teeth and flailing hooves, she explained that she would be the boss, after John and Bart, of course. A bell mare is essential to a wilderness expedition such as we were planning. Her importance is based on the fact that mules will stay with a mare. By attaching a bell to her when the animals are turned out to graze in the evenings, the wrangler can hear the location of the stock.

Each mule also had to be taught that bucking off the pack is not acceptable behavior, and that it is to come when called, halt instantly at the word "Whoa!," and not express its frustration in any manner other than an occasional bray. In return for carrying heavy loads over long distances, for great patience and fortitude, for standing around in hot sun and dreary, cold rain, each would receive a half-bale of hay, which it had to carry, and a ration of oats, which it also took along.

It doesn't take much deduction to conclude that the mules were getting the short end of the deal. They seemed to know it, too, as they plodded on resignedly, sad-faced, heads drooping in weariness, to the jingle of the bell mare's lead. Despite the vast meadows and apparently abundant food, the grazing of pack stock must be greatly restricted. When the long winter rolls around and the herds of deer and elk are forced out of the high country, there must be food available. So the mules had to pack their own food, and ours, too.

I did not consider myself a wrangler. Even the practice I'd had packing for hunting trips did not qualify me as a horse and mule trainer. I've been kicked a few times, stomped on a little, bitten on occasion, and watched the hard, hard ground come up to meet me a good many more times than I'd like known. Having fallen off my first horse at the age of three and been kicked in the belly at five, I don't even remember when I was first bucked off.

A wise old saddlemaker who lived on the south shore of Flathead Lake warned me right off: "Never trust anything you can ride. Surprise a horse and he may kick. You never surprise a mule — he kicks because he intends to." I'd been around mules only enough to tell that he knew what he was talking about. This was sufficient knowledge to keep the reflexes fast and eyes wide open, and to recognize that working inside a pole corral with a dozen or so wild mules would be a little risky. My first observations on the secrets of survival had been: don't trust anything; keep your eyes swiveling; jump fast; and keep a bale of hay or a tree between you and any mule that is not your friend. Still, the nagging thought remained: who's being trained —mule or man?

We were faced with a difficult assignment. Mules are more intelligent than most men, by some people's reckoning, and they also have a reputation for stubbornness. I doubt that they are necessarily stubborn; sometimes they just don't agree. To my way of thinking there are two methods of training, and the only way that has any chance of success is convincing the animal that this sort of thing was what it wanted to do all the time. Most of them are pretty congenial animals.

"Twelve hundred pounds of mule against 180 pounds of man isn't exactly an even contest," wrangler Bart began. "You gotta be smarter, and with a mule it ain't easy." Just then this long-legged, long-eared mule named Big Red casually eyed me, carefully measured, laid back his ears and, quick as a wink, spun around to aim a pair of large, economy-size hooves my way. I dodged successfully. It reminded me of a story my grandfather used to tell about the time he was in Kansas City at the livery stables when a gentleman who had been swigging too freely from a bottle of double-rectified corn squeezings staggered in between the mule stalls. He either fell or leaned against the rump of one of the animals. Lightning-quick, the mule lifted the drunk with his heels and deposited him at the heels of another mule across the way. Equally quick, before the man even touched the ground, the second mule returned the serve. Grandad said that the poor fellow never came close to the ground as half a dozen mules joined the fun, volleying him back and forth before the horrified crowd of onlookers could react. When the rescuers finally got him out of the aisle of the barn they figured he must be dead. He merely stood up, brushed off his clothes, and staggered out. Everyone agreed that had he been sober it would have killed him.

The training corral where we were working was fair-sized, constructed of lodgepole pines. The horizontal rails were about seven inches in diameter and well secured to vertical pilings at eight- to

ten-foot intervals. A well-plowed garden adjoined on the north, pro-
viding soft dirt to cushion the spills of man and mule. A doe-eyed
Jersey cow stood in the middle of the runway of a private airport for
hours at a time to watch our operations. John's mobile home was on
the west. The view to the east was of dense woods sweeping up to
the grandeur of the Swan Range, which would be our destination
with this wild-eyed bunch of four-legged, short-fused dynamite
charges, as soon as we had finished convincing them to do things
our way.

To train a mule you must understand him. Every one, just like a
man or a woman, is different. Some are placid, some lazy; every disposition you can find in humans is stowed away in some animal, and
in many combinations. But as with most humans, the best way to
start is by showing them that you mean no harm and will keep their
bellies full. The second thing is to teach them to wear a halter; the
third objective is to teach them to carry a load while following the
lead animal single file. After that, everything else is polishing the fine
points.

When we were in the second phase, teaching about halters and
their purpose, I met Tim Dalton. Tim was a quiet sort, not a bit
aggressive but filled with strength, both kinds. He and his family
were to accompany us during the filming; his wife was good-looking,
his kids attractive. Besides, they had their own horses. Tim and his
brother were stone masons, among other things. I'd heard rumors
about Tim's strength: he and his brother were reported to have picked
up a thousand-pound mantel stone and lifted it to the top of the fireplace; they didn't like the way it looked, so they picked it up again
and reset it.

One day I was busy wrestling with Big Red, a handsome critter
with a bit of fire in his eyes. He was doing pretty much as he pleased.
Every time I reached for Red's halter, that mule would sling his head
back. Tim was standing nearby, leaning against the corral, watching.
"Give me a hand, will ya, Tim?"

Tim reached over the logs and took hold of the halter. Big Red
started to pull back. Tim locked his thighs under the horizontal rail
of the corral, and using both hands pulled Red's head down, meanwhile bending that seven-inch rail upward about six inches, thus
convincing Red who was the stronger. We never had any trouble with

Red again, but if anyone ever says "strong as a mule," I know what he is talking about: almost as strong as Tim Dalton.

During the training period, there came a rainy spell, one of those long-term sessions that just kept at it till everything was one big sea of mud, especially in the corral where the mules lived. Earlier John had been bragging, with ample justification, about his property. Among the things he had done was to sink a new well and he insisted first thing that we taste the results, so that we could appreciate really good water. It did taste good, clear and sparkling, and he proudly pointed out the site of the well, in the center of the corral. As I looked, all I could see was a lot of mules standing rather dejectedly, knee-deep in black, squishing mud. Water was streaming off their bodies, dripping, splashing into the dark deepening pools. Suddenly the water didn't have its original appeal. In fact, my imagination began to run rampant, and Mary, not wanting to insult John's pride and joy, called me aside in a moment of privacy and suggested we start drinking coffee. This sounded like a great idea, so coffee was the requested refreshment. The weather soon cleared and the sun came out. Wrestling with mules is hard, hot work. The days grew warmer. Dessie, John's wife, a very kind and thoughtful individual, decided that it was just too hot for coffee, as indeed it was. One day she came out to where we were sweating profusely over the training and presented us with tall ice-filled glasses of lemonade, clinking sweet coolness. Mary, concerned over the possibility of mule sweat and the like, helped serve. Her typically ingenious solution was to excuse herself, take my glass to where our van was parked, and lib-erally sterilize the lemonade with alcohol (bourbon, if memory serves me correctly).

No one seemed the wiser, and the training sessions became much easier; in fact, they became downright pleasant. Bart began to show some curiosity and kept an eye on Mary, apparently wondering why she always took my lemonade to the car before serving it. I'm sure he did suspect something, for shortly he approached her and asked if she just might have some brandy to dampen his Skoal a bit. Whether the well water was a hazard was never resolved, but I noted that neither of us had any problems. Whatever worked in Bart's Skoal seemed to work for me, too.

We were having a great time. It was work—hot, hard, and sweaty labor—but we were slowly convincing the mules that it was to their advantage to do things our way. We would work them over the soft garden where a fall couldn't hurt them. One mule in particular had in mind taking off whenever he felt like it, and I learned it is impossible for a 180-pound man with only two legs to hold a 1,200-pound mule equipped with four, especially when he is already in gear by the time he comes to the end of the rope. This mule knew enough never to try it when tied to a post, or even snugged to another horse, but would take off for distant pastures nearly every time someone tried to lead him afoot.

It was a losing battle. Then I remembered a trick I had seen a long time ago called the "Running W." We would put on a pack saddle, or just a wide belt with three cinch rings around the belly of the mule. One end of a strong but soft (to prevent rope burns) rope is tied to, say, the left side of the cinch, then led through the ring of a leather hobble strap worn on the right forefoot. The rope then leads back from the hobble ring to the ring in the center bottom of the cinch, down again in the same manner through the other, or left forefoot, hobble ring, and then back through the left-hand cinch ring and thence to the trainer. It's a neat trick: you start out leading the animal, he takes off in his customary way, then, as he's just about to snatch you loose from the halter rope, you simply lean back and dig your heels in. As the rope comes tight it pulls up his forefeet and he lands on his chin, unhurt but for his pride, and wondering what happened. Two or three such episodes cure any tendency to take off without permission.

The shoeing as well as the fitting of pack saddles also had to be attended to. Each mule had his own saddle, adjusted to his particular contours, with the leather harnesses fitted. Of course, the riding animals were put through their paces at the same time. Things got smoother and smoother as each animal began to find his place, and we all got to speaking, if not the same language, at least so that we more or less understood one another.

From a couple of dozen available mules, Mary and I drew for our own use a fast-walking female for her and a long-legged, sleepy-looking gelding for me. I was skeptical of my mount at first. He was a homely critter, and I figured he had a streak of mulishness in him

until Bart demonstrated the mule's performance and his own skill
by riding around the pasture as he stood atop the saddle drinking a
milkshake. Mary's great for naming animals, not being content with
just saying, "Whoa, mule!" She named hers Rosinante, which she
quickly shortened to Rosie. After Rosie kicked Bart the first day on
the trail he referred to her as "Rosie-Damn-You." However, at the end
of a week of good behavior he conceded that Mary was right in calling her "Rosie-You-Sweet-Old-Thing." Bart soon concluded that Mary
and Rosie had reached an understanding, for whenever Mary approached, Rosie would begin to talk to her in a sweet and low tone
and would soon be chewing on the brim of Mary's straw hat before
she could dodge.

My animal had to be named, too, and Mary dictated that his
name henceforth would be Wilbur, "because he looks out from under
his eyelashes like Wilbur-What's-His-Name does." I didn't remember
Wilbur-What's-His-Name, but it did make me wonder. Whenever
Mary wasn't around I preferred to think of the mule as Old Tripod—
for I found that I could leave camera, film, sandwich, or anything
else in the saddle for thirty minutes at a time and Wilbur would not
budge.

I stopped him once with his left hind foot on a boulder. After
a while I concluded that I should move him, for I doubted that he
would have got around to moving on his own. I tested him once by
aiming him at a wall. He proceeded till his nose was less than an
inch from it, stopped, and seemingly went to sleep. I really think he
just didn't give a damn. He had seen it all before. He never kicked or
bit, yet when coaxed out of a walk into a gallop he would breeze past
the other animals in an apparently effortless lope. He was as sure-
footed as a fly, and so easy to ride that I could spend the entire day in
the saddle without strain.

Calm and collected, only twice was he ever startled. Once we
were leading a string along a mountain trail when, rounding a blind
corner, he came nose-to-nose with a hiker before either saw the other.
I don't know who was the more surprised. Wilbur just sat down on
full power brakes and was ready to switch ends and unload heavy
artillery before he realized what the apparition was. The hiker was
equally scared when he looked into a black face that resembled a

cow moose with a wad of tobacco in her cheek. The other time that Wilbur was upset was when his saddle slipped, but that story comes later.

Within a week, we hoped, we'd be heading into that primeval million-acre forest called "The Bob," to sample the cutthroat and the rainbow, spy on the grizzly, and watch the mountain goat clinging to the cliffs. There, we would be living and working in another world, of original wilderness unaltered, unpolluted by man.

4.

On the Continental Divide

Our caravan to The Bob left Swan Valley and proceeded to Hungry Horse, where a dirt road takes off to the southeast, following for twenty-five or thirty miles the rim of the gigantic reservoir that fills what was once a rich wildlife wintering range, sacrificed to an arguable need for a dam and more electricity. The road terminates at Spotted Bear Ranger Station, the northern entrance to the wilderness. At a wide spot laid out for parking—no motorized equipment of any sort is permitted beyond—we unloaded the stock trucks and automobiles and began to pack the mules. Our first day on the trail would be up to Meadow Creek where it branches, then a dozen or more miles to Gorge Creek and along its banks to our campsite. A Forest Service ranger station built of logs is the last stop, and when its flag disappears from view, you are on your own, for here is the line where the wilderness begins.

The Bob Marshall Wilderness extends over nearly one million acres of wild mountains, ranging to nine thousand feet in elevation and including sixty serpentine miles of the Continental Divide, great gorges and heavy timber interspersed with open meadows. It is immense beyond comprehension: according to legend, only one person has ever hiked it all, and that was Bob Marshall himself. He was among the greatest of conservationists, a professional forester who saw the need for preserving more than a sample of the land in its original form for both man and wildlife. He wrote that it is not sentimentalism that makes a virgin wilderness such a delight, but the physical demands of the trail that produce an élan unknown in man's normal surroundings. Cursed by the few who saw it their duty to eliminate all that is natural or wild, he was the prime force in the founding of The Wilderness Society. I find him in the same league as Leopold, Allen, Muir, Thoreau, Carhart, and Murie. He recommended that nearly all roadless areas of more than ten thousand acres be classed as "primitive," and at his own expense inventoried for the Forest Service all roadless areas in the United States exceeding three hundred thousand acres. The Bob is his, and America's, crowning glory.

We found the trail shaped to accommodate perfectly a mule and its packs. It was lined with tall trees, a dark, shadowy world that gave way to great open, grassy meadows, where elk were grazing in the distance, bulls with their antlers still in velvet. The path itself was little more than a foot wide, once a game trail, and had become well used from heavy traffic by vacationers, outfitters, and their pack strings. The Forest Service blazes, the smaller one above, the larger below, seemed hardly necessary. Red, lushly ripe thimbleberries lined the trail towards Black Bear Ranger Station. John leaned from the saddle to scoop up a few, while Snip, his stallion, snatched mouthfuls of berries, leaves and all, as they set the pace.

A little pond edged with cattails lay near where we stopped for lunch. Tufts of aquatic grasses and weeds formed tiny islands, and the entire surface of the water was dotted with ducks. Spring comes late in the high country: coots, wearing black coats and white faces, were busy courting and defending territory. We watched them squaring off at one another. Heads down, bills dragging the water, they made short charges that ended in confusion and explosions of spray. Ruddy ducks bobbed about, feeding, preening, and courting. The ruddy drake, so readily identified by his brilliant blue bill, bright cinnamon back, white face, and black hat, courted the female by pressing his bill against his breast, fanning his tail, and following the rather drab gray female. She responded by paddling into the bush with her head lowered to water level. Mallards were abundant. It looked like a good year for waterfowl.

Rain had begun to fall, and soon water was streaming from our slickers. In order to anticipate filming possibilities, Wilbur and I took the lead. Behind me, trailed by John, was the pack string of seven mules, plodding on, dripping water, their packs spattered with mud. Behind them, the rest of our party: Bart riding a mare, Mary

aboard Rosie, and the Daltons—Tim, Lola, and their sons, Tim, Jr.,
and Zach, ages thirteen and nine. Though more interested in having
just turned sixteen and possessing a driver's license, John's son Kert
also deigned to join us. Jack Mudgett was our indispensible camp
cook, and more.

Our trail grew steeper, skirting boulders and following the bank
of the flooded river that roared ceaselessly while cutting its way
through the bedrock towards the valley below. We reached Gorge
Creek, a seemingly bottomless stream bed that had carved its course
a few hundred feet deep through solid mountain. The trail had deteri-
orated, part of it having already been washed into the gorge by winter
storms and spring runoff, but by the time John had dragged seven
mules through an alternate route, we had a new trail that could be
considered almost passable.

Our first day's ride was not long. Getting the animals transported,
packed, and under way was a time-consuming test run. During the
rest of the summer we would be riding twice the twelve-mile distance and taking it in stride. Thoroughly soaked and exhausted from
the day's efforts, we reached our first campsite in communal misery.
Tents were set up and tarps stretched to keep off the worst of the
rain. Lodgepole pines furnished ridgepoles and awning supports. As
soon as the stove was unpacked, Jack started a hot meal. As official
cook, he went nowhere without a huge chef's knife, a sword of Ex-
calibur dimensions that was off limits to everyone else. Nor was he
ever found to be without his fishing rod.

One of the world's great wonders is the morale-restoring benefit
of a good meal. Eating in the wilderness consists of a big breakfast,
usually pancakes and bacon and eggs washed down with lots of
steaming coffee, but this would occur only after rounding up the
stock, feeding and tending them, and otherwise getting things in
shape for the coming day. Lunch was seldom honored and could
range from a candy bar or peanut butter sandwich to a corned beef
sandwich and coffee from a can. Supper might sometimes be late,
but it was the main meal of the day and always hearty. While Jack
and his appointed assistants prepared the food, the rest of us finished
the camp chores, set up tents, gathered firewood, and fed the stock
and tended their needs. No matter how wet, cold, tired, and sore the
crew, or how dark and wet the night, the horses and mules must be

unsaddled, unpacked, fed, and watered first. Then and only then can the needs of two-legged folk be considered.

Sunburst Lake lay another five or six miles beyond our Gorge Creek campsite. It was a sapphire set in an emerald-ringed basin. The reflection of the ice fields of Swan Glacier high above glittered under the blue skies of summer. The lake was fed by a half-dozen waterfalls that drained the icy waters from the melting snow only a short distance above. As a result, even in mid-summer, while the rest of the world sweltered, this lake remained thoroughly chilled. Early the following morning, as soon as we could finish breakfast, a mule named Josephine was given the honor of carrying our raft from campsite to lakeside. The raft was a stout twelve-foot Avon, designed to handle the rough rivers of foaming chutes and hidden boulders which we expected to encounter that summer.

On the rock- and log-littered shore of Sunburst we first found a shady place, well back from the water, where Josephine and the other stock could wait for us in relative comfort. Then we inflated the raft and launched ourselves onto the clear waters of the lake. Slipping along the shores, we could see great boulders 30 to 40 feet below the surface, and suddenly we were over a chasm of cobalt blue like that of the Gulf Stream—the lake is said to reach depths of more than 240 feet.

Beside a waterfall was where the fishing started. It seemed logical that the fish would be feeding there. Mary chose for her fishing site a large rock near one of several cascading waterfalls. The flattened boulder, fifteen or twenty feet across, jutted into the lake like a natural pier, backed up to dense thickets covering a steep slope. Beyond a rock slide, almost out of sight of Mary, Tim and his family chose an overhang from which to do their fishing. A brown ice fly with a round head, like a jig with a fly-tied tail, created just for the trip by Jack, proved to be the only producer. And such a producer! Big cutthroats rose to almost every cast of our ultralight tackle. The strike was light, but the fight came quickly, and lasted. As I was filming, I found myself thinking that these were among the last truly native fish—at least they fought like no hatchery-raised models in my experience. Bart and John were fishing from the raft and Bart caught the largest fish of the day. I'd guessed its weight at well over four pounds when he announced he could eat the whole thing

by himself. Bets were made immediately, and Bart accepted the
challenge.

With the day drawing to a close and long shadows beginning
to reach across the lake, we gathered up our gear for the ride back
to camp. When we crossed the lake to pick up Mary, Tim, and his
family, I noticed Mary looking a little pale, and quite anxious to see
me. She was glancing nervously at the underbrush.

"How was the fishing?" I asked.

She answered softly, "It was big!" I thought she meant the fish,
but she was talking about a bear. "I could hear it breathing, it woke
me up! I'll tell you about it later. I'd like to get back to camp."

Jack was first on the trail. Though a competent horseman, he
prefers to hike in tenny runners and always carries his fishing rod.
He had taken off at his characteristic half-lope, saying he'd have
supper started by the time we got Josephine loaded. We took special
care this time with the oars, for their rattling had upset her on the
way in and set her to bucking.

The forest was dark and dense. Great logs, undone by some long-
forgotten storm, lay crossed and heaped in various stages of decay.
Small streams meandered among the rocks, forming bogs and small
pools. The animals threaded their way along the trail through a
jumble of boulders and jagged slabs of rock. Small warblers flashed
in sunlit openings and stopped to sing. Huckleberries, large and
luscious, lined the trail. Ahead was a burn of several hundred acres,
covered now with tall stems of bright pink fireweed, green bear grass,
purple thistles, and flame-red Indian paintbrush. Over all towered
the gaunt skeletons of once-magnificent trees a hundred feet tall,
their branches dead, their golden bark burned black, thanks to a
careless hunting party that had left a campfire smoldering a few years
before.

Just as we topped a knoll, Jack reappeared out of the timber,
panting. On the run, he waved his arms for us to stop. "Grizzly
ahead!" He gasped his story: "About a quarter-mile up there I came
over the hill and this boulder stood up and started moving towards
me. I damn near ran into it before I saw it. It's at least eight feet tall!
I didn't stop to see any more."

We held a council of war—nowhere to go but ahead, for the route
back was fifty-four miles over the mountains. The women and kids

rode in the rear and sang, half-heartedly but loud, for we wanted the bear to know that we were around and not surprise it again. The armed men took the lead, I with a camera. I was also carrying a .38 special, which until then had seemed rather formidable as handguns go. Somehow, just thinking about the bear's towering presence, I felt as if the barrel had melted and become about as effective as a three-inch pocket knife with a rubber blade. Tim followed with his .357 magnum and Jack wielded his spinning rod. Mary said our procession made her think of *Peter and the Wolf*.

We gave that bear every opportunity for dignified retreat. I figured that it could have had any one of us if it had so chosen—Jack, or a mule, or little Zach's pony. By the time we got to where it had been surprised by Jack, the bear was gone. Oversized tracks and territorial marks were everywhere, torn logs and a big area cleared of huckleberries. That day was my first introduction to grizzlies. We were glad that the animal had opted for a meal of fresh fruit.

Supper was a little late, but fresh trout was the main course, well fortified with side dishes. With much encouragement that evening under the stars, by the light of Coleman lantern and campfire, Bart ate his four-pound fish. It was served on an old military stainless steel mess tray about eighteen inches long. Both head and tail of the fish hung over the ends. He ate it and we confirmed that he had eaten the whole fish. So we paid our bets, and he moaned in his sleep most of the night.

That night, after Mary and I were snug in our own tent and sleeping bags, I asked her about the bear she saw at the lake that morning.

"I was fishing and lost the only lure I had. I was a little tired, so with the warm sun and all, I thought it was a good time to take a nap. I put the life jacket down as a pillow. It was so nice and warm, and with the sound of the waterfall, I dozed right off. Next thing I was aware of was this heavy breathing. I didn't think I breathed like that, so I just kept my eyes closed and held my breath. The heavy breathing kept on, right over my head! I didn't know what to do, with everyone else gone, you off in the raft fishing and the rest all the way down the gorge. I thought about escaping by rolling over into the lake, but I knew it was so awfully cold that I couldn't last long even if I could take the life jacket with me, so I didn't move, just froze, hoping it would go away. After a bit the breathing didn't seem so heavy, but there was the smell of a wild animal. I opened my eyes very carefully, in time to see this big bear with a hump ambling away towards the bushes. He disappeared in moments, so I started breathing again, just before you came back to pick me up."

I was happy that I still had a wife.

The day that we decided to photograph mountain goats, three of us were on the trail earlier than usual—John, Bart, and I with one pack mule—up the slopes of Inspiration Point a few miles above Sunburst Lake. We had sighted goats in that neighborhood previously and thought that by reaching the top early enough, we could get some film of these rockhoppers. Having a touch of acrophobia, I become really nervous in high places and break out in a sweat just at the thought of setting foot on a fire escape or climbing a fire tower. Still, I felt confident that I could photograph a goat from a friendly ridge without difficulty, if I didn't think about it too much. The weather outlook was good; it was clear and hot. No chance of rain, insisted one of the party, "We've had all the rain we're gonna have this summer." Though a high, thin layer of cirrus clouds gave me some doubts, I kept them to myself. Who was I, the Carolina dude, to contradict the Weather Service, the radio stations, and our guide?

We located the site of an old hunting camp in late afternoon, after a long, hard trip. Though it had obviously been in use the previous winter, the camp looked as if it had been abandoned in a hurry. Firewood was still stacked, and there were remnants of a temporary corral and some moldy hay. Staking the stock, we dropped pack and saddles, dished out a quart or so of oats to each of the animals, and got a fire going. The tin can that we'd used to measure oats we rigged with a wire bail for a coffee pot, for we were traveling light. As it boiled on the coals we dug into the saddlebags and procured a can of meat and some bread for a complete supper.

By the time we had finished eating, darkness was obscuring all but the red glow of our campfire that reflected off the trees and clumps of beargrass. A thin overcast denied us anything but the palest light from the heavens. No matter where we looked there was nothing but blackness. The feeling of wilderness was all about, and we heard no sounds but the sigh of wind, and now and then the stamping or shuffling of horses' feet. We were too tired to sit up for long. While Bart was making a final bed check of the animals, I secured the cameras in case of rain, and remembered John's mention of having seen grizzlies in this immediate area the last time he was here. I suspected that John was a little apprehensive, too, for he was insisting that a defense circle be set up. Wilbur, my mule, stood to the northeast of camp and Snip, John's stallion, to the northwest. Jack, the pack mule, had the southeast position, while Lady, Bart's bay mare, guarded the southwest. The outer defense was duly warned that, if they expected to be alive tomorrow, they'd have to let us know in plenty of time should a bear show up.

I'd slid into my sleeping bag, rolled up my shirt to serve as a pillow, and was dozing off to a lullaby of wind in the trees when the first big wet drop hit me. With great haste we rigged ponchos, manties, and poles into a shelter, prayed that the wind wouldn't blow too hard, and turned in again. The rain spattered off and on all night. Dawn broke with a magnificence of red-tinged black clouds piled on the horizon. Soon shafts of light from a warm golden sun were caught in the raindrops dangling from spruce needles. A small pond below glittered its reflections. I stirred up the fire and was coaxing the coffee to a boil when a slight movement caught my eye. Our mounts were all standing alert as bird dogs, ears cocked forward. They were watching a five-point elk, antlers in ragged velvet, observing our camp from less than fifty yards away. I tried to get hold of the camera, but as I moved ever so slowly towards it, the elk faded into the trees. Oh well, there'd be another time.

After quick rations to the horses and ourselves, we hastily threw everything into manties, and packed and saddled the stock. Heading up the trail to the pass where the goats were known to hang out, we followed a steep, rocky ridge where you could spit a thousand feet or more down either side. We tied the animals in a clump of spruce on the edge of a wide-open mountain face. Because of his crippled foot, John stayed to guard them while Bart and I took off on foot to investigate other rock faces for signs of goats.

It wasn't an easy trip, and signs were few, but Bart knew what he was doing and kept insisting that there were goats around. By midmorning we came upon fresh tracks and a clump of white hair clinging to the brush. Just then a billy got up leisurely from behind a rock not seventy-five yards away and meandered up the rock face, as if more bored than disturbed. He was big, all creamy white, with gleaming black horns. Our strategy was to get above him for filming. Soon I found myself standing on a tiny foothold on a vertical rock face, filming the antics of a goat directly below, the camera lens pointing between my feet. The big fellow wandered along what appeared to be a sheer cliff, nibbling at tiny clumps of vegetation and finally jumping from rock to rock in his descent to a pool three or four hundred feet below us. So engrossed was I that I was no longer conscious of my surroundings until, looking up at the bottom of Bart's feet, I saw that his boot tips were barely clinging to a rock as he pulled himself straight up. The top of the cliff was still another hundred feet above him.

How do we get ourselves into such scrapes? Of course it's because of an overwhelming interest in the subject. I was now very much aware of my untenable position, but I could not afford to allow my natural cowardice to take command. If I had, I suspect that I would still be there, frozen forever against the cliff. Passersby, if ever they should wander that way, would see the petrified cameraman too scared to live, a permanent blot on the mountain face. As it was, one crack at a time, sometimes backing and altering course, we worried ourselves upward. There was no way down.

Not until we had scrambled, sweating and exhausted, back to the ridge top that we could follow back to the horses was I in a position to notice the weather. It was clouding up, and in almost no time the distant sound of thunder began echoing among the peaks. We hurried as fast as we could to where John and the horses were waiting, but the storm was moving up the valley even faster, obscuring distant mountains with rolling clouds of black and gray, their brilliant white tops boiling and jagged shafts of lightning dancing within. The first gusts of wind were rattling the trees and sending the dry forest duff whirling when we got back to a worried John. It was too late to move to a more protected place. The storm was upon us.

I tried desperately to recall the proper thing to do in a thunderstorm. There were fractured trees all about, and every one of them looked like a successful lightning rod that had been scarred and burned by a thousand bolts. The horses were in the only copse of any size and that wasn't much. I glanced at them, their tails tucked under, sterns to the wind, and knew that it wasn't a safe place.

Neither was the rock face, where already we could feel the growing electricity in the air and smell the ozone as the rock-busting lightning danced closer and closer. All I could think to do was to keep as low as possible, off any exposed area, except that it was all exposed, and out from under any trees. In a shallow dip in the rocks was a cluster of fallen trees, lying in criss-cross confusion. We headed for them, hunkered up on them while keeping as low as we could, but still off the ground, hoping that they would furnish some insulation as the first blast of sleet and rain engulfed us.

The fury of a mountain storm comes from a collision of titanic forces. I have dodged tornadoes and ridden out hurricanes, but when the mountain gods get to quarreling and throwing their fire shafts, the battlefield becomes an indescribable confusion of lights, sounds, and sensations. You feel the hair on your body stand, and the very rocks seem to tingle with blue voltage. Every sense tells of disaster and the feeling builds with the hissing of lightning that explodes in great sheets of flame, above and below and all about, sending shards of shattered rock or tree fragments sizzling through the air like artillery shells bursting.

Sleet and icy rain came in slashing deluges, sheeting the world in grays and whites, while uninterrupted rolls and crashes of thunder shook the earth. The mountains seemed to rock and shudder. Already deafened, we could feel the drumming pressure of the sound. Even thunder can be only so loud when each crash is echoed and its echo repeated, rumbling through and across the valleys. Between gusts and blasts, we could see the horses, tied in the scant shelter of scrub cedars, their backs humped to the storm and glistening wet with sleet.

The gods were kind. Perhaps they had only issued a warning to the trespassers caught in the realm of the mountain kings. The storm passed down the valley and we watched it below us. It was filled with firebrands, shorting circuits, complete with smoke and flame. I believe that all of us were surprised to find ourselves still among the living, and thankful to discover that the horses had survived. We slung the soaking packs on the mule, cinched up saddles, and headed down the muddy, streaming slopes. We were wet to the skin, chilled by the sleet and wind; we had water sloshing from filled boots and running like ice down our necks, backs, arms, and legs. I was wearing a wool shirt and gloves. The gloves looked like the udder of a cow, full to bursting. Only under the wide brim of my Stetson was there any semblance of dryness. The others were, if possible, even more miserable, wearing cotton and polyester, and John's black hat dribbled long black streamers of dye down his face and shirt. It was twelve long, cold, and wet miles back to camp, where dry clothes, tents, and warm food waited.

When it was time for the Daltons to return to home and jobs, we all came out, to ship film to the processor, pick up fresh supplies, and take real baths. Immediately six of us—John, Bart and his wife Shirley, Jack, Mary, and I—headed back into the hills, the understated name given to the back country by those to whom it is a second home. If there is a single trail that will expose one to the maximum of The Bob, it would be the most used one, which follows the South Fork of the Flathead River. From Spotted Bear it wanders south-southeast between the Swan Range and the Continental Divide through the heart of the wilderness. Our pack string of mules was doing pretty well by now, getting along with one another and with us, but there were still a few rough spots.

We had unloaded our new provisions from the trucks, made up the packs, and had the mules loaded and ready to go. I was repacking the camera and new film and everything was just about set when John, a little impatient, decided to start the string down the trail to keep the restless animals from getting tangled up. My dependable mule, Wilbur, was standing nearby, patiently waiting while I tinkered with my gear. Bart had put on Wilbur's saddle and was just saddling his mare when from down the trail came a shout, "Hey Bob! Come a-runnin'! I got troubles!" Figuring that some one of the string had decided to go on the wrong side of a tree, I dropped what I was doing and, snatching the reins, took a flying leap onto Wilbur. It was a mistake. Bart had saddled, but not tightened the cinch—something every rider must check for himself. As soon as my foot hit the stirrup, the saddle slid under the beast, and I found myself lying in a pile of rock rubble under Wilbur.

The combination of my rush, leaping aboard, and the slipping saddle scared the reliably placid mule. He went sky high. Although I was able to get my foot out of the stirrup, the rocks prevented me from rolling out of the way fast enough, and all thousand-plus pounds of Wilbur came to earth at the junction of my hip bone, belt buckle, and belly. I faintly remember seeing him disappearing into the woods in a series of high jumps, the saddle ricocheting beneath his belly. The next thing I noticed was that I was hurting, staggering around in circles, thinking, "At least my hip isn't broken or I wouldn't be standing." Mary and Jack helped me onto the bunk in our van. Bart, seeing that I was in good hands, rode off to help John.

Now I was wondering what was inside me that could be ruptured. While I was getting my wind back, pulling the parts together, and checking for blowouts or leaks, Jack had sprinted to the creek to get water for tea. As soon as I'd downed that, he insisted that I try walking. Then Mary pulled out of my vest pocket the shattered remains of my light meter and Jack picked my .38 revolver out of the dust. The force of the blow had burst every seam in the holster. It was fortunate for me that I was wearing the gun, for it helped spread the force of the blow.

By this time Bart had got John out of whatever predicament he was in and had caught and calmed Wilbur. The rest was up to me. Though hurting, I was about fifty miles from the nearest hospital, and thus far I couldn't detect any major interior disruptions. After a few minutes of self-reassuring, I decided that we could continue. I was aware that I couldn't walk very far, that the only choice was to ride the next fifteen to twenty miles to camp. Eventually I turned purple from navel to knee, but was able to stagger around and got out of a lot of chores for a while.

Living off the land that summer was no hardship: we had cutthroat trout, a few whitefish, and an occasional Dolly Varden, locally known as bull trout. And then there were huckleberries. Along the trail Mary described a dozen ways to prepare them, not including just standing in the patch and feasting. Plenty of huckleberries had accounted for fewer than usual bear raids on campsites, so said the Forest Service. Still, there were many signs of bear all around.

One argument that many conservationists wrangle over is that Montana still allows the sport hunting of grizzlies. This great and endangered beast, which once ranged over almost all of the western states, is now limited to a relatively small range in three ecosystems. One is the Yellowstone area, another is the Cabinet-Yaak, and the largest is the area where we were, the Northern Continental Divide:

from somewhat south of the Bob Marshall Wilderness north to include Glacier National Park. Some groups contend that the bear must
not be hunted, estimating that there are probably no more than 400
grizzlies outside of Glacier in the hunted ecosystem. Montana's Fish
and Game Commission is said to argue that management of the bear
is complex, and the reason that they have been able to maintain a
healthy population is that they are able to open and close hunting
seasons according to immediate needs. It is pointed out that man
and bear have traditionally conflicted only when the bear has inter-
fered with human enterprises. Consideration of private land owner-
ship is important, and the compatibility of man and bear behavior.

It has been noted that in nonhunted areas like Glacier and Yellowstone parks, fifty-nine people have been killed or injured in the past
twenty years. Outside the parks, including all the Lower 48, Canada,
and Alaska, thirty-three incidents, with thirty-five injuries, have been
reported in that twenty-year period. It is in the best interest of the
bear that the killings of humans stop, for every time a human is killed
retribution is swift—one or more bears.

It is the unhunted bears, especially those within the Yellowstone
and Cabinet-Yaak areas, that are in the most danger. Almost all of the
bears killed in these areas were killed by a government agency, and
most of them had already been handled by man—often in the name
of research by well-intentioned individuals. Understandably, researchers are forever trying to learn all there is to know about bears,
and they do so with all their high-tech ability. An animal is trapped,
drugged, collared, weighed, measured, tattooed, radio tracked. The
bear, though immobilized physically by drugs, is very much aware of
what is happening; he isn't stupid. After such an incident he knows
that the man-animal is not going to hurt him, therefore why be afraid
of man? This is the same lesson he learns in the parks. On the other
hand, those animals living in the wild in hunted areas learn very
quickly that man cannot be trusted and should be avoided if at all
possible.

In some ways it seems as if man, in order to protect the wild,
insists, usually in the name of science, on removing as much wild
as he can. In a sense, it is a case of emasculation of the wilderness
to remove any mystery, any danger; this is especially notable in the
national parks. Here, some of our more misguided public servants

seek to remove all possible threats to man, while retaining only the appearance of wilderness. To me, "wild" means to live and compete and adapt with chance, for only those animals and plants that can survive on such a basis can be truly wild. Hunting, if managed with the long-term interests of the species in mind, can be beneficial, and keeping the population within the carrying capacity of its habitat enhances the possibility of species survival.

This aspect is often overlooked by well-meaning people who worry a great deal about an individual being and in doing so condemn a species. Of course the whole problem of endangered wildlife is still tied to habitat, and thus we find that it is an endless cycle. Many an individual can recall the slaughter, some years back, of approximately fifteen hundred elk by government hunters in the Yellowstone area, a sanctuary that prohibits hunting in order to protect the animals. The excessive killing was the result of an overpopulation that had occurred because a basic tool—natural predation—was left out of management. I doubt that the elk preferred government hunters over natural predators or private hunters.

It hadn't taken us long to become fully settled into the routine and to look for photographic opportunities and wildlife. The camp consisted of two large wall tents erected back-to-back, one filled with sleeping gear and shared by the crew. The mess tent for cooking and supplies, with an attached fly for shelter while eating, was the center of camp activity. Mary and I had our own backpack tent, set up separately. Nearby was a hammock I'd brought along for necessary siestas. Soon I found that I had to get there fast to claim it. On cold mornings, the favorite place to stand was near the little wood stove, with its ever-present pot of coffee. By the time sun hit camp we'd be moving out on the day's work. Fishing was superb. It was ego-satisfying fun to catch a big cutthroat and have to release it because it was too large for the pan.

The Flathead River's South Fork dwindles during late summer to a relatively quiet mountain stream. The onrushing torrents of the spring thaw's melting snow, uprooting trees and tumbling boulders, no longer prevail. Now it is a peaceful valley of woods and meadows. of mountains and overhanging cliffs; a green-clad retreat where elk peer from stands of lodgepoles while enjoying their midday siesta.

A reluctant bell mare throws her pack and refuses to cooperate

On the trail: an alpine meadow, Glacier National Park

Mary Simpson pauses to get her breath, near Boulder Pass

Flight of geese, on Missouri River

Sunrise, from tent along the Continental Divide

Royal Brunson and Bob Makala with deer in canoe, Judith Basin

Mule deer on ridge, Judith Basin

Breaking camp at Gorge Creek, Bob Marshall Wilderness

Franc White bringing trophy antlers back to camp, Ontario

Denali, also known as Mount McKinley, on a rare day when the whole mountain is visible

Reflections off Alaskan lake

Here, where a lone eagle soared high above us, and a goat climbed easily to the highest crag, was an idyllic setting for floating the river in our raft, to fish the pools and watch the scenery drift by. Bart packed the raft on one of the mules and headed upstream to a flat; John, Jack, and I followed close behind, toting fishing gear and cameras. Bart then returned with the stock to a pickup point downstream. Jack, by now acknowledged as the master fisherman, was testing some of his newest fly designs. John and I prepared the raft and regarded Jack's success with envy.

The river was glass clear, a mingling of quiet pools, of polished rocks, of wavering green mosses tossing in the current, of drifting fish and a panorama of passing beaches, forests, and rocks. There was the constant murmur of the shallows. Then we'd be caught suddenly in the current and swirled downstream, dodging boulders and logs, to be deposited into another quiet pool. A few moments of casting into every crevice, and abruptly another chute, and we were whisked past a gravel bar, whipped around a bend and into more riffles. Innocent trout leaped clear of the water in their eagerness to seize a fly; next we'd see the stunning but brief reflection of a snow-topped mountain in still waters, before a flash and the roar of wings as a wood duck took flight before us.

The unceasing murmur of the river became a rumble, and the rumble grew louder. As we slipped along, the river narrowed and picked up velocity as it snatched us through a narrow cut. We pulled up to a convenient gravel bar, where I stepped out. Jack and I studied the situation and agreed: maybe we ought to hand-line the raft around the fast water. John laughed at our doubts; after all, had he not skippered boats in the sounds and off the feared Carolina Capes in all weather and spent a bit of time in Alaska's waters, too? He was full of confidence. I picked up my camera, Jack his rod. I was willing to film John's expertise. Jack preferred to fish.

John shoved off. The spray flew as he deftly guided the raft into the mainstream, fairly flying. He aimed between a snag and a boulder, and the current caught him, tossing him sideways. Control lost, the raft slammed against the boulder, sliding up its side. The raft hung there a moment before the water cascaded into the interior, pinning it like a leech to the moss-beslimed boulder. John, with a notable degree of haste, scrambled to safety on top of the rock, and we watched helplessly as the water plucked out the contents of the raft. Oars and life jackets bobbed downstream. Camera case and film bags floated after, followed by lunch box, Thermos, pumps, more life jackets, and an assortment of clothing.

The whole flotilla, except for the raft and John, disappeared around the bend. John was stranded, and looking around we discovered that we were, too, for we were on an island, civilization eighty or so miles away. John was trying to salvage what he could. The creel, loaded to capacity with fish already dressed for supper, was lodged against the seat. Grabbing a strap, he hauled it out. "At least we can still eat!" He heaved it towards the bar where Jack was waiting. Too heavy, it fell short and the swirling stream swallowed it. Teetering on the edge of the raft was my tripod; that rescue was successful. John saw a leather strap flapping underwater, snagged it, and pulled out my tape recorder, sloshing full of water, and tossed it to me. A long nylon line was secured to the bow. Jack, up to his chest in the rushing, icy current, hooked it with his fishing gear, landed it, took a strain, and John pried at the raft. They couldn't budge it until I was able to get a firm hold on Jack. Finally were we able to worry it off the rock.

John was too slow to jump aboard and he was stranded. So we dragged the raft back upstream and let it float down at the end of the line. As it swung by the rock John flopped aboard and we swung it ashore. It was at least another five miles to camp, where Bart and the rest were waiting, and the raft was the only practical way to get there. Oarless and gearless, we set off, poling and paddling with the tripod and a stick. Ahead, we saw a life jacket, then an oar, and another jacket. For the better part of the next two miles we were retrieving gear, floating or lodged against the banks. The last thing we found was the camera case, complete with film, lenses, filters, and sundry sodden objects. Nearly submerged, it bobbed before us, awaiting rescue.

The sun was setting behind a blue-gray ridge, its rays filtering through tall spruce and fir, before we spotted the orange and white tents of camp. The women were sitting before the fire tending something, and Wilbur, my forgiving and forgiven mule, brayed his greetings as we made for the beach. We were cold and wet, hungry and tired, but very happy to be back, even though we had lost both the day's catch and the day's film, except for what was in the camera.

After we had finally secured our footage of The Bob, life was pretty much of a letdown, especially with the prospect of several thousand feet of film to edit, which was not our preferred way to approach Indian summer. But we still needed elk footage. Not that we hadn't seen and photographed them; but to get really good wildlife action on film is far harder than hunting them. We knew that a few were in Glacier National Park, but access would be difficult. Another possibility was Yellowstone. But the best prospect was the National Bison Range near Moiese, Montana. It wasn't far from our headquarters on Flathead Lake, and big bulls shouldn't be hard to find.

Around four o'clock one frost-kissed morning, with every blade of grass seeming to glisten white under the stars, we loaded Snip and young Johnnie's gelding Thunder aboard the truck and started down the east shore of the lake. Mary and John's wife Dessie followed in our van with provisions. The valley lay dark except for a scattering of ranch lights. A quarter moon hung low over the Mission Mountains and cast a cool bluish glow over new-fallen snow. The yellow light spilling into the darkness from windows of the Bison Range office told us that the manager was waiting for us. I could smell his breakfast cooking, bacon and eggs and coffee, even before we knocked at the door. I never cease marveling at those who are always impatient for dawn to break and are at work long before the sun gives so much as a hint of making an appearance. We joined him for coffee while he outlined the rules for riding on the range and gave us a few suggestions.

His first warning was to stay clear of the buffalo, but if we found ourselves near the beasts, the most important thing was to keep ourselves on the uphill side. A buffalo is fast, but lazy. He can keep up with and even outrun a horse, but he won't pursue uphill unless forced. We hadn't come to film buffalo and even hoped to avoid them, but it seemed like a fair warning, for several hundred were in the neighborhood. I knew that he understood what he was talking about, having watched the range personnel riding the annual roundup. For excitement and danger there is nothing like being pursued by stampeding buffalo, and stampeding them was the only way a roundup could be managed.

We'd seen horsemanship in that roundup in a class apart from the best rodeo riding. The procedure was to crowd a small, manageable band of buffalo along a fence line leading to the corrals. We could hear and feel them first, the ground quivering under the thunder of hooves, then a tower of dust rising above a knoll just before the huge animals came into view. They roared past us, the horsemen riding flat out, one in particular close on the heels of the racing buffalo. All we could see in the commotion was a dozen or so of the lead animals, but we could hear and feel the rest of the herd following. Nearing the corral, a heavily built wall of large logs, the brown mass of horns and fury turned into the enclosure, and the lead rider set his horse sliding on its heels. Nearly hidden in the cloud of flying dirt, the horse was still moving as the rider leapt clear of the saddle to slam the massive corral gate shut before the buffalo could circle inside and escape. When the herd was contained, he remounted the excited and dancing horse at what seemed a full gallop. It looked like a good way to commit suicide.

Horses unloaded, cinches tightened, we rode up the steep, dry hillsides in search of elk as the first rays of light were burning across the rugged mountain horizon. It was still too dark for filming, but we figured we had better get on location and find some subjects before the sun was too high. The air was sweet and cool with the scents of mountains and sage. A golden eagle soared above the next ridge and a nervous band of antelope watched from across the draw. Though I was shivering a bit in the crispness of the day, the horses were soon sweating. We had already kicked out some mule deer with racks big enough to pass for elk. Pausing to let the horses get their breaths, I dismounted, pulled the movie camera from my pack, checked the light meter, then unscrewed the cap from the zoom lens. I was ready.

By now the sun was casting its warmth across my shoulders, and it felt good. Ahead was a dense thicket of ponderosa pines and shoulder-high brush. John saw the elk first, just the glint of white-tipped antlers. I was below the bull and had to get above somehow without disturbing him. Unlike my mule Wilbur, Thunder was no tripod. John and I consulted in whispers. Often elk are not spooked by a horse or even a man riding one, but I had to get close. Even riding, by the time I could get off the horse, set up the tripod, and locate the animal in the viewfinder, he would be long gone.

It occurred to us that if I kept behind Thunder, walking, the elk might not notice me and spook before I could set up the camera. We decided to try it. I had forgotten one thing—how blasted steep the trail was. Only a few feet of trying to keep up with a healthy range horse heading up the mountainside took my wind. Desperate, I grabbed Thunder's tail and let him haul me up the slope. I could see the elk watching, half hidden in the shade of some brush, almost invisible. At last I reached a screening bush that allowed me to let go of Thunder's handle, jam the tripod legs into the ground, and swing what I hoped was still a prefocused lens to where the beast lay.

It was a beautiful piece of film, if I do say so. The scene opens with a view of mountains, trees, and a dark shadow beside a jumble of boulders and bushes. Then, slowly and dramatically, the shadow, a great seven-point bull elk, rises, pauses, and steps out at gradually increasing speed, his hooves sending out little puffs of dust and rolling rocks. Accelerating among the trees scattered along the dry hillside, he reaches the crest and runs parallel to us, head thrown back, the massive antlers lying along his back as he continues in perfect silhouette against the skyline before finally disappearing. It was all the footage we needed.

The rest of the day we spent riding about looking for more opportunities, shooting a few feet here and there. We had completed the film. It was now just a matter of editing, polishing, and writing the narration. Mary and I would spend the next few weeks working undisturbed in a small cottage beside Flathead Lake to complete our part of the job. Later, Chet Huntley would do the narration and the film eventually would go public as *Escape to the High Country*.

5.

Along the
Wild Missouri

After a summer of working, our labors consisting of camping, fishing,
riding, and hiking, Mary and I felt that we needed a vacation, a
chance to go out and relax, maybe do a little camping, fishing, hiking, and riding, and see some more of the lesser-visited countryside before settling into our film editing. By this time Royal and Bette
Brunson had finished Royal's stint as naturalist in Glacier Park. They
too wanted a break before he resumed his duties at the university. He
suggested a float trip down the Missouri River, and it seemed like a
good idea. Mary and I had our blue canoe, in addition to the raft that
we had used while filming in The Bob. The season was drawing to a
close, but there was still a bit of summer left to be enjoyed at the
lower elevations.

The historic Missouri River Breaks is a wild and isolated region
of rugged barrens and water, a fantasy land of towering white cliffs,
of rapids and cottonwood groves. These badlands of the West were
so remote that from the time we left Fort Benton there would not be
another town for at least 200 miles. Three small, seasonal cable
ferries, a few lonely ranches, and one bridge more than 150 miles
downstream—that was all. Here Lewis and Clark made their way
upstream in 1805, the first white men, probably the first men ever,
to cross the western plains and mountains. This portion of the river
has remained virtually unchanged since then.

We carried copies of a somewhat later expedition's charts, drawn
in the 1890s, that seemed more accurate, more useful than modern
charts. On Deadman's Rapids we found a raft pontoon—from an
expedition that had failed? Maybe the party was still wandering

around, looking for civilization. There was no reasonable way out, I figured, once committed to the river. It was about 250 miles from our departure point, Fort Benton, to the next town, Fort Peck, with a total of five crossings between.

Fort Benton was once the head of navigation for mid-nineteenth-century river traffic, where the explorers and fur traders landed, calling it "the Chicago of the Plains." It was also the starting point for the historic Whoop-Up Trail. In the mid-1800s the Missouri was the most important of all western routes. Beginning at St. Louis, steamboats transported supplies, ranging from plows to powder, upriver every spring flood. The river above was blocked by "the great falls," so described to Lewis and Clark by the Indians. The falls proved to be an insurmountable obstacle to further navigation. At Fort Benton the supplies were unloaded and several trails, including the Whoop-Up, led out of this boom town of the northwest. The Whoop-Up was the major route into Canada. Western gold seekers and cattlemen used Fort Benton as a supply point. It was the only early trading post in Montana to become a town.

The fort and the little settlement have been immortalized by the Western artist, Charles Russell, in *Wagon Master*. They still retain the flavor of the trailhead of the Old West, in the heart of Blackfeet, Piegan, and Assiniboine territory. Just north of us, the final major Indian battle was fought in 1877 and the last native Americans subdued. Chief Joseph had led 250 Nez Percé warriors in holding off 5,000 troops for five months, losing 239 of his people in their desperate flight to the Canadian border.

In Fort Benton, before we got under way we had been briefed on sites of old forts and outstanding landmarks by Gail Stensland, a vocational education teacher engaged in a river float venture. With our 1880s chart, we were in business. The current, though considerable in September—upwards of four miles an hour—was much slower than during the high water of spring runoff. After the Marias and Teton rivers drain the northeastern slopes of the Rockies, the Missouri broadens to some three hundred feet. Laden with minerals, it knifes the plains and picks up the soil that gives it the name "Big Muddy." Some river lovers wonder why the Mississippi, rather than the Missouri with its vast drainage of mountains and plains, was designated the "Father of Waters."

The day that we launched into the Missouri the river soon turned rough, with whitecaps and flying spray. The canoe was getting harder to control by the minute. Behind us an enormous cloud of dust was smoking down the deep canyon, and the wind was carrying tumbleweeds high above the whitewater. Bette and Royal, ahead of us in the raft, were carrying the bulkier items of the outing, with their water-loving dachshund Chamois tied short atop the duffle.

I yelled at them, but they couldn't hear above the roar of wind and water. Remembering the whistle attached to my fishing vest, I blew a blast. When Royal looked back, I motioned towards the menacing black cloud. They dug in their paddles, and the raft skittered across the river. Paddling frantically now, we tried to make shore through short, steep waves that were slopping over the sides of the canoe. I steered towards a sheer cliff with a fringe of rocks. Hoping that we wouldn't hit any submerged rocks as we raced along the shore, I shouted to Mary, "Take a line and jump!"

She bailed out, slipped and, despite anything that I could do, the canoe slid across her legs as she lay half out of the water, still hanging onto the line. She crawled ashore, and I back-paddled. But still the canoe slammed into the rocks, and a wave or two swept aboard before we could haul it clear of the raging river. The winds were lashing at us in a hurricane frenzy by the time we could secure the craft. We scurried behind a boulder and watched the wind pick off wave tops and scatter them like puffs of smoke. The raft had disappeared down a river blanketed in clouds of dust; Bette and Royal were nowhere to be seen.

Trying to reassure ourselves with the thought that the raft was the safest place they could be, we waited for the storm to abate. In thirty minutes or so the wind had eased enough for us to sponge out the canoe and start our search for the others. Perhaps a mile downstream we spotted the raft on the beach. Our friends stepped out from behind some willows, where they claimed to have been napping, and asked where we had been so long.

Stars were shining through the cottonwoods, fire flickering red against their deeply furrowed bark. Coyotes sang in faraway hills. An owl answered, the last thing I heard until I awakened. The moon was still high when a fiery red and black sunrise came up behind black buttes. A rustle in the tall grass nearby, and the biggest buck antelope

I'd ever seen was parading a few yards away. The base of his horns was the size of my biceps, which might not be much on me, but was a whole lot on him. His harem had been broken up during the night. We'd seen him guarding twenty-four does as the last light faded. Now, lying in the tall grass, scanning the herd with binoculars, we saw only three does. Mary fancied that the buck looked bewildered. I reminded her that antelope can't count.

To watch an antelope round up his girlfriends is to witness a demonstration of hot pursuit: he selects a doe—so do several other bucks—and the chase starts. Now the antelope is surely the fastest animal I know, cruising at forty miles per hour even over rock- and cactus-studded plains, and when flat out he makes a roadrunner look like a sleepy turtle. Miles later, tongues hanging out, the other bucks have dropped out of the race. The doe, exhausted, stands spraddle-legged, hiding behind a boulder. Then the two dance back and forth till she gives up and is herded off to the rest of the harem, which meanwhile other bucks have been raiding. Fortunately the rut is of short duration, for even an antelope couldn't survive such antics for long.

After the buck had strolled by, there was a thumping behind us. A pair of yearling does had spotted us and were nervously stamping their feet, making short runs, trying to identify us. Maybe we looked like prairie wolves, or worse. Soon, curiosity satisfied, they raced off, and Royal started banging the coffee pot around, hinting that it was time for breakfast. Sausage and eggs, biscuits and honey, all washed down with coffee. Then to shuffling and packing gear, and we shoved off to get some mileage before the heat of the day burned too bright.

Cruising the Missouri is like no other experience. Some say that a river has a soul, and indeed this one must. You soon feel it: tall hills, some covered by grass and sagebrush, some black, appearing volcanic, others steep slopes of clay and rock, still others white cliffs looming far ahead. Wide, serene waters bubble along; racing rapids, roiling with white water, cascade over hidden boulders. Strange formations of gleaming white sandstone have evoked names like Cathedral Rock, Citadel Bluff, Burned Butte, Pilot Rock, Crooked Coulee, the Pinnacles, Eagle Rock, and Steamboat Rock. There are flat dark boulders balanced on slender white pedestals that tower high on a hillside. Sheer walls form a medieval fortress, complete with spires and buttresses. Ridges emerging from flat land resemble garden walls and backbones of dinosaurs. Any description whatever seems to fit these incredibly bizarre formations.

Almost every evening, mule deer moved away from shore as we stopped for shelter in some cottonwood grove. Daily, Canada geese, all dignity, barked at us. Beside driftwood fires we toasted our next day's journey with steaming chocolate, unrolled sleeping bags beneath cloudless skies, went to sleep to the river's murmuring and a half-moon's late rising. We wakened to coyote yodeling or antelope hoofbeats.

As the tiny cluster of outbuildings at the P and N Ferry landing loomed ahead, we thought it wise to lay in a supply of fresh water. A little red-headed girl met us, barefoot, brushing the hair out of her eyes and smiling bashfully. She introduced us to her three-legged dog, old Sal. Soon a woman came out of an unpainted house, wiping her hands on her apron. A couple of horses watched hopefully from a log corral. Somewhere a radio played. We filled our water jugs. "The Mister" was up somewhere bucking hay.

It seemed a lonely life, in a country God had forsaken to some, beautiful to others who add, "no fumes or factories, clean air, where you don't feel like you're trespassing." But whether you consider it God-forsaken or beautiful, "big country" does describe this vastness that is Montana, where the horizon is unlimited except by clouds or the purple haze of some distant range. The clarity of the air reminded me of a time when we were hiking in the Chisos Mountains high above the Rio Grande and a Mexican with us observed that with such a view one could see riders three days before they could arrive. Here, too, you feel that you can look into the day after tomorrow. No road signs, just wind-blown grasses and sage, high-flying falcons, and eagles soaring on a thermal. Cowboy artist Charles Russell saw this land diminishing three generations ago and painted *When the Land Was God's*, recording the history perhaps better than anyone.

Back in the canoe we drifted on, stopping here and there to climb a cliff, explore a cave, or brew coffee over a fast-burning driftwood fire, until we reached the end of our trip, the ferry crossing at an arbitrary point seventy miles from the town of Big Sandy and thirty-five miles from the small settlement of Winifred. The ferry tender lived alone except for the companionship of two horses and two dogs. Home was a vintage trailer on the river bank, where the dirt road that comes precipitously down the Breaks is impassable in wet weather. Leading a life even more lonely than the little family at the P and N, this red-faced, lean and lanky fellow in a western hat ferried across one to three cars a day, sometimes none for a week at a time. Most were oil prospecting crews. From May to December the cable ferry, a thirty-foot float on pulleys attached to a wire cable across the river, was a single-car operation. The rest of the time the road was closed and the river frozen.

With no phone, the tender was always glad to have company. Over coffee, while we waited to be picked up, we discussed the river, he indicating that river folks feel very strongly against any dam: "Would flood all the good land, and we don't need it." At the same time, they doubted that the Park Service should have to take so much bottom land to protect it. Still, they preferred a park to a dam, but why must there be a choice? Why not just leave it alone? "They don't want dams or people. They've got along without either for a long time. They can't see why it should be changed."

Returning to Missoula to collect our mail, we were still so stimulated by our float trip on the Missouri that it seemed a good idea to see and film this great river from the air. Del Bloom was quick to offer the services of his plane, and I was even quicker to accept. Perhaps we could work it in with an antelope hunt, Royal had suggested. In the glorious last weeks of Indian summer, the cattails that fringed the ponds were already going to seed. Birds were massing in trees, lining up on utility lines, getting ready for the tourist-class flight to Mexico. The high country had a covering of white, and the coats of horses and dogs were thickening noticeably. A bleakness was settling over all, but it held a certain beauty, even with cold, wintry clouds racing by, gray on gray.

Recalling the magnificent buck antelope that we'd seen on the Missouri Breaks, I had signed up for an antelope permit. In due time it had come, good for one antelope, either sex, Area 69. Hastily, I searched the map: wrong area. The buck of my choice was south, across the river, and my permit would allow me to hunt only on the north side. But Brad Huffman, the Brunsons' son, was ranching on the north side, not far from the designated area. I could meet Royal there and we'd all hunt together.

In a matter of hours I was returning to the Breaks, climbing above Missoula smog so dense and layered that Del had to go to ten thousand feet to find clear skies. Only then could we take a course towards Helena. Cruising above snowy peaks, looking for elk in case of a future hunt, we discussed the barren slopes where clearcutters had been at work. Untold acres had been cut, leaving the steep mountain sides naked to the elements. Hundreds of logging trails criss-crossed, and it was easy to see where the unprotected soil had washed into the valleys and streams below. At Montana's state capital, where, some claim, the streets are built from gold ore, we refueled and took a heading for Winifred, south of the crossing where we'd come off the river earlier.

I was enjoying the ride and the photographic opportunities until Del asked, "You don't happen to have a compass, do you?" Watching the antics of Del's compass as it swirled wildly caused me to quit sightseeing and start looking for landmarks, almost as scarce on these plains as in Carolina swamps: a few canyons, fewer ranch houses, but nothing to fit the chart. At last we spotted an elevator and circled until we made out "Farmers Exchange Co-op"—one in every town. Finally, by flying slowly through Main Street, such as it was, we spotted a road sign that read "Denton," a name that was on our chart. Putting the sun behind us, we set course for Winifred, with the fuel indicator quivering towards empty.

Winifred's air facility consisted of a dirt strip and an expired gas pump, the kind with a glass crown on top. No one was there, and the facilities looked abandoned. Well, one thing at a time. I hiked a mile or so to town: two gas stations, one grocery, a school that was preoccupied with holding a football game, and three saloons. One gas station was in operation, and the attendant helped lug the fuel in five-gallon cans to the waiting plane. Back into the blue sky; this time our destination was Big Sandy.

The Missouri River starts as wild mountain streams on the southeastern slopes of the Rockies. The accumulated drainages of the Madison, Jefferson, and Gallatin rivers meet near Three Forks to form the Missouri and flow north and northeast, as if destined for Canada, until about eighty miles beyond Great Falls. Just east of here, near Fort Benton, the river changes its mind and turns south and east, cutting into the soft earth and creating the wildly magnificent Missouri River Breaks. They are abrupt. From the air there is the impression of unlimited prairies scored by dusty trails, of river bottoms that are suddenly slashed through with purple gorges, eroded hills, and wind-carved buttes. Then the blue strip of the river appears in the midst of a wrenched and twisted land. Words cannot soften it, or describe adequately the savagery of the landscape. Bleak, beautiful, awe-inspiring, the untamed wilderness tolerates the scattered strips of wheat land only on the outermost edges, reserving the rest of the land for those free from civilization.

We flew on to Big Sandy to rendezvous with Mary, the Brunsons, and the Huffmans. There Del refueled and, just as in a Western movie, flew off into the sunset. We spent the night at the Huffman ranch, where long before dawn Royal, stumbling around with a cup of coffee, called me from my dreams. I splashed water on my face and shaved—thereby, he said, jinxing the whole expedition. The tantalizing aroma of bacon slithered down the stairs from the ranch-house kitchen. Connie Huffman, bless her, still sleepy-eyed in a bright pink robe, had decided to cook for us, despite the unreasonable hour and her claim that the mere thought of food so early made her sick. As for myself, there is something about getting up early, seeing the eastern sky grow light, turn pink and red-gold, and finally, watching the red blob of sun come over the horizon, that makes me feel downright virtuous.

Brad was soon in his pickup and calling us to come on. I was grateful that he was driving, for roads in the Breaks are, first, unpaved; second, ungraveled; third, ungraded; and fourth, nonexistent. What passes for a road is the path dragged out of the sod from one barbed wire gate to the next. After several miles and a couple of gates I remembered an old saying in the West: never be the outside passenger—it's the gate-opening seat. By the time we had reached our area the sun had scarcely lifted itself from behind the distant Little Rockies, but Royal's keen eyes spotted the spice-brown and white of a band of antelope grazing up a wide draw.

The wind was south, behind us, so we'd have to make a wide circle across the valley and start the stalk behind a range of hills to the west of the animals. A nearby wash afforded cover. After a mile or two of hiking we bellied up to the crown of a hill, hiding behind a clump of sage before trying to sight the animals again. They were gone. Cautiously we worked back another mile, west and north towards a remote draw. I had eased out into the open to peer around a hill when Brad hissed a warning. There was the whole herd, and there I stood for all to see. Trying to fade, I felt like an elephant seeking cover behind a sapling.

Earlier we had flushed a trio of mule deer. They had crossed the valley, and the antelope were watching them instead of us. This was our chance: we had only one small open space to cross. It was a steep slope shaded by a hill. I stretched out on my belly and slid down, pausing to watch from behind a clump of sage. Here I peered through the scope to see if the sentry was looking. She was. Her black face was aimed directly at me, her sharp eyes having spotted something new at three quarters of a mile. I froze, and waited till she relaxed her vigil and glanced away.

The stalk is the hunt. It's then that nerves begin to flutter. Buck fever may set in, and doubts: Can I get close enough? Hold the rifle steady? What if it sees me, or moves? As the doe looked away, I slid ahead a few feet. She looked back. I froze. Time crawled on. She looked away again, and I slid into a hollow. Safe, I breathed. Brad soon joined me.

"Where's Royal?"

"Heading down the draw to get a running shot when they go by."

We were within three hundred yards. Shooting a scoped .300 Browning rifle, I was within range, but determined to get closer. An antelope is a small target, with the vital areas less than a foot in circumference. It is too easy to only wound the game. I'd rather miss entirely. There is little reason for any shooting at more than a hundred yards, for it is not the kill that is important, but the skill that comes in the stalk. Perhaps this is why many skilled hunters sooner or later turn to the bow.

We edged up to a small ridge covered with rock outcroppings and pines, slid our rifles into position. The big buck on the right was to be mine; Brad would take the one on the left. The only problem was that the buck was facing away, and the crosshairs fell on his rump. I waited for the angle to change.

From across the valley came the rattle of rocks. The herd came alert, preparing for immediate flight. Still a bad angle, but the best I could expect. "Ready," I signaled Brad. The herd took flight as I was realigning the crosshairs. The rifle slammed in recoil. I rammed another cartridge into the chamber, but the buck was down. Brad had fired a split second later, making a clean miss. Throwing on the safety, I rose and raced to the spot, aware of a herd of deer running by. Brad came up, "Danged deer spooked 'em!" We looked at the buck, killed quickly by a shot through the backbone. The herd was already close to a mile away and disappearing. Royal hadn't had a chance. "Biggest buck deer I ever saw spooked 'em just before you fired!" They went off to get the truck, and I turned to the job of field dressing.

This was not to be our only hunt on the river. Bob Makala, a former student of Royal's and by then a teacher in northern Montana, was also interested in hunting mule deer in these parts. He had done considerable hunting, occasionally with Royal, but he had never floated the river. Our stories of all the game we had seen inspired him. As for Royal and me, we needed no further stimulation to return to these hunting grounds, which is one of the finest in my experience. Not that there is more game than in many other areas, but I like it for its remoteness and the feeling it imparts of isolation and wild serenity.

So it was that another time Royal, Mary, and I were crossing the great expanse of plains again, to rendezvous with Bob Makala at Big Sandy and head south to the bluffs where the river waited. Abandoning the pavement, we took up a graded gravel road for twenty or thirty miles, passing winter wheat fields and sagebrush barrens, an occasional ranch house and isolated windmill.

Strangely, when the Breaks began to show, the road—now a one-lane dirt track—meandered in a big loop. It isn't easy to lose a river, but somehow I was beginning to think we had. In some desperation we stopped for directions at a ranch house not many miles off the road. A youngish fellow, apparently dozing, with broad-brimmed hat pulled over his eyes, was leaning against a pole corral. A big dog lay nearby, one eye open and watching us. Bob Makala hailed the man. The dog had now opened both eyes enough to measure us. After a long pause to size us up and study our rigs, the rancher didn't move, but reckoned that if we would take the road down across the wheat field and hold south, we'd find it. He was still leaning against the corral when our departing dust obscured him.

The road was no more than a pair of ruts through a substance which, when wet, becomes impassible gumbo. Scattered dark clouds to the west urged us to hurry; this was no place to be caught in a rain, when movement would immediately become impossible. On an antelope hunt a few years before, we had first encountered "gumbo." We were camped on a dry river bottom in eastern Montana when a light rain began just before dawn. In icy wet darkness we threw our sleeping bags into the car and headed for high ground, but it was almost too late for escape. The first drops of rain promptly turned what had been hard-baked clay into a slick grease that stuck to everything it touched. Feet and wheels were spinning, the car skewed sideways back and forth all over the road, and all hands but the driver were pushing. We could manage to go only a few yards at a time before having to stop and scrape the accumulated mud off our boots—boots that had soon grown as large as snowshoes and heavy as lead. The gumbo also clung to the tires, building up in the wheel wells and soon locking the wheels. We had to pry away the mud with a military trenching tool before slithering along for the next hundred feet. We made our getaway at last by leaving the road and driving across the grasslands, where the vegetation kept the tires relatively free of this slick, gluelike material. I recall Jeff Miller's returning to our car, where Mary, under most adverse conditions, was creating coffee and other sustenance. In his haste Jeff had failed to pull on his boots. Mary and he spent the rest of the morning pulling out prickly pear spines, removing mud, and administering first aid to the cuts and bruises on his feet.

Our trail this time twisted off across a rolling landscape of cactus and whispering grasses, barbed wire fences and cattle guards. Then it dropped steeply into an arroyo, clinging stubbornly to the hillside only to dive over a ridge and into a gully. After a tortuous route through the tumbled wash, it abruptly spit us out into full view of the river. Wide and peaceful, the mighty Missouri mumbled along between cottonwood-studded banks dwarfed by towering white cliffs. Our arrival was duly noted by prairie dogs whistling from mounds nearby, and by a magpie, flashing black and white as it changed trees for a better look at the intruders.

But it was already mid-afternoon, and there was not enough daylight left for talking to prairie dogs and magpies. We dumped the two canoes from atop the VW van and heaped our gear haphazardly against a cottonwood log. Moments later, our two vehicles were trailing great palls of dust back over the breaks. The plan was to leave one car at Brad Huffman's ranch. He would meet us in five days in the Judith River basin, at the ferry landing where the Judith joins the Missouri. While the pickup car was being delivered, Mary and I packed the canoes for the trip down river.

So we were back on the wild Missouri again. While nothing like the River of No Return, it does not graciously permit the trespasser to change his mind. Once more we were out of touch with civilization—not even a ferry before the Judith—no telephones, only abandoned ranch buildings, desolate plains, steep cliffs crumbling on the river's edge, deep canyons, and scattered wildlife. With canoes on the beach and gear stowed, we were ready to shove off as soon as Bob and Royal returned. "I think we've forgotten something," Mary kept saying. There was no time to go back and fetch whatever it was, for though our first planned camp was only a few miles downstream, the bluffs were already casting long shadows.

While supper cooked on a narrow bench just above the river, the fire flickering off the sheltering branches of a giant cottonwood and the coffee bubbling contentedly, I sat on the bank watching the river go by in the gloom. The moon, full and hazy with the last heat of fall, was rising out of a notch in the distant Breaks. Clouds drifted along, black with moon-brightened white edges. The soft white haze around the moon ended in a slightly pink ring, portent of a weather change ahead. Jagged breaks downstream, softened by darkness, became irregularly moulded forms. The river was silent, though flowing smooth and swift, gentle ripples and upwellings blurring perfect reflections of moon and clouds. A high cirrus layer was backlit by the moon's blue-whiteness. The shining mirror face of the river stretched southward between dark banks, fading into blackness that reflected where a star hung, glittering just above the horizon.

The campfire smoke smelled good. I could hear the dry leaves rustling as Mary prepared supper and the others set up their tent. Mary and I planned to sleep in the open, with the big cottonwood to deflect some of the frost, so that we could see the sky, breathe deep of the pure air, and hear the rest of the world sleep. Behind camp the white cliffs glowed phosphorescent ivory in the moonlight. There were no lights but the moon, stars, and our small fire. A splash in the river. The distant call of a wild goose, and an owl replying. The fire popping. Relaxed laughter at some old joke. The clatter of a leaf falling. Then Mary rolled over and announced to me in a clear and distressed voice. "I knew we had forgotten something. We didn't bring any sugar!"

A coyote, away off, howled its lonesome song. Too bad there was no sugar. Only Royal required sugar in his coffee. I drifted contentedly into deep sleep.

A gentle crunching, scraping sound wakened us in the darkness. The moon was still up, spilling its cool blue light across the land, and a slight pink grayness in the east foretold the dawn. We slid out of the warmth of down bags, fumbled for boots in the pale moonlight, and went to investigate the noises. There was a silhouette high in the cottonwood, a fuzzy ball like an oversized bird's nest. The flashlight beam revealed the green eyes of a benign-faced porcupine. Unconcerned with our curiosity, it resumed its scraping at the tender bark.

It was time for a breakfast fire. A great horned owl called three deep-throated questions that echoed off the white cliffs as I arranged firewood gathered the evening before. A single match set the powder-dry twigs to popping. A curl of blue smoke, then a steadily growing flame. The coffee pot, well blackened and battered, perched on the rocks. It was absorbing the heat while our still-sleepy party began shaking out sleeping bags, rolling up their tent, and packing the canoes. Across the river four does, almost black in the early light, waded into the river. Catching our scent or sound, they stopped, looked alert, then, in the characteristic bounds of mule deer, cleared the bank as if on giant coil springs. They paused just for a moment to look, then, unconcerned, sauntered back to the river.

The plan was for Royal and Bob to search ahead for deer, with Mary and me breaking camp and following, since I wasn't hunting. Through the day we'd bring up the rear, so as not to disturb the game, then speed up to make camp ahead of the hunters. The river appealed to our sense of history, and we liked to camp on or near one of the Lewis and Clark expedition's sites. One night we picked Pablo Island, just opposite the site Lewis and Clark had used in 1804 on the north bank of the river. On that same low bluff, too, the artist Karl Bodmer and Prince Maximilian made camp some decades later when they retraced the expedition's route to record the grandeur of mountain and river on canvas. The Missouri River Breaks look much the same today as then.

We counted lots of deer in the Breaks, but while we were on the river the female of the species seemed to have taken over, for the first twenty deer we sighted were all does. The twenty-first was a spike buck. Number 32 was a big buck that eased up a branching arroyo before Royal or Bob could get near, and not until Number 37 did another buck appear. This one, too, was disappearing up a dry wash in a long narrow canyon. Royal and Bob took up the stalk while I followed with a camera. Mary stood by the canoes. We had climbed maybe four hundred feet above the river and marked the deer off as a lost cause when Royal spotted the animal sneaking into a brush-filled draw. Royal dropped him in a clean kill with an offhand shot that would make anyone proud.

Those who haven't hunted in this kind of country might think that the hunt had ended. Perhaps it had, but the work was only beginning. After field dressing, Bob thought that he could carry it. He did manage a hundred feet or so. Then the two tried to drag it down a wash. Two hundred feet later they were lying on their backs exhausted, trying to get their breaths back, with a mile still to go. Meanwhile, a dark cloud had obscured the sky and the wind was picking up considerably. I wanted to get out of that gumbo canyon before it rained. I'd never seen the deer that I couldn't carry, as long as I could get it onto my shoulders. They hoisted it aboard. I did pretty well for the first couple of hundred feet, but after that I, too, was exhausted, stumbling and staggering between the rocks and sage clumps that seemed to snatch alternately at the antlers or my feet. The wash was too narrow for two men, and too steep to climb out. Finally in desperation, we cut the deer in half. Royal and Bob dropped the hind quarters over my shoulders, and they took the antlered end. Soon sweat-blinded, I ricocheted from bank to bank till at last I staggered down to the river shore, dropped my burden, and reluctantly went back to meet the other two and help them with theirs.

At the same time Mary had her hands full looking after the canoes, for while we were gone the wind had risen and was now howling down the canyon, carrying clouds of dust and stirring the river to whitecaps. Despite being fully loaded, the canoes were in imminent danger of being blown downriver, and waves were already slopping aboard. She had managed to drag them higher onto the shore. A vee of Canada geese swept by. They seemed to be escaping from the storm and urging us to do the same. We already knew the disposition of the river when sudden howling gales make up. Now the dust-laden winds were flinging tumbleweeds into the air and turning placid waters into white foam and rolling seas. Then, as quickly as it had come, the storm subsided into just a nice whistler that sang through the gorge, leaving the golden cottonwood leaves still trembling and the river settling to a mild chop.

The game loaded, we set off again to race with the wind still fresh at our backs, pushing us downstream. I was dreaming of the ultimate camp supper, fresh deer liver, until I discovered that my biologist companions didn't share my tastes and had left all the choice parts behind. They gave me their eloquent food-chain lecture about all the sanitarians of the wild that by morning would have removed every trace of the kill. I was not convinced about the plight of the coyote, the badger, or the golden eagle. I was talking about the victory supper, not sanitation.

It was a luxury not to hunt but to rediscover the personality of the Missouri, as different from other rivers as a mountain stream is from the blackwater creeks of the Carolinas. About all they have in common is running water and that strange phenomenon that all streams seem to have, best described as a destiny. A free-flowing river compares with a dammed river much as a free-flying eagle with a caged eagle. Unfortunately, when man finds a river, he feels obliged to make it "good for something," by channelizing, damming, or otherwise altering it, compelled to destroy what he loves the most— or does not understand. If he does not find reason to change it, and somehow realizes that it is beautiful, unique, or useless enough to keep as scenic or wild, he still cannot resist "developing" it by making it more accessible. The upper Missouri remains unchanged only because it has been isolated from the mobs that are seeking escape from themselves. As it joins the other wild and scenic areas it will suddenly have to justify its existence and the various agencies will justify their existence by advertising and increasing the usage, thus destroying much of its real value.

What to do with the Missouri River Breaks has long been a con-
troversial topic, with at least three schools of thought: dredge, so that
boats and barges can haul cheap cargo, because railroads have failed
to provide adequate service; dam, for electricity, flood control, and
irrigation—the "golden key to progress"—though most of the dams
already existing on the river have failed to stimulate progress. The
third plan, calling for recreational use as a scenic river, introduced by
Montana's late Senator Lee Metcalf, assures that the river will remain
as it is for future generations to see and enjoy. I prefer the river folks'
view: just leave it alone. But this seems impossible in our world, and
the Breaks will never be the same wildly mysterious place that it
was when Lewis and Clark found it, or even as it was when we first
explored its reaches. So today the Missouri has a keeper, a river
warden. At least part of its beauty will be retained. Contrary to those
who thought it was a barren and uninhabited land, it never was. It
is teeming with life, and unsurpassed beauty. No, God never did
forsake it.

6.

Franc Gets
His Moose

One year Franc White asked us to join him on a moose hunt in
Ontario before we went west. Franc is also an outdoor writer, who
produces a very popular sports show for a whole mess of television
stations. He was interested, not in going west, but north, beyond
Georgian Bay, into the lake country about a hundred and fifty miles
north of Sault Ste. Marie. There the moose were allegedly so thick
that they were hiding behind nearly every bush.

To hunt in Canada, tradition almost demands a canoe. Our friend,
the late Jim Emmett, then boating editor of *Outdoor Life* and dean of
anything on or near the water, had suggested that we try an almost
indestructible type, made of Royalex material, fabricated in Wis-
consin by Thompson Boat Company. A phone call or two revealed a
dealer in Buffalo, New York, with one of the right size in stock, and
we stopped there to pick up a bright blue canoe en route to rendezvous with Franc and Lois in Chapleau. A glance at the map suggested
that an interesting trip might be a shortcut by ferry across Georgian
Bay. The ferry was late docking because of a storm, which, according
to one of the crew, was so severe as to leave hoof prints of the cattle
cargo on the overhead. They were canceling that afternoon's trip but
"not to worry—the weather will be better by morning."

All that night a full gale howled across the torn waters. We
decided to spend the night sleeping in the van at the ferry slip, to
be first aboard in the morning. This was a mistake, for the car shook
and rattled so much that once or twice in the night I got up to make
sure that the emergency brake was fully set and the transmission in
low gear. Around midnight I slipped chocks under the wheels,

reducing our chances of heading out to sea without benefit of ferry should the gale grow any stronger. Sleeping conditions were poor that night; it was a little like sleeping in a concrete mixer, I thought. By ten the next morning the storm hadn't abated much, so we took the long overland route, hurrying in order not to miss our rendezvous early the following day.

Loaded with supplies, we joined Franc and Lois at Kutner's Lodge in Chapleau for final instructions from outfitter Hugh Kutner. Later in the day we found ourselves about to board a White River Flying Service bush plane. It was a DeHavilland Beaver, an aircraft of uncommon strength and dependability and very popular as a freight hauler in the Canadian bush country. Our pilot, Del, a young man full of confidence, had immediately set about loading the cargo, which consisted of all sorts of fishing, filming, hunting, cooking, sleeping, and surviving gear, stacking it here and there, wherever there was space in the plane. As a final gesture he lashed the two canoes securely to the struts where the floats are attached to the fuselage. Satisfied, Del climbed aboard, revved the engine, and we waddled down the river. The pontoons were slapping the water like a skipping stone until, at last, we bounced into the air with a roar. We were bound for some vaguely described lake shore somewhere in the bush, to spend two weeks away from any civilization, on our own, scarcely knowing where we were or what was ahead.

The Canadian North Woods is big, seemingly without end. The horizon unfolding below us only revealed more of the same dense, dark forests interspersed with countless lakes, each glittering in the brilliance of the autumn sun, reflecting the blue sky, the white clouds, and the vast forest. The lakes seem tied together by myriad streams, with pale green bogs wherever beaver blocked the waters, white rapids and waterfalls interlacing and disappearing beyond the rim of the earth. As lake after lake flashed by, the pilot would call out its name, as if all were old friends. North by northwest, we winged our way towards a destination we had seen only as a blue spot on a forestry map.

Abruptly a wing dropped, and we made a fast circle of a lake. Del pointed at the water below us, "There is your home for the next two weeks." I peered out, hoping to see some significant landmark, a campsite, or anything that would help us survive. The plane splashed down, skimming towards a small cove, until just at the last moment, the throttle cut, and the pontoons sank into the water, effectively preventing us from piling into the shoreline. It took only a few minutes for the cargo to be dumped on the beach. We heard Del's passing farewell, "Someone will come by about Tuesday to see if you are okay. Have fun, and good luck!" Then the engine roared and the plane was enveloped in a cloud of spray. Within moments, even the sound of the plane had faded across the endless forests. We were on our own.

The first order of business was to set up camp and get a pot of coffee boiling, then assess the lay of the land. We were on a narrow, gravelly beach that was only slightly higher than the swamp behind us. The lake, maybe three-quarters of a mile long by half a mile wide, seemed shallow, with a large snag near the middle. All else was black conifer forest and the exposed granite of the Canadian shield.

We'd noticed as we were landing that there was a river to the south and west that offered possibilities for hunting, but because this was where the pilot had dumped us, our present location must be the best camp site available. The two pop tents were quickly erected, the gear stored, sleeping bags unrolled, firewood gathered. We were ready for two weeks of concentrated moosing in seemingly complete isolation. We were alone in the wilderness. But just as we were finishing our evening meal we were greatly startled by a soft voice from the darkness. "Hallo there! May I join you?"

A short, wiry, gray-haired man appeared out of the gloom, standing at the edge of the firelight. "I am your neighbor, Magnus Nyman. I am a trapper and you are welcome. My cabin is on that hill. Are you hunting? Perhaps I can help you."

We introduced ourselves, and thus became acquainted with one of Ontario's legends. He suggested several likely places where we could hunt. Though he had a hunter to guide at the time, he would be glad to assist us in any way. That night Franc and I studied the map with a great deal of interest, and realized that it was a long way to anywhere. It was reassuring to have a real woodsman in the neighborhood.

Franc's canoe was the larger, an aluminum eighteen-foot cargo model with a square stern, steady, easy to paddle with lots of room, but noisy. Every slap of the waves, rub of a branch alongside, or touch of the paddle sent sound waves echoing through the woods. Thereafter I referred to it as the kettle drum, and we soon switched to our sixteen-footer. Slightly more tender, even a little cramped after a full day of travel, but silent as a ghost, it would forgive scraping and gouging and could slide through brush with scarcely a sound. It was an ideal hunting canoe, and incidentally, the plastic did not transmit the cold of the water nearly so quickly to the bottom of the feet.

A routine was quickly established. Long before daylight we'd eat a hasty breakfast. By the time the faintest hint of light shone across the waters, we would have shaken the frost from our gear, turned over the canoe, loaded it, and slid it into the water and begun the search for the monarch of the North Woods. Bundled to the ears against the cold, we would set off across the lake, usually following a nearby stream past several beaver dams towards a succession of lakes. More than once I found myself with the thought of how cold those waters would be in case of an upset.

There are other residents of the North Woods besides moose, hunters, and trappers. They are the mosquito and, wherever there is fast water, the invincible black fly. Much smaller than the ordinary house fly, triangular in shape, it is capable of driving any warm-blooded animal insane. And thick! The classic journal of the Voyageurs noted, "The mosquitoes were here in such clouds as to prevent us from taking aim at the ducks, of which we might else have shot many." This was written in 1775, so a reader might think that the infestation was a thing of the past. But Franc swore, after watching me search behind a swamp for some sign of game, that he could trace my every move simply by watching the clouds of insects that were forever hovering above my head. Good repellent, the type that contains over 70 percent active ingredients, was fairly effective.

Normally, the woods are quite free of such pests after August, but one warm day the black flies descended. In a long-sleeved shirt that was a little skimpy in the sleeves, my unprotected wrists proved uncommonly attractive. It wasn't the loss of blood, it was the after-effects. For the next four nights the only way I found to cope with the intense itching and burning of the resultant oozing sores was to put my hands outside the sleeping bag so that the freezing night air would numb them enough for me to sleep!

Nature gives us many significant warning signs, if we are able to interpret them accurately. A common example is in the reliable old saying, "Red sky in the morning, sailor take warning." There are others, of course. We were sitting around one evening enjoying the warmth of the fire, recounting the day's activities, when I noticed a frog hopping past the fire. I paid scant attention, for we were listening to wolves howling in the distance, and watching the firelight dancing among the trees. In the midst of pouring ourselves another round of coffee, a second frog hopped into the ashes and, confused, jumped into the fire. Surprised, we were commenting about it when still another went by. Then Mary, returning from the tent, noted a movement underfoot and called our attention to still more frogs. Curious, we began looking around. The ground was alive with them, a continuous migration of what appeared to be green mink frogs. Why were all of these amphibians migrating past our camp? Ignoring us, the fire, and all other obstacles, they were moving out of the swamp behind us, crossing the narrow sand bar where our camp was situated, and heading towards the lake.

We took it as a warning: those frogs must know something that we didn't. Probably they were responding to some barometric change, or perhaps to a combination of factors. Either way, such a phenomenon can fill the mind with apprehension. The next day was windy and wet, and by evening the temperature had fallen. The following morning we awoke to find that my long johns, soaked by the previous day's rain and hung by the campfire to dry, were frozen stiff. For the rest of our stay they hung there like boards, white and useless, for snow, sleet, and icy winds had taken over. Our igloolike tents were gradually collapsing from the weight of snow and ice, no matter how often we shook them clear.

By now we had discovered that our companions were less familiar with cold-weather living than we, and weren't faring as comfortably as they should. Lois made some comment about her cold, wet feet, but added that it was only to be expected, for of course everybody camping in such weather had cold, wet feet. It turned out that her waterproofed boots were soaked, the felt liners soggy. She thought that this was the way things always were for those who go into wintry woods. Further questioning brought out that they hadn't slept warm since they arrived. Not complainers, they were toughing it out: after all, while we had down mummy bags, Franc had announced that they had Mummy and Daddy bags of genuine kapok.

Raised in Alabama, they had never camped in really cold weather.

It was up to us, then, to straighten things out quickly, for comfort is essential to outdoor living. I'd learned about drying boots by heating grain and dumping it into the boots to absorb the moisture, but we had no horses, therefore no grain. Sand, a poor substitute, would have to do. First, we heated some gravel till it was just a little warmer than comfortable in the hand and dumped it into the boots, shook it about, and repeated the process. It pulled out the moisture, while the liners and socks were baking dry at a safe distance in front of the fire. Too much heat will quickly ruin any leather; it is also guaranteed to shrink wool, leaving one worse off than before.

The next problem was their bed. It was built upon some boughs, which was fine, but they had placed an airtight "space blanket" over their sleeping bags. It is sometimes difficult to remember that cold comes from below. Even though it is true that heat rises, the logical place for the waterproof blanket is underneath. I had learned this the hard way in Texas a few years before when, one cold and windy night, sleeping on the open plains, I wrapped a poncho around me and my sleeping bag for wind protection. I had awakened in the early hours to find that the sleeping bag was frozen solid around my midriff. Later I learned that the human body loses a pint of water or more through perspiration in a night, even during sleep, and the sweat had condensed on the poncho, soaked the sleeping bag, and frozen. The weight of the body tends to crush any insulation from below, which is where most of the insulation is needed. That is why a closed-cell foam or insulated air mattress is so efficient.

The wind can also be a major problem, and that is the main reason for insisting on a windproof cover for a sleeping bag. A tent serves the same purpose. Unless the weather is wet or snowy I prefer a large (10' × 12') waterproof nylon tarp most of the time. Also, sleeping with a companion adds a lot of warmth. Companions of the opposite sex make camping far more comfortable and, if selected with care, have other desirable attributes.

Icy sleeping bags and cold feet at night are effectively cured with a heated and wrapped stone or a hot water bottle or canteen. In this instance, a whiskey bottle, emptied of antifreeze and filled with boiling water, tightly corked and wrapped in a sweater, provided an almost immediate cure for Lois and Franc. There is a distilled truth, fitting every kind of expedition: a belly full of good food, a good

solid night's sleep, and dry feet will solve almost any problem before
it has a chance to arise. A few years before, while riding in the Sapphire Mountains of Montana, a couple who were with us began to
bicker, then quarrel, which was not at all their usual behavior. My
wife suggested to them that she needed a break and, pulling her
horse alongside mine, whispered, "You take her horse while I get
them something hot and sweet to drink." I caught on immediately
and, as soon as we halted, I dismounted and took the friend's horse
while the husband took Mary's. Meanwhile Mary had taken a flask
of brandy from her saddlebag and slipped each of them a draught on
the sly. Without either of them being aware that the other had had a
drink, the calming process began. It was soon confirmed in camp by
solid food. There was no more bickering. Something sweet, preferably
hot but mainly immediate, almost always has a calming effect; even a
sweet alone will help restore strength and tranquillity.

Hunting moose or any other kind of game isn't always the lead-
pipe cinch that we tend to believe from reading the outdoor books.
To be sure, the goal is to score, though many writers claim you can
load up with nothing but the biggest and best bulls with the best
racks in the world if you simply do as they say. The real world isn't
like that at all. It is sneaking around through the woods, tracking,
looking for signs, usually for days at a time. When and if you do spot
something, chances are it is a doe, a cow, or a spike, especially if you
are looking for a bragging trophy. Some hunters score regularly every
year, but they are the exception. Depending on the game and the
area, the scoring average varies, but if you figure the odds are eighty
to one against you, you won't be far wrong.

After a week we had pretty well covered the surrounding territory
for the elusive moose. We'd found some fresh signs scattered here
and there, but for the life of us, after a week of searching up and
down the lakes, the connecting rivers and streams, it appeared that
if we expected to take meat or photographs home the expedition was
going to fail.

About the eighth day the weather began to improve. Hunting in
a mixture of rain, snow, and storm isn't the best way to get game, for
they, too, tend to stick to their bedding at such times, but now the
sun was breaking through fast-moving clouds and by noon even

knocking a little of the chill from the air. Encouraged by what looked like promising weather, we set off even earlier that morning, determined to hunt what I called Number Eight lake, so named because we would have to pass through seven lakes first, including two or three portages.

Looking over our gear, rifles, ammunition, a sack of lunch, life jackets, matches, it seemed that we had all that was needed. We shoved off with dawn just breaking. Franc, being a little heavier than I, took the stern position. We had worked up a nice rhythm and were able to make good time without tiring ourselves too much, so that in a day's paddling we could cover many miles.

Traveling quietly, with only the sound of dripping water and a slight swish at the bow, we glided across the lake to the shore opposite our camp, then turned up a long finger to where a series of beaver dams blocked the feeding river. Here we had to lift the canoe over four-foot piles of branches, mud, and all the construction material that a family of busy beavers had assembled before we could set out again. Following the main river channel to another lake, we skirted the shoreline until we came to a long portage over a rocky trail. Generally I carried the canoe and a pack while Franc hurried ahead loaded with the rest of the gear. We launched into another river, which forked within a short distance. The water was much faster here, and, bucking our way upstream, we could hear the sounds of a waterfall to our left telling us to keep to the other branch.

The forest was in full autumn colors. A different sort of light, common to these parts, seemed to intensify everything: the towering conifers, the jack pines looming green-black, the sky filled with the closeness of outer space. It was a window to another world, where the frost-licked meadows that ringed the beaver pond had taken on the gold of aspen. Sunbeams flashed in a mix of silver broken by the black of fast-moving water. Beneath us, as clear as North Country air, the river rushed on over blue-green depths. Every boulder, submerged log, or cluster of waterlilies clinging to the edges stood out clearly. The shores, lined with bulrushes or muskeg, glowed in the greenish tans of vegetation already brushed by the frost that had settled in the lowlands. Beyond was the dark, limitless forest where trees were sometimes growing out of, sometimes bypassing and surrounding, the exposed black granite that makes up the Canadian

shield, that portion of the earth's crust dating back to the Pre-
cambrian era.

I found myself remembering lines I read years before by William
Faulkner, something to the effect that the Lord created this earth,
and said that it was right. Then He made man to be the overseer of
His domain and the animals on it, a servant assigned to do the work
of the Lord. The land was not for man himself, but he was charged
to be its steward, to hold it intact for the welfare of all mankind. In
exchange for this honor he was to pay in humility, virtue, strength,
tolerance, and the sweat of his brow. But when man failed his stew-
ardship in Europe, and as he was quarreling over the bones of that
continent, explorers were discovering the new America. Now, those
of the same persuasion are seeking to divide America's carcass among
themselves alone. In our greed for possession, we often overlook
what the true value of the land is, and that our wealth is only that
of the community in which we live. Even bucking the current, I felt
very wealthy.

It was afternoon before we finally pulled the canoe up onto the
shore of the final lake, Number Eight. A faint trail near where we
beached the canoe seemed to lead into the bush. We followed it,
moving slowly and quietly through the woods, among fallen trees
and clumps of brush. Old signs of game were plentiful, but, save for
the ever-present pine squirrels and the squall of ravens passing overhead, the sigh of the wind seemed to be our only company. By now
Apollo, the sun's charioteer, had whipped his team well along on the
downward trip towards the evening stables, and there was a hint of
color rimming the edges of low-lying clouds.

"We'd better be heading back. It'll be after dark before we get
there, even if we leave right now," I reminded Franc.

We were both standing on the edge of a beaver pond staring
across the vastness, trying to let soak into our memories every facet
of this unlimited wildness. Franc was a couple of yards to my left,
and I had just turned to leave, thinking that he was close behind me,
when I heard the slap of a beaver's tail. Then BLAM! BLAM! BLAM!
BLAM! BLAM! The crack of gunshots nearly burst my eardrums.
Had Franc gone mad? I was ducking for cover with the echo of five
shots, fired as close together as possible, reverberating across the
marshes.

"I got him! I got him! I got him!" My partner was dancing around as if he'd been standing too long on a fire ant mound. He was waving his rifle in the air and shouting over and over, "I got him! . . ." There, on the far bank across the beaver pond, settling into the stump-filled muck, was a bull moose. Quickly I ran along the shore and raced across the top of the dam to where he lay. He was breathing his last in steamy puffs and at the same time struggling to rise. I heard Franc calling from across the water, shouting alternately, "Don't shoot him!" and "Don't let him get away!"

Meanwhile, I was holding the rifle pointed at the bull's head and trying to decide if another shot was needed. It wasn't, for he was in the final death throes.

I looked back to see where Franc was. He was convulsing on the shore, as if out of control. Frightened, I yelled at him, "What's the matter?"

"I'm having a heart attack!"

"My God, lie still! Don't move!"

I was scared. My mind was racing—It's three or four hours from camp . . . it's getting dark . . . several portages, that long one through thick country. . . . Franc is six-four and weighs more than two hundred pounds. And the canoe, too! "Franc, don't move! Lie down and hold still!" What's the first aid for heart attacks? Even if I get him back to camp, what then? It must be eighty miles to the nearest hospital by air, and the plane won't be back for at least two more days!

I'd forgotten the moose and was racing back towards Franc when he seemed to calm down. Sitting on the bank he called out, "I'm all right, I think I'm just having palpitations. Take care of the moose." A little confused, considerably relieved, and hoping that what he'd said was so, I watched him for a few minutes. He seemed to be recovering, so I turned back to the moose. It was dead, the first shot had hit in the neck, apparently breaking the spinal column. I didn't notice where the other four bullets had gone. I suspected that he'd missed, but Franc claimed that they'd all hit the same spot.

Palpitations brought on by the excitement must have been Franc's problem, for in a few minutes I looked up to see him approaching, apparently well enough. Now new problems faced us. The moose was lying in a foot or two of water and wedged against a stump. I grabbed a leg and tried to roll him over. I might as well have been trying to pull up the stump by hand. We had to turn him over and get him out of the water in order to do any field dressing. Franc was at first too busy admiring his trophy to address the serious issues. Admittedly, it was a trophy; the antlers, if I remember correctly, were fifty-four inches across. This was a big, prime bull, but that didn't ease the work ahead.

Using our belts and the slings from our rifles, we managed to get sufficient leverage to roll the moose into ankle-deep water and turn him on his back. It was nearly dark when we both set about removing the guts, liver, and heart. Thinking back, it was a bit frightening, too, for more than once I heard and felt the blade of my razor-sharp knife clicking against Franc's as, like blind swordsmen, we hacked away at arm's length trying to sever some part deep within the body cavity, in what was now almost total darkness. I still don't know how we didn't cut each other, even as we tried to be cautious.

Leaving the dressed-out moose to cool, we took the heart and liver, slung the rifles over our shoulders, and headed back, feeling our way over the beaver dam. By the time we had crossed we couldn't see each other, so one would advance, feeling his way, then the other would follow in a parallel path. We were searching for the trail, a faint path scarcely a foot wide. Whenever one of us came to an open spot he would stop so that the other, when he found an opening, could head towards his voice to verify that we had indeed found the trail before crossing it.

Once I noticed Franc's voice seeming to come from below me. I paused, felt around with my feet and realized that I had inadvertently walked up a large log and was four or five feet above the ground. Finally, we connected with what appeared to be the game path. Taking turns, one advancing while the other waited as a guide point in case the first strayed, we found the lake, and soon, our canoe. We had no flashlight, but I did have two short candles in the pack in the canoe and plenty of matches. There was still sufficient light to differentiate between water and land, so with the occasional lighting of a candle, especially on portages, we could make our way.

It is difficult at best to remember every step and turn of a three- or four-hour passage. There was some concern, when we heard the roar of a waterfall, that we had taken the wrong branch, especially when we felt the tug of fast water. Finally arriving at the last long portage, I found my way along the trail with the aid of the candle and was able to set it at the end as a guide and return to help carry the canoe and gear. Following an unfamiliar rocky trail while carrying a pack and a seventy-odd-pound canoe without falling on your face once or twice has very little in common with strolling down the primrose path.

At last we were in the home stretch. After dripping a bit of wax to affix the stub of the candle to the bow to guide us, we dipped the paddles deep and the water sluiced by. We rounded a point and there, a faintly gleaming phosphorescence in utter blackness, was the flickering of our campfire. We paddled still harder, and though the night and water were dead still, the candle was hard put to stay alight. Suddenly, looming out of the total darkness, white arms were grabbing for us. So surprised were we that we nearly capsized before identifying them as the snags of the tree that resided in the middle of the lake.

It was an exhausted, excited crew aboard the blue canoe as it slid onto the shore in front of our camp. Franc lolled back in the stern, held the dripping liver aloft and proclaimed, "Mama, I feel like I just shot Stonewall Jackson off his horse on the square in Nashville, Tennessee!"

Back in camp, Franc's shots had brought Magnus, our newfound friend, from his cabin on the ridge above our camp. He surmised that we were too far away to field dress and transport a moose in the remaining daylight and would make camp. "They do have an axe, don't they?" Lois pointed to the woodpile, "There's the axe." "Oh—then you'd better build up the fire." "So that's what we did all those long hours of waiting," Mary told me later, "we kept a big fire going. And every little while Magnus would come down from his cabin to reassure us."

The hunt was a success, though the real work was yet to begin. The butchering and hauling of probably a thousand pounds of meat, bones, and hide would keep us busy the next couple of days. The following morning we took our wives to the scene so that they could participate until all was safely hung from the trees by our camp. Not wishing to make more than one trip, we took both canoes. Here the big aluminum cargo canoe showed its worth. Both were loaded till the gunnels were dangerously low. By evening we had made the long run back to the last lake. Now things got hairy, for a strong head wind had blown up, sending whitecaps racing along the water. Trying to stay in a lee, we found the last mile a matter of keeping the bow into the wind and heading into the waves as carefully as possible in order to keep from swamping. I estimated that we had a nine-hundred-pound load in a sixteen-foot canoe. It was too much, but by luck, the next evening we were feasting on roast heart of moose, stuffed with rice and garnished with bacon strips.

The day of our prearranged departure dawned full of dark clouds, and though a scant two weeks had passed, the beautiful autumn we were enjoying when we entered the bush now had turned to winter. All day the sun hadn't managed to do much more than ease the worst of the gloom. When the plane had come in a couple of hours earlier to take our wives out, the flying conditions were, in my estimation, unacceptable even then. They were far worse now. Dusk was settling in and the snow was falling, heavy and wet, leaving a feeling of foreboding as we sat on a poncho covering our wet pile of duffel stacked on the lake shore. "It's too late now. He won't be able to find the lake, much less land in this mess," was Franc's contribution. It had been bad enough to watch the seaplane loaded with our gear and women roaring across the black waters and disappearing into the blinding snow. At that time I wasn't sure that I hadn't just lost my wife and full-time companion, and I suspected that Franc felt the same way.

This looked like the worrisome ending of an otherwise very enjoyable, though strenuous, two weeks of moose hunting in Ontario. There was more to the expedition than that, of course, for Franc had badly needed footage for his television series of outdoor programs, and I had new material and background for some of the newspaper columns and outdoor features that make me my living. We had got what we came after, but this weather was of much concern.

I looked around for a place to set up the tent again, aware that it would be a long, cold night, and it might be several days before the plane could return, if the weather continued foul. It wouldn't be too serious a problem, for we still had the tent and the sleeping bags, and a moose for food. Besides, Magnus's cabin wasn't far away, and we seemed to be on pretty good terms with him. Still, it was a bit of a nuisance not to get back to base as soon as we had planned.

I wandered off into the woods a short distance looking for a better place to reestablish camp. A small clearing with a minimum pile of rocks and timber was nearby. I kicked aside a few rocks, then noticed one of them in particular. It was crumbly, laced with dark, bluish metallic lines. Upon closer examination, after scratching and chipping, I confirmed to my satisfaction that it was either silver- or lead-bearing ore, and a rich piece at that. I dug a bit more and there seemed to be plenty wherever I looked. Returning to where Franc sat on the duffel waiting, I showed it to him. He seemed uninterested, so I put a few samples beside my gear for later scrutiny.

"There is no way that plane will get in tonight. Let's go up and see Magnus and con him out of a cup of coffee. We can set up camp afterwards." It was so cold and wet that coffee seemed like a good way to raise our morale. Magnus's cabin being such a short distance away, we could smell cookies baking. A shout got us past his big dog and put a cup of coffee in hand. Magnus had been a trapper all his life and was now in his early sixties. At sixteen he had come from Finland—Lapland, actually—where he'd lived and worked in the woods and herded reindeer. If ever there was a professional outdoors-man, he certainly filled the bill.

Just as Franc and I took our first swig of coffee and were reaching for the cookies, the distant throb of an engine began to swell, then grew into a roar as our transportation cleared the treetops. We raced back towards the shore, and the plane faded into the snowstorm, only to reappear, popping out of the falling snow to skim the stark blackness of the lake like a water-skiing ghost. There was a hasty loading in the dark of wet tent, sleeping bags, and duffel, my canoe strapped to the struts. With the moose, in quarters now, piled on top of our other gear, the plane was filled to capacity. Then Franc squeezed in on top of the wet and musky-smelling moose. Waving good-bye to Magnus, who had followed us down to see that we got off, I slid into the copilot's seat, the engine revved, and the laden Beaver wallowed out into the snow-filled night.

The plane trembled, the engine, at maximum throttle, roared and shook, and very slowly we began to move across the lake. It seemed as if we would never get off. I could think only of the big snag that Franc and I had run into with the canoe—it was somewhere about where we were. Gaining speed, now lifting just enough to splash a bit, the plane rose and splashed, bounced and skittered along the wave tops. We were fast running out of lake. There was no way we could get up enough air speed. We bounced again. Peering into the snow streaming past us I imagined that I could see the snow-covered forest marking the opposite shore. It was not my imagination. I'd been told that your life is supposed to pass in review when you are about to cash in your chips. All I can remember thinking was, "Mary must have made it; otherwise the plane wouldn't have come back. I'm sorry that we didn't have more time together. I hope she gets along all right without me."

The trees, black with outlines of snow weighting their branches in heavy droopings, were flashing by the left wing as the plane turned and made a final bounce and lifted. I could see trees off the right wing tip streaking past. Ahead was darkness, then the white of the rapids.

Del, the bush pilot, had turned downriver in a last effort to get takeoff room. Now just skimming over the rapids, trees looming on both sides, he was following the ravine, over the beaver dams, lifting ever so slowly as the engine snarled and roared us upward, inch by inch, it seemed. Either the terrain lowered as we followed the river or we gained altitude—I suspect the former—but at last we were skinning just above the treetops. Now the pilot was able to ease the throttle back just a hair. If that engine had so much as missed a beat, there is little question that a lot of trees and ground would have been displaced.

For the next fifty minutes the stall warning kept buzzing. Below, snow-burdened trees stood with dark circles beneath them while all the ground was white. Countless lakes appeared and vanished beneath our wings, their black open waters surrounded by closing rings of ice and snow. The potholes where the beavers had dammed the inky ribbons of streams were outlined in white. The heavy snow that had been streaming past the windshield in a gray blur was lessening now, to be replaced by utter darkness. Only the green lights of the instruments, the red glow of the compass, and the blue of the engine exhaust pierced the night above the snow-laced forest.

Then in the distance the soft glow of a village, the twinkling of street lights, and buildings came into view. Almost home. "We've made it!" A wide circling bank and the plane was aimed for the black void marking the river winding through the village of Chapleau. The throttle chopped slightly and with full flaps extended we started to descend.

Suddenly out of nowhere, great white forms, like giant snowballs, dozens of them, swept past the windshield. Snow geese! We were flying through an entire migrating flock of hundreds of them, each big enough, if we hit one, to smash engine, wings, and windshield into bits and wipe us out in an instant. Del twisted the plane towards the thinnest line of birds and somehow missed total catastrophe. Making a wide circle, we came in. Slipping down between the buildings and missing little things like steeples and wires seemed child's play, except for the complete darkness. Not until the pontoons touched the surface of the river could we actually see the black and icy waters.

Limp, exhausted, we taxied up to the seaplane docks to secure for the night. Our wives were waiting. Never has the pleasure of a hot bath, after the two weeks of smoke, chill, rain, blood, sweat, and just plain fright, felt so good. It was some time later before I remembered that in the frantic rush we had forgotten to load my precious ore samples. Probably it was just as well, for they might have been the final ounce that would have done us in. Some day I may go back to the source of that mother lode of silver ore that is still waiting in that secret place; but I'm in no hurry, at least not until I run out of small change.

7.

Of Mountains

Mountains seem like bindings that hold the earth together. Look at a map or a globe: starting in Spain, an almost continuous ridge of high land begins at the Pyrenees, runs eastward to include the Alps, swings into the biblical lands of Iran and Afghanistan, continues eastward, rising and falling across Mongolia and Siberia to include the sky-scraping peaks of the Himalayas towards the icy roof of the world. Where the seas have broken through or the earth has cracked are only short pauses in this mountainous belt until it regains its majesty in the Brooks and McKenzie ranges to form the backbone of the North American continent. Not yet finished, it continues south, creating Mexico's Sierra Madre and the mountains of Central America. Nor does it terminate with the Andes, but carries through the highlands of fire to the Straits of Magellan.

Throughout these thousands of miles of mountains is a similarity: their harshness. Be it the windblown steppes of Mongolia or the storm-wracked Himalayas, the parched bleakness of Afghanistan or the snow-covered Brooks Range, mountain land is generally inhospitable to man. There is also a pervasively savage attraction, for these rocky crags are host to a wildness to be found nowhere else. Here thundering waterfalls cascade, alpine lakes glitter like gems, rushing rivers course through what seem like bottomless canyons, and ice-capped peaks punch holes in the clouds. Among cliffs scoured by wind and rain and in the jumbles of rock-strewn slopes may be isolated bands of mountain sheep and blue-green glaciers groaning over icy cracks and crevasses. Vast, barren moraines and milk-white glacial streams speak of the extremes of nature, and are among the few remaining wild lands, for such places as these man tends to avoid. They are the final retreats of many hard-pressed animal species that cannot coexist with prolific man as he seeks room to expand.

A few wise people of foresight, particularly in North America, realized that some of these extraordinary areas were worth preserving in their natural splendor, at a time when most of the wilderness that white man discovered and that natives took for granted was fast disappearing before an ever-spreading nation. The mountain West—much of the area included in the Louisiana Purchase and the last portion of the United States to be settled—held in many ways the least desirable lands of this new nation. Here and there, true, were apparently unending forests, large deposits of various minerals, and scattered rich valleys and meadows where homesteading could take place profitably, but for the most part these were well picked over as—and often before—the new western states were created. Vast holdings were donated to the railroads to encourage development. As much as 25 percent of the land area in some states went to single corporations. All the best resources were well divided before any lands were set aside in the public domain to be kept as national treasures where we might seek refuge from the increasing pressures of a burgeoning industrial society.

If we compute man's life expectancy at the biblical three score and ten, or seventy years, and use this as a scale of time, the initial invasion of North America by the European surpluses in their earliest settlements occurred not much more than five and one-half full lifetimes past. The real deluge of population got under way about two hundred years ago. With the defeat of the native inhabitants, the West was settled within recent memory—I can remember my grandfather telling me of his encounters with hostile Indians in the Dakota Territory. Americans were still engaged in homesteading fifty years ago, and the practice did not end until the Taylor Grazing Act of the early 1930s. Today there is very little public land left to give away. Even so, the Department of the Interior lately has been putting Bureau of Land Management holdings on the auction block.

Our nation averages around sixty-five souls per square mile, which we must share with birds, bears, and fishes. Very little of our land area has been kept preserved in its pristine condition. Less than a tenth of one percent of the original grasslands has been kept free from the plow. For the most part those areas that have not been altered or converted to something other than the original usage are those "locked up" in virtually inaccessible areas, such as mountain tops and pocosins. By a stroke of foresight, a few miles of oceanfront have been reserved for all of us, to be developed as National Seashores. The key word here is "developed"; almost none has been retained in its original wild condition. In similar context, virtually no virgin forest remains in the United States except where it is economically unfeasible to remove it.

We Americans are heirs to some of the most spectacular mountain ranges in the world. These ranges, born uncounted eons ago, are ever shifting, ever changing. The melting snowfields, spring runoffs, and resulting floods are forever altering the land, washing away the debris. All the while, amid volcanos and storms, living things grow, evolve, move, and are absorbed into their vastness. Let's hope we have the good sense to hold onto what remains ours.

It is not strange that Mary and I found it increasingly difficult to stay out of the back country once it got into our blood. Whenever we had the chance, we would figure a way to spend a little time in the bush. Perhaps one of our most memorable hikes was with two Marines, Randy Miller and Chuck Borsani, who had just returned from spending weeks, months, behind enemy lines in Viet Nam. They were even more eager than we to find some peace and relaxation. For this venture we had decided to backpack from the western side of Glacier National Park over the Continental Divide, working our way north into Canada's Waterton National Park.

We started one afternoon at the southwestern tip of Kintla Lake in Montana, a long finger of water between Starvation Ridge and Parke Ridge. The trail leads northeast, following the north shore and continuing to the smaller Upper Kintla, where we camped surrounded by dense, dark lodgepoles and glowered at by stony-faced mountains. Chuck unlashed a fishing rod and immediately hooked a Dolly Varden trout, while Mary sat by the fire nursing sore muscles and a couple of blisters. My second cast netted an eighteen-inch Dolly. In fiction the sun sinks slowly in the West; here it plummeted behind a mountain. We sat around the campfire, its orange light causing black shadows, the lake making soothing sounds on the rocks.

Randy predicted a bit of a climb the next day. By that afternoon we were sweating up and up the switchbacks of a west-facing slope, a fierce sun baking our backs, while, in the distance, the sound of inaccessible cool water plunging two to three thousand feet down a mountain face taunted us. We caught glimpses of brilliant blue-green lakes. An occasional grouse took flight with a thrum of wings, and a bald eagle soared overhead on wings of gold. We saw a fresh bear track on the trail, one of the largest I had ever seen. Finally, dripping with perspiration, we emerged onto an ice field at close to eight thousand feet, where a fresh wind brought its full refrigerated force into our faces. The sensation was one of having reached the top of the world. We had scarcely paused for breath before the wind had sucked out the sweat and body heat, as if we had stepped into a deep freeze.

The trail led along the base of Boulder Glacier, and now the chill bit deep. As rapidly as possible we crossed the ice field and made a hasty camp. Mary was feeling the effects of hypothermia. While I was stuffing her into a sleeping bag inside a windproof mountain tent, Randy fired up the pack stove and boiled water for his special concoction, hot Tang, a wonderful restorative for hypothermia, having both heat and sugar to bring the blood up to quota. We remembered another of its miraculous effects from canoeing in Ontario, where Franc White sometimes mixed gin with Tang for a breakfast eye-opener. Franc's tactics had certain merits, though we prefer such mixes after the sun has crossed the yardarm.

Far below us we could see a lake of wind-rippled blue, deep greens, and rocky shores. Standing there amid the thrones of the gods is to feel oneself at the heart of a different world, where the sky is a glorious blue and the horizon reaches out forever. Here cotton balls of clouds slide by, glancing off the grays and yellows of the upthrust mountains. We were relieved to be resting weary muscles after a couple of thousand feet of uphill hiking, and even a little proud of ourselves until we saw above us two mountain goats grazing our way, their creamy white coats blending with the snow fields behind them. A great golden eagle circled a while, then swept downward towards a towering cliff and disappeared. We watched a departing sun dip behind snow-tipped peaks across miles of blue mountains, its remaining fire flashing on the ice fields. Then the intense blue of unshielded space darkened into a star-crowded night.

Down bags held the bitter cold at bay and our sleep was deep, broken only by the flare of a red-faced sun framed by the tent flaps the next morning.

We picked up the trail again, past more cooling ice fields towards Lake Francis. But we were soon sweating. In this rarified atmosphere the sun was burning right into our skins. Around a bend, a cascade of white water foamed down the rocks, thundering its way to the valley far below. The water was still numbingly cold, direct from the melting of last year's snow and ice. Purified by the ultraviolet rays of the sun, aerated from being dropped thousands of feet over water-polished rock, such a drink has no near competitors.

All through this high mountain country, from valley floor to the foot of a glacier, are flowers—pallid yellow columbine, waxen sego lilies, the ubiquitous wake robin. Up the slopes march the white plumes of beargrass; blue penstemon crowds the edge of the trail, and Indian paintbrush ranges from deep rose to orange. There is the purple of heath, and the gold of arnica gives way at higher elevations to the equally brilliant yellow violet. Even in the glacial moraine small sedums appear along with the willow shrub that nourishes the goat.

Our trail took us through a high valley that twisted and turned along the backbone of the continent toward our destination in Canada, and from each turn another view unfolded that no words in human vocabulary could adequately chronicle. Pocketed on a mountainside, a melting glacier dropped a veil of water, only to have the winds toss it back to the lip of the mountain. We were now hiking at an elevation of around seven thousand feet, at about forty-nine degrees north, which though not extremely high put us well above the timberline. It was a climate where trees had given up the struggle, and the other alpine vegetation had only a few weeks at most to emerge, flower, and make seed before a brief summer ended.

Before this hike we thought we had seen all the spectacular scenery that could be composed. On the other side of this same range, hiking towards Grinnell Glacier, we had paused long enough to catch our breath, and looked down on Grinnell Lake to see a rippled milky emerald surrounded by the deep green of spruce and pine and the glitter of aspen. On the far side of the lake a cow elk grazed while her calf paid a call at the dairy bar. We had climbed to this glacier, the color of aquamarine, that gleamed as if lighted from within by some strange, cold electrical fire. In that high, thin atmosphere, dwarfed by mountain ranges that faded into blue horizons, the glacier, although a mile square, seemed but a few hundred yards across. Above us loomed the Garden Wall, a thin ridge of the Continental Divide extending north into Canada and on to the edge of the world. It is the same sheer formation known in The Bob as the Chinese Wall, and now we were looking at the other side of it.

Weather changes make up quickly in this region: fast-moving fronts sweeping in from the Pacific and whirling across these ranges, then stalling or tripping on the peaks, to drop their moisture in snow, sleet or, if the hiker is lucky, mere rain. It seemed no time at all after we noticed clouds gathering on the western horizon that a sleet-laden gale was howling. The wind whipped at our ponchos, screamed down the draws, picked up gravel and sent it rattling among the rocks. We made a hasty camp beside Lake Francis, securing our tents with rocks and deep-driven stakes, then crawled inside.

This was no quick-come-quick-go type of storm; it seemed determined to stick around. Time passes slowly in a tent 4½ feet wide and 7 feet long with sitting headroom only at the center. It was cold and damp; cutting sleet alternately froze and thawed, as if unable to make up its mind. We waited, drank hot tea and Tang, waited, and told stories, till cabin fever set in. What else was there to do but go fishing?

Fly fishing in a gale that's sweeping in from behind makes a back cast a bit difficult but it does aid greatly if distance on a forward cast is the goal. The thin ribbon of icy water plunging into the lake from a glacier must have stimulated the fish, for almost immediately I hooked and landed a fine rainbow. Now came the problem: eating dehydrated precooked food makes a cast iron skillet unnecessary, so we had brought nothing large enough to accommodate a big fish. The solution had to be to roast it over hot coals. In gale and rain, with legal firewood almost nonexistent, this can be difficult, but we were serious enough to find a way. I ran a sharpened stick through the fish lengthwise, pinning the belly flaps together with a twig. Then I salted the trout liberally and roasted it slowly. It made a superb treat.

The rain was easing somewhat, and we were mucking about, debating whether or not to break camp, when we discovered that we had not been alone. Fresh bear tracks were all around. Where we had camped so hurriedly was obviously a bear crossing. But it was late and the rain was picking up again, and we decided to spend the night before leaving the site to the bears' exclusive use.

That evening when we came out of our tents to huddle under dripping ponchos, eat rain-diluted rations, and stare into the smouldering fire, Randy related a tale that he claimed was told to him by "Smoke" Elser, a well-known Montana guide who operates from the Rattlesnake area. A man who worked for him was telling a client why he would never again hunt bears. He had nearly met his match with a grizzly. "Nearly got kilt one time," he said. "That bear was a'mighty quick. We were huntin' and stopped to look over some sign when I first saw him. He was hidin' behind a big log, waitin' to ambush me. Now I know they're mighty smart, but he didn't figure I knew he was there. All I could see at first was his eyes. Then here he come, jumped over that log with a wild roar and opened his mouth so wide all I could see was teeth. Quick as light I threw up the rifle and shot him right smack in the tonsils. That bear swapped ends faster'n grease, 'n' I ain't dared look no bear in the tail since."

"Why? What happened?" The guide spat in the fire and paused to recollect. "Why, when he swapped ends he was so fast that bullet took my hat off when it came out the other end."

The rain began to fall a little heavier and we called it a night, to crawl back into damp tents and sleeping bags and dream of bears.

It was a soggy, bearded, muddy crew that finally descended from the high barren rocks to the dense woods and emerged on the shore of Waterton Lake in the Canadian Rockies. As we came out of the dripping darkness of sodden forest we met a group of tourists being escorted around the lake by a park naturalist. Having just been led on a hundred-yard walk along the lake shore, they were again boarding a dry, comfortable, enclosed boat feeling as if they had been on a great adventure. Among them was a stout matron who, upon meeting such exotic creatures as we who actually went out into the woods just like wild animals, began to gush over us, especially Mary.

Mary's response was solemn, "Oh, wait till you see the seventy-three-year-old woman who just came down from Stoney Indian Lake! She's right behind us."

Even so, we had promised one another certain rewards for completing the course: Chuck would treat us to passage across the lake, Randy would buy a round of beer, and Mary and I would take care of dinner.

The Prince of Wales Hotel is a beautiful, ornate, and rather plush structure designed to separate tourists from their dollars. It stands near the northern end of Waterton Lake. We were still in hiking clothes, having failed to carry city clothes on the trail for such occasions. We had set down our packs and were standing in the lobby where a string trio was swinging into its first light classical selection of dinner-hour music for the bored palefaces sitting about. The same matron entered, the one who had been gushing over us on the boat. Now fashionably dressed in a manner to reflect her husband's success, she waddled by, pausing long enough to lift her glasses, the kind affixed to a long handle.

Mary spoke to her, and the grande dame responded, "As my husband and I were coming down on the elevator I remarked that the inn here is not the sort of place where one just drops in off the highway." There was a long pause accompanied by all the hauteur she could muster: "But I see I was wrong."

National parks and wildlife refuges are the best places to observe wildlife under natural conditions. Probably the greatest concentrations of native American game can be found in Yellowstone Park, followed by Glacier Park and the National Bison Range in Montana, and Custer State Park in South Dakota. My friend Royal Brunson was for several seasons a naturalist in Glacier. Even with his background as zoologist and hunter, his knowledge of wildlife still seemed uncanny, the more so to a tenderfoot like me. Al Robinson, who used to take me tarpon fishing in the Florida Keys, could not only catch tarpon, seemingly at will, but predict the actual time when they would bite. Royal was much the same; from his knowledge of the various animals' habits, he knew just when and where to be for observing wildlife. So when he asked, "Did you ever see a wolverine?" I fully expected to be led to one.

In legend and in fact there is but one animal that fears no other, and that is the wolverine. A large musk-bearing mammal, heavily muscled, it is feared and respected by trappers for its cunning, ferocity, and incredible strength. Pound for pound, this relative of the weasel is said to be the strongest and fiercest of animals. Reportedly, it has attacked and killed moose, elk, and deer. It can run effortlessly over any terrain and climb any tree. Woodsmen have told of its forcing a grizzly bear to give up the trail rather than tangle with it, for the animal always seems to be spoiling for a fight. Perhaps the only fur-bearer considered more fierce is the Tasmanian devil. Yet the wolverine is rare, and, though elusive, it has been extirpated from most of North America. Extinct east of the Rockies, the species has very few survivors south and east of Alberta, though trapping records show that around a thousand hides are sold by Canadian and Alaskan trappers each year.

If Royal could show me a wolverine, I'd be glad to accept his offer. The departure point would be where Going-to-the-Sun Highway tops the divide. There we'd take the trail that leads north from Logan Pass towards Granite Park Chalet. The trail follows the backbone of the Continental Divide, a path, none too wide, that leads along the west face of the sheer cliff called the Garden Wall. We pulled on jackets and checked to see that we had film, camera, and lunch before setting out.

It was still early morning, and an icy wind whistled along the face of the cliff, knifing to the marrow. Very shortly it became apparent that Royal had introduced us to a place specially designed to scare the wits out of those who suffer from acrophobia, that paralyzing fear of high places. Nor is it for those clumsy with their feet, for the trail, only a few feet wide, leads over apparent voids where, if you dare look down, you will see far below a narrow line that marks the highway. And those little bugs crawling on the line, about a quarter- to a half-inch long, are buses, campers, and automobiles. Here and there park officials had thoughtfully provided lengths of garden hose. The hoses concealed steel cables secured to the cliff that rose perpendicular towards unseen heights on our right. They were designed to hang onto for some false sense of security while negotiating the rock-strewn path. With a death grip on a lone patch of slippery bear grass, I dared to look at the panorama unfolded below, of streams winding into eternity, and above, of snowfields that had resisted the brief, intense heat of summer, perhaps destined not to be melted, but to form the beginning of another glacier.

The trail widened slightly, the near cliff no longer absolutely vertical, merely almost so. Abruptly Royal urged me to take the lead. "You might get your camera ready," was all that he said. Just then I saw a movement on the trail ahead. Somehow I had started thinking about this being grizzly country, and what we would do if we met one, when here came a critter, dark, with a massive head of merging blacks and dark browns, loping along the trail towards us at a mile-eating gait. It was on all fours, and its shoulders looked as if it were wearing football pads. Short forelegs appeared bowed, like a bull-dog's. Its paws were large, ears short and rounded—all bear in appearance, but it had a long bushy tail. It wasn't a grizzly or even a bear, but it had every appearance of being able to wrestle one.

I aimed the camera. The animal was perhaps sixty feet away and closing fast when it heard the shutter click. It stopped and seemed even larger as it looked us over, then advanced slowly, eyes cold, fierce.

I was in a quandary about which fear to respond to. There was no retreat, no side trail, no trees to climb. The cliffside was vertical above and there was only a yawning vastness below. To run would simply invite attack, I feared. Climbing was out of the question. Even if there had been an escape for me, Royal and our wives were on the trail directly behind me. There was no choice but to bluff it out. If that failed, camera and tripod would have to serve as a last-resort defense.

Closer and closer it came, with no sign of turning. Then it paused and stared at us—we were four—as if figuring the odds. Which would it choose? It jumped up on a rock, studied us some more, then casually turned and faded into a draw that we had not seen, a cut in the rocks knifed through by centuries of spring runoff. In a few moments we saw it again, standing on a boulder looking at us, perhaps making a final assessment of our strength relative to its own, before it loped off along a ridge towards where some mountain goats were feeding. As it disappeared into a jumble of rocks I resumed breathing.

Royal laughed. "You must be a mean-looking hombre to scare a grizzly-eating wolverine off the trail. Of course, you know, they never attack man unless cornered or trapped. At least no one has lived to tell about it."

A sickly giggle came from Mary. "Gee, I'm sure glad it wasn't a Tasmanian devil!"

A few nights later, lying in my sleeping bag, I was listening to a creek hiss and rumble its way down a canyon in the Bitterroots, thinking idle thoughts like, If I knew just how far it is to the base of the cliff I could figure how high it is—maybe a half-mile, because the North Star is riding like a beacon atop the sheer rock face. But that wasn't really important. What mattered was that the cliff was there, and I was there, and I could see the entire face, washed a blue-white by the moon and its craggy features accented by tall ponderosas clinging to the cracks. A dying fire was flickering alongside Mary and me. Overhead, the tall, straight trunks of spruce and pine reached into the dark sky. There was a light, sweet scent of wood smoke, but better than that, the clean, cold air, filtered by miles of wilderness, with perhaps a hundred miles of mountain and forest to cleanse it before it reached the next permanent abode of man. Animal smells, woods smells I can live with, but man—and I'm one of them—has a smell of his own, whether it's his cars, his factories, or his person, and it's nice to get away from it.

Immense as a wilderness can seem when you're in the middle of it, only a very tiny portion of the continental United States (Lower 48) is designated as wilderness today. I'd like to see a lot more wilderness areas scattered throughout the nation. It may be because wilderness stands for freedom, something that means more to me than power or wealth. To some, freedom means less work. My freedom means more work, but of a different kind. I'd rather chop wood to keep warm than work for the money to pay for electricity or oil, and I get the fun and exercise of chopping my wood. Don't get me wrong. It's rather nice to have those who think differently punching a time clock so that I can enjoy the fruits of their labors. I wouldn't change places with them for the world, but I'd be glad for them to have a slice of my freedom.

In no time at all it was sunrise, the air crisply cold and the fire a bank of cold ashes. The tops of the mountains, pure gold in the first rays of sunlight, gradually took on the white glare of day. As the sun reached them the trees above us had a turn, too—golden green at first before paling to ordinary spruce and pine colors. I looked to my fishing tackle: it was still there, but sometime during the night something had visited our camp, likely a mouse, from the way wrappers were chewed.

I was reminded of a friend who was on a fishing trip with two of his buddies. In the middle of the night he was wakened by a strange noise. Next he heard snickering from the pickup, where his friends had chosen to sleep. "Porky-pine, chewing up Doc's boots!" "Heh, heh, won't he be surprised in the morning!" Doc looked at his boots beside him; they were intact. He waited a few minutes before shining a light on the boots and the porcupine sitting on the tailgate of the pickup. It was a few seconds before screams and curses of "Them's my boots!" were followed by blasts from a gun that blew Porky and boots off the tailgate. No one could hear Doc's snickers.

Recalling his last laugh, I picked up my rod and wandered down to the singing stream where some beavers were building a dam. Maybe I could get a fish before breakfast.

Thousands of people have tried to answer the question of why man goes fishing—escapism, reversion to more primitive instincts, attempts to prove oneself or find oneself, relaxation, or communion with nature—all have been offered as reasons. For some the element of profit enters, while still others use fishing as a stepping stone to promote themselves in the eyes of their peers. I've questioned myself many times as I've sat in a canoe on some remote north-woods lake while listening to a loon laugh, or cry; or waded the noisy gurgling water around the boulders of a cold mountain stream; or ridden gentle swells in a skiff in the Florida Keys, seeking tarpon but watching roseate spoonbills probing the mangrove flats. I've questioned the great attraction of angling while standing on a Carolina fishing pier crowded with spot fishermen, or waist-deep in the crashing surf along the more remote strands of the Outer Banks. Was it because of an innate desire to prove myself that I cast for bonefish on the flats of Florida Bay? I doubt it whenever I think of once fishing for king mackerel while seasick enough to conclude that my own eyeballs were counter rotating and unable to focus on either the rod or the fish that was struggling for its life.

There is no single answer, not even the one attributed to the alpinist who climbed Mt. Everest "just because it's there." I think man fishes mostly because he thinks the fish are there, and it is part of his primitive hunting instinct to pursue and attempt to possess a form of life that has the ability to escape. True, it is reinforced by the food-gathering urge, and the ego boosting does not interfere. The taste of fish is secondary to the surroundings. It is a time when the pressures of the world loosen their grip, are put aside for a moment in favor of the arch of a flyline, the call of a bittern, the sight of a golden eagle hovering on an updraft, or the flying fish skittering all blue and silver across glass-clear waves above cobalt depths. Perhaps the reasons are too complex for me, but more than likely it's that I have a continuing romance with wilderness and the fishing is just an excuse to be there.

Undisturbed beavers have been known to create, though inadvertently, a paradise for trout fishermen. Gene Tingle and Ed Drake had guided us to such a hidden bit of heaven for some applied fisheries research. I won't reveal the exact site, but we had started by heading towards Salmon River country, then turned off where hot springs burble out of the bowels of the earth and followed a dirt road until it ended and a horse trail began. In the depths of this rather steeply walled canyon, where the waters seem to talk their way over moss-backed rocks that have been tumbled through the centuries, the beavers have accomplished what man can only imitate. Yet to be discovered by eager trappers, they had built their dams of logs and chinked them with branches and twigs. In the brilliance of that late Indian summer the sunlight rippled across gleaming ponds, reflecting all the autumnal golds and reds that nature could command. Deep emerald pools told us to forget the season, for we could see living shadows wavering among the aquatic grasses that swayed with the currents. Already turned by frost to yellow with bronzed edges, leaves showered down on creek and forest floor from the light puffs of wind that sniffed through the valley. The banks, steep and brush lined, were thick with alder and willow.

I could hear the fish calling me, so, pulling on waders, I made my way towards the sound of falling water. Ed had already announced that he would work downstream, and Gene had determined to investigate the stream above the beaver ponds. I plunged into a criss-cross of sloughs and channels at times waist deep. Through mazes of fallen timber mingled with abandoned dams and waterways I made my way cautiously. The water was icy, the cold quickly penetrating all my insulation and numbing my feet. I chose to ignore it. Whenever I reached reasonably open water, I'd flick a fly as far ahead as the brush permitted. There was no response until, finally locating the main stream, I could see ahead a clear stretch where the water poured over a spillway into a deep hole, then spread out to fan over the shoal in bubbling rapids. With short casts I proceeded to work the fly at the base of the rapids, then lengthened the casts until the line was snaking over the deeper water and the lure settling easily on green water at the intersection of a rock and a sunken log.

It floated there a moment as the current snatched at it, then a swirl of water and a form rose like a gray-green ghost. The trout slammed at the lure, water erupting in a rainbow of spray. It discovered its error when I lifted the rod tip and set the hook. The contest was on. Diving madly towards the deep hole carved beneath the log by the fast water, the fish in its rush bent the rod in a deep arc before the pressure turned it aside. I was using an ancient and very light rod of split bamboo. It was as if the wand were alive, the fibers protesting, the tip quivering under the strain. The fish gave up on reaching deep water and surged over the rapids. Keeping up the pressure, I again turned it from the faster and deeper water until, at last exhausted, it allowed itself to be led to a gravel bar in midstream. The brilliant red gashes under its throat identified it as a cutthroat. Bronzed green sides held a dash of yellow spots, and its belly was creamy pink, twelve inches of beauty, fat with the riches of fast water, still pools, and all that the mountains could provide.

For a moment I wanted to return it to its haunts, so that its unexcelled beauty could continue to enrich this stream, so that it and all that it stood for could live on and on. But my companions were expecting fish for breakfast; this was part of the chase; this was what I had come for. I slid it into the creel, somewhat haunted by having removed this living thing, yet knowing that nature favors no one, that each is part of the life system of another.

I flicked the fly again, and again, repeating the search from shallows to deep holes, behind rocks and logs, as I waded up the stream, pausing only to take in the colors, the dancing light, to watch the fish scurrying underfoot and the clouds reflecting on the quiet pools. It was not difficult there to take the limit, even though releasing all of the smaller fish. I kept only those that would fit a twelve-inch frying pan. Yet it was not my skill, nor the superiority of my equipment, that produced those fish for us to catch. I credit the beavers: those eager engineers, those nonunion craftsmen that can create unsurpassed habitat, prevent floods, and hold water for all forms of wildlife—deer, fish, birds, man, and moose—to use at no cost to the taxpayers. If only the Corps of Engineers could say the same!

It was late before I climbed the banks and returned to camp where Gene, Ed, and the women were gathered around the fire. Mary had baked cornbread in a Dutch oven, the coffee pot was simmering at the edge of the glowing coals, and Marion Tingle and Trixi McCormick had the rest of supper waiting. Among us, we had enough fish for breakfast. After supper, sitting around the crackling fire, we felt the cold of the mountain high country beginning to slide down into the valley. It caused us to move closer and closer to the flames as we shared tales of hunting trips and big fish we'd known, of trails followed in the wilderness by horse, canoe, and on foot. Ed had been raised in the far recesses of the mountains, living off the land for extended periods; Gene and Marion, ranching for many years, knew the open range as well; Trixi, ranch raised, had known a different world, too, in show business as a trick rider.

Procyon was rising above the peaks before Mary and I slid into down sleeping bags that we had laid out under the protective branches of a spruce. Long ago we'd discovered it to be several degrees warmer under a tree, the branches also keeping off dew and frost. Tall grass will do an admirable job of deflecting the wind. I pulled a watch cap down all the way to my eyes and wormed into the sleeping bag with only my nose out. Behind us, the fire was showing its last pale yellow shafts of flame above glowing coals. Overhead the unending canopy of stars moved on. I tried to stay awake long enough to see Orion rise, but failed. My next awareness was of dawn coming late into the valley and the sound of rushing water. I rolled over in time to see a puff of smoke. Ed was kindling the morning fire.

Breakfast was cutthroats dipped in seasoned cornmeal and cooked in hot oil to a golden brown. Potatoes and onions were prepared with bacon on the lid of an old Maytag washer, a Western outdoorsman's most treasured piece of equipment. Scrambled eggs rounded out the menu. Speak not to me of cholesterol: these gave us the strength to drink the fresh-boiled coffee. Where the sun doesn't lift above the ridge before ten, there's time for a second cup, even a third. We could take our time preparing for another bout with the fish in a valley where the fish do not get up at dawn, but keep bankers' hours—not biting before 10:00 A.M. and quitting by 4:00 P.M. The sun was just reaching camp when I slipped out of my down jacket and donned my waders. It was time to go back to work up at the beaver ponds.

Wild country to a fisherman is a succession of streams and lakes put there just for his pleasure. I remember one fall when we were on one of the blue-ribbon streams found at the edge of Yellowstone Park, hoping for a last fish fling before the ice locked in the stream for the winter. The evening chill was moving in, and there was not much light left. With enough fish in the creel for supper, I lay the rod down and started looking for a convenient place to clean the fish. All the time I had been fishing I had thought myself quite alone, but in the wild things are not always what they seem. The sun had dropped behind the mountain, and the afterglow cast a pink haze over all. We were looking at boulders on a distant hillside, dark lumps among the sagebrush and brown grasses. Then the boulders moved! I fished pocket-sized binoculars out of my shirt and focused. Elk, dozens of them, were grazing on the slope, the golden, heart-shaped rumps identifying them.

Soon the Mad Moon of November was spilling its fullness into the valley. By its brilliance, I began studying the herd for bulls. Then I heard a small noise nearby, like someone blowing his nose. I turned very slowly to see, perhaps ten yards away, a big cow and a calf nearly as large puzzling over the strange creature leaning against the rock. The baffled look was evident in the dark faces framed by ears now cocked forward. The cow continued to study me, but the calf, already bored, rubbed its head against her flank. She must have caught a hint of something foreign, for, gracefully and noiselessly she eased past in a semicircle, assessing me. How an animal of a thousand pounds and more can walk through thick brush, trees, dry grass, and rubble without a sound is beyond my comprehension. She seemed to float like a dark shadow, fading ghostlike into the draw.

The Mad Moon of November is so called because it is the season
of the rut. It occurs earlier in some places, this time when wild animals like the buffalo and elk of the plains, driven by the mating
instinct, lose all sense of caution. It was the moon when Indians
could safely lay in their winter meat supply, dried and smoked into
survival food. It was a time of feasting, too, and food preparation,
such as dried fruits and berries being mixed with rich buffalo suet
into pemmican cakes. New robes and blankets were tanned and softened. Surviving the coming winter depended on this exciting moon
of madness.

By the time the full moon had lifted over the mountains, reflecting off snow-tipped peaks and throwing a full blue light on the hillsides, I'd counted more than sixty head of elk feeding down the
slopes. There were few bulls to be seen. The rut was about over.
Most showed the long, skinny spikes of two- and three-year-olds,
but we were treated to the magnificent sight of an occasional senior
bull carrying a majestic rack with all the dignity of royalty. Now
their winter migration would begin, when high country snows
forced them towards the valleys and towards waiting hunters.

It had been a great day. Earlier we'd wandered up Yankee Jim
Canyon alongside the Yellowstone River, where in nearly every bend
and backwater we could hear the geese gabbling and see them feeding on the flats. There were swans and Canada geese, rafts of bald-
pates and shovelers, and a generous sampling of other waterfowl.
As we approached one backwater with long-lensed cameras in hand,
there was an explosion of hundreds of birds bursting into flight simul-
taneously—the roar of wings, the honks of alarm, the splashing of
water. Then, rising, wheeling, and forming lines and vees, they moved
into organized flight patterns to sweep past peaks and over draws,
above grazing cattle that dotted the river margins, past clumps of
brush and trees, to glide downward and settle in a safer section of
the river.

As the moon rose the temperature kept falling, with a keen wind
adding to the chill. It would be a cold night in the mountains. Pumping up the tiny pocket stove, we put the fish on to cook, then brewed
a hot drink. After eating we filled a Thermos in preparation for morning, laid out sleeping bags, and slipped into them to wonder at the
stars, the brilliant moon, the sounds of wind and water, the scent of

sage, the far-off sounds of geese, the wind moaning among trees and rocks.

The moon was still high when the sun put a rosy wash on the mountains. Two mule deer wandered by casually, seeming to know full well that they were safe from this hunter. Mary enhanced my sense of well-being by handing me coffee even before I could get out of the sleeping bag. We broke camp and packed the car. Frosty fog filled the valleys, but the ridges were bright. We glanced up a game trail leading into the rocks: a coyote, already in winter dress, was sitting in the sun, yawning, eyeing us. Aware that we had seen him, he winked and disappeared. It was as if he understood our feelings, perhaps better than we did.

8.

The Road
to Alaska

One of my fondest dreams, ever since I was a toddler, had been to visit Alaska, and when I read about the Alcan Highway I knew that it must be explored, and by me. All summer Mary and I had been camping and fishing throughout Montana, but it was a dry summer and forest fires were wracking the state. Most of the forest land was now closed, with a pall of blue smoke lying over the hills and valleys like a shroud. Mary agreed; this would be a good time to go north and west, to the land of gold and salmon, where the moose are as common as deer, where the beluga whale and the walrus wander. I packed up my gold pan and put a new set of tires on the old van, for I'd heard stories about rough roads, blowouts, and being stranded in the wilderness. These essentials taken care of, we figured we were ready.

Of the many border crossings into Canada, the one we chose had the most propitious name: Eureka. Very few restrictions are placed on the American tourist visiting Canada. There are several requirements, such as some kind of identification, and a few questions asked: What kind of things do you intend to sell? Have you more than three days' food supply? How many cigarettes do you have?

But one thing obsesses Canadians: they trust no American with a handgun. They will ask, and repeat several times, do you have any handguns? They had no worries about rifles or shotguns, for they understand that those are for hunting. By contrast, a Mexican border official told me that he considered shotguns and rifles were for killing people, adding that anyone who uses a handgun for anything but self-defense must be crazy. It's all in the way you look at it. There is a provision for taking handguns to Alaska by having customs seal them in a box that cannot be opened until back in U.S. territory, with exceptions for bona fide shooting matches and competitions. Otherwise there is no alternative but to leave any handguns behind.

I asked the customs official why the fuss? He stiffened. "Handguns are for killing people." He added that he had served many years in the Canadian military, during which time he had killed many people, and he didn't carry a pistol now. I wanted to ask him if the Canadian Army issued pistols instead of rifles. If I were in the killing business I certainly wouldn't want a pistol. But it didn't seem the appropriate time to get into such a discussion. Besides, my wife, anticipating the worst in me, turned on the tape deck, which blared forth "Oh Canada!" The customs gentleman straightened up, clicked his heels and snapped to attention: "Have a good trip, sir!"

We drove on, aliens in a foreign land, somewhat. To be sure, there are a few other pecularities, among them that below every official sign in English is the French translation. I told my wife that I thought it very nice to be so considerate, but what about the other people, such as the Spanish, the Greeks, the Russians, the Chinese, and all? She answered, a bit huffily I thought, "Well, there are a lot of French-speaking Canadians." Now I know a bit of history, too. Back in the 1700s the French lost Canada to the British. I understand that some of the French are still sore about it and refuse to learn English. Suppose the Indians had felt the same way? My wife chose not to hear me and we drove a few miles in silence.

The romantic in each of us wants to fall under the spell of the Yukon—without getting cold, of course. Robert Service and Jack London deserve much of the blame, but Kenneth Roberts and a host of others who wrote of or searched for the Northwest Passage, and scores of cheechakos who kept diaries to hand down to their grandkids, share the awesome responsibility for feeding the urge for northern adventure lying buried, sometimes deeply, in all of us. Mary and I are no different. And, though we had crossed the Canadian border often, we had still felt a tingle of excitement when the crisp customs official said, "Have a good trip, sir!"

We'd been informed that, no matter how magnificent we'd found the mountain ranges of Glacier, they are as nothing when compared with the Canadian Rockies. When it comes to mountains, Canada has some whoppers. In the series of national parks that runs through the heart of the Rockies—Waterton, which joins Glacier at the border, then Kootenay and Yoho and Banff and Jasper—each in turn is more impressive than the last. The rugged backbone of a continent rises to even grander proportions here.

Some of the North American continent's more famous tourist traps are included in these parks, among them Radium Hot Springs. It's a big swimming pool filled to capacity with lobster-hued people in skimpy swimming suits, fat, skinny, all simmering cheek-to-cheek. Restaurants are similarly crowded. Canadians must be loaded with Christian charity to put up with us Yanks in tourist form. If they charge higher prices it is little enough compensation.

Clearly, nothing will deter Americans from vacationing when and where they wish. Distance, time, and trouble seem to be no consideration. Surely no one who can afford it stays at home, for the resorts are chock-a-block, elbow-to-elbow with vacationers, all pushing and shoving. Many youths hitchhike, toting bedrolls. Others ride motorcycles, and surprising numbers are to be found bicycling. Their outfits identify them. Bare legs and a rucksack mean bicycle, unless they also carry long ropes and ice axes and wear big clumsy shoes. Then they are, or would like to be, mountain climbers. Ordinary blue jeans and denim jackets designate hitchhikers; down jackets and bright colors usually mean a car. The most popular place in town is not the bar, but the self-service laundry. Indeed, that is what has put America on the road today.

Canadian national park campgrounds are no different from those in the States: the name of the game is cozy—a thousand square miles of parkland, and they crowd the campsites so close together that you can hear your neighbors snoring on all sides. Luxury motor homes run generators that sing you to sleep mechanically, so that you don't have to listen to squirrels, birds, and that everlasting wind in the spruce trees. Roughing it is when the TV set doesn't work. Then the so-called camper can't stand being confined with his kids and boots them out to help me shave or drive tent stakes. One night per summer in a campground is about our limit—we like our fellow man a bit more scattered.

We came upon a crowd of cars and, sitting serenely by the roadside, efficiently combing the bushes with long claws, raking in paws-full of berries, a black bear. A few yards away another bruin was grubbing busily under a log. Surrounding the two were the tourists, Instamatics clicking furiously. Luckily the species is generally peaceful by nature. When the berry picker wanted to escape the surrounding hordes, it uttered one "Woof!" and waddled towards them. Women screamed, children cried, and men fell over themselves in mass clumsiness. Canada has set aside several of these seemingly endless tracts where man can take a real vacation from the pressures of his day-to-day environment. We can hope that Canadians have learned from our mistakes that even this rugged land is fragile and that there is an end to "endless."

But whether they see it or not, the scenery is what most people come for. Leaving behind the Columbia Ice Fields and the parks area we headed northwest, following the Yellowhead Highway. Behind us were the tall mountains, sheer, snow-clad crags jutting thousands of feet above dark green forests. Wild, foaming rivers, spilling over high cliffs in cataracts and falls, spray reflecting rainbows in the mist, white clouds clinging to black peaks. Fantastic but real glaciers between towering walls of rock, deep crevasses glowing with that unearthly, yet intense, blue-green of glacial ice. Glacier-nourished lakes, deep and clear blue gems rimmed by the golden green of marshy meadows, these outlined by the black-green of northern spruce. To the fisherman, the final lure is to see such a gem dimpled by the rising of a hungry trout.

With range upon range of mountains disappearing into blue-gray ahead of us, we found the scenery gradually changing as we followed the Fraser River towards Prince George. From northwest Montana we'd felt that we had a good running start, but after several days of travel and finding ourselves still in Alberta and not yet on the Alaska Highway, it was tempting to forget the goal and just launch the canoe into the nearest stream and follow it, no matter where it led. From Prince George the road meanders northeast towards Dawson Creek, the real beginning. You don't think of your trip as starting until you've knocked off the first thousand miles. Then there's that uneasy feeling that you have indeed arrived at the jumping-off place, when your heading is west-northwest again, so you stock up as if you were a sourdough headed for the Klondike.

The road was called the Alcan when construction began in 1942, and finished for wartime use before the end of the same year. It's 1,523 miles from Dawson Creek, British Columbia, to Fairbanks, Alaska, about the same distance as driving from the North Carolina coast to Minneapolis, but on rough roads. The highway ranges from superfine dust to pavement, from mud to rock. It's full of curves and surprises, yet passable for almost any vehicle from eighteen-wheeler to bicycle. It's the hitchhiker's Everest. By taking it easy, you can drive the Alaska Highway in a comfortable five days, Dawson Creek to Fairbanks. Going faster means more broken trailer axles, flat tires, and damage to windshields.

The more leisurely pace gives better opportunity for sightseeing—there's plenty to see if you like trees, rivers, and mountains as viewed through a mud-spattered, rock-crazed windshield. At halfway point our score was only five holes in the windshield. Keeping the rear window clean was a hopeless goal, to be abandoned almost immediately. Besides windshields, the most common casualty is smashed headlights (ours wore plastic contact lenses), followed by getting stuck in the mud, followed by flat tires.

Plenty of facilities are to be found along this highway, but it was only after we had passed Dawson Creek that we began to feel free to slip off into the bush for wilderness camping. The Canadian sun was setting over the spruce forests when we found a stream of shining silver undulating into a deep valley. Here we made camp, our only company the trees and the loneliness. Thinning gray clouds scudded by, pausing to adhere briefly to distant peaks, then tearing on to rejoin their kin. The undersides of some were alight with yellow and fiery orange, promising a fair tomorrow. The forest floor was deep, a mixture of moss, fallen needles, and moldering logs, beneath sentinel spruce with spiraling bark marking their reach for the sky in this harsh environment. Slender lodgepoles stood shaggy and unkempt. It was quiet, except for the whisper of a breeze through the treetops of a forest calm in its depths. Breaking in was the coarse call of a low-flying raven heading towards security for the night. The smoke of our campfire settled like a light fog in the narrow river bottom. Flickering orange flames warded off some of the descending chill. Mary, sitting on a log at river's edge, was watching the advancing darkness, sometimes playing a few lonesome bars on her concertina.

The Far North is a strange land. The summer night is subdued twilight, rivers fed from great glaciers run milky white, and bull moose stand on highways challenging trucks. Its early fame was of gold, and the fortune fever still exists. Anticipating the probability of finding our own gold mine, we were making it a point to check any streams that might be in the vicinity of wherever we stopped. It was possible that gold seekers had missed one. The idea had been nourished further when we encountered a Volkswagen bus with a big box on top, a washtub in front, pick and shovel in the rear, stopped near where we were parked for a coffee break. The bearded driver, we concluded, must have been a geology professor on sabbatical from some eastern college. He saw me eyeing the rig and volunteered that the box strapped to the top of the van was a sluice he had designed, a rock washer contrived to separate the gold from its company. He figured that there was still a lot more gold to be discovered in the North, and I agreed. Mary, skeptical, surmised that he, too, had fallen under the spell of the Yukon, but she concluded some of his spell may have been helped along by a heart-warming brandy known as Yukon Jack. We did admire his spirit, though, and his rig made us feel like tenderfeet.

The road follows sprawling valleys, skirts around the ends of mountain ranges. Occasionally we saw a moose as it disappeared into the bush; more often we saw a dead one by the roadside. Far to the west loomed the coastal mountains, high and forbidding, snow on top, anchored in dense forest. Giant river bottoms, looking as if they had been bulldozed out by raging floods, chewed at the road flanks. The roads were puny scratches alongside gargantuan forests, mountains, and rivers.

Long before we set up our first camp in the Yukon, we had begun to realize that just seeing and feeling this land is the real treasure. We were going north to meet autumn. The snow on the mountaintops was fresh, and nightly the frost was creeping lower into the valleys. Aspens and willows were turning bright gold, scrub growth was scarlet, and fireweed cerise to royal purple in a kaleidoscopic brilliance enhanced by the atmosphere of the northland. The yellow-greens of marshes surrounded ponds and rimmed rivers. An incredibly blue sky was reflected, glittering, from still pools and the shoals and rapids of countless streams. In this truly primeval land the dark greens of forests extended beyond time and imagination, and there was the inescapable feeling that something still more special was waiting just over the next rise, around the next bend.

The night was cold, and our down bags felt good when the frost settled on them, catching the starlight. We wondered how long any of this wildness would last. We had already seen in eastern Canada how the Indian is caught in a dilemma: whether to retain his tribal heritage of hunting and fishing while the women cook the meals and prepare the skins and furs, or join the system and work for wages, getting hooked on the need for electricity and television, for cars and roads, for snowmobiles and stereo, only to be informed that he's not happy and should go back to the old ways. Either way, he'd be disillusioned. So progress crunches on, in the form of bulldozers and mines, of necktied passengers in company helicopters flitting in and out of the bush. Northern Canada, too, is a paradox. Travel promotion releases praise the boundless wilderness, across which gas and oil lines are marching; the wildlife is confronted by roads and grand-scale logging; and the incomparable fishing in creeks and rivers is muddied by dragline operations. Mary summed it up with her favorite line from Oscar Wilde's "Ballad of Reading Gaol": "Each man kills the thing he loves . . ."

Until we began to discover northwest Canada, the Territories, and Alaska, our experiences with "big" had been Texas-big. Now we had looked down on rivers longer than any we'd ever seen, gazed upon mountain ranges that seemed to have no end, regarded ice fields and glaciers from above, below and alongside, all of which gave us a top-of-the-world feeling.

The geography changes but little on the Alaskan border. The changes were in the road. Suddenly everything was paved, a new and shiny pavement that rolled and heaved like being at sea. It was the ever-present battle with permafrost.

We camped beside the Tanana River and feasted on a fine supper of Mackinaw trout, having no further thought than of a good night's sleep, snug in our down bags, breathing the clear, frosty air. The North Star seemed almost overhead. Then it began: as if just for us, a welcoming to another world. In the northeastern sky an eerie band of light started to build across the heavens. In strange yellow-greens, flickering, writhing shafts of lights soon reached out of sight to the northwest, pulsating strongly in pastels, disappearing and coming on again in white. The vibrant colors filled the sky from horizon to horizon. It was the aurora borealis of the arctic, and we could only stand in awe. The vast fields of everlasting ice and snow to the north seemed larger, colder, closer. The mood of the arctic was upon us.

I remembered those days growing up in the Dakotas when the sun was but a frosty glare reflected off the snow if it did appear for its short stab at daylight around noon; the long, glittery nights of squeaky snow and frozen breath; and the brilliant stars in a brittle black-and-white world. Fierce as it was, it hadn't been all bad, and there was no denying the astonishing beauty, even with the promise of harsh penalties that allowed no mistakes in thirty- and forty-below weather.

So, fresh from the country, we drove into Fairbanks and began looking for sourdough pancakes, which seemed fitting for a proper celebration of our safe arrival. A suspicious policeman followed us for some distance before stopping us and asking why we were going the wrong way on the town's only one-way street. No ticket, after we explained that there was no sign where we entered and no way to turn around, and that we had got off as soon as possible. Sad to say, we found no palatable sourdough pancakes in this land of alleged sourdoughs.

Fairbanks' history is fascinating, but today, at least at first glance, it is only a replica of a thousand other towns outside, with the inevitable fast-food emporiums, shopping centers, and car sales lots. The exceptions are its university, its wildlife research areas, its airport, and the fact that it is located at about sixty-five degrees north latitude, or only a little more than a hundred miles south of the Arctic Circle. The latter distinction makes the airport the obvious gateway to the arctic. There we could look into the past and the future at once, in the terminal where security guards searched passengers, among them young and eager engineers, bound for Prudhoe, Fort Yukon, and Barrow, along with a patient couple carrying two new axe handles, their purchase in the white man's village. It made us wonder if hijackers were present even in the arctic. We found that the airport was a sort of launching pad for miners, explorers, geologists, anthropologists, and arctic researchers, a place where oil-rig construction workers mingled with missionaries and where Eskimo and geologist rubbed elbows.

Our plans included meeting Bette and Royal Brunson in Fairbanks. They had taken the ferry from Prince Rupert to Haines earlier, driving on to Fairbanks so that Royal could make a caribou hunt in the Brooks Range with Don Klepper, a former graduate student from Montana who was teaching in Alaska. We found them at Don's home, where they were skinning out their game, which would be the Klepper family's winter meat supply. Caribou are to the arctic as deer are to rural Pennsylvania. It is estimated that there is a native Alaskan population of more than sixty thousand of these animals today, though in the Yukon Territory's Whitefish Office of Game and Fish we had learned that an estimated one hundred twenty thousand were in the process of crossing the Porcupine River.

Another native of the Arctic Barrens, and rather rare, is the musk-ox, not often sighted today and even less frequently hunted. There is a government-sponsored breeding farm near Fairbanks where they can be seen. The populations are growing now after being nearly wiped out by hunting. Admiral Perry wrote that on two occasions his finding a herd had saved the lives of expedition members. A relic of the Ice Age, and first reported in 1670, the first live animal was brought to a zoo in 1899. The musk-ox looks somewhat like a small buffalo, about five feet at the shoulder, with massive, broad-based horns, somewhat like a slicked-down hairpiece. A better description might be, a dust mop on legs with horns on one end, for its thick layers of hair almost sweep the ground. If it weren't for its horns you couldn't tell which way it was going; even with the horns it's not easy. Experts claim that biologically they are more related to goats and sheep than to buffalo or cattle.

From Fairbanks we were to head southwest towards Denali National Park in the Alaska Range. Three major mountain ranges dominate this northernmost state: to the north, the Brooks Range directs the final destiny of the Yukon River and faces the Arctic Ocean and Point Barrow. The Alaska Range arches around the Gulf of Alaska to the south. The Aleutian Range is the spine of the Alaska Peninsula, that long finger of land pointing far out into the Pacific, separating it from the Bering Sea. Other important mountain influences are the Kuskokwims in the heart of the southwest, and the coastal series including the Wrangell, Talkeetna, Chugach, and Saint Elias mountains.

I had always wanted to say that we unrolled our sleeping bags north of the Arctic Circle, but at that time there were no roads, and it seemed foolish to take a plane, so we settled for the Nenana River before taking a course south. The caress of night air carried the refreshing scent of spruce as we put our foam mattresses and sleeping bags by the fire and rigged a light shelter from the dew. Sleeping under the stars erases the barrier between man and heaven. Being enveloped in the depths of a warm down bag beside the fire on a cold night is an indescribable physical pleasure that reaches into the soul. It means listening to wind in the trees, a loon laughing back as if to an hysterical world, and, with luck, a wolf howling or a flight of geese announcing their course across the velvet midnight sky. Insomnia disappears, and the long night of sleep is as blank ecstasy.

We woke to the sun striking a cluster of golden aspens on the opposite slope, and stamping feet on my sleeping bag. Well, more of a scratchy hopping. Cautiously I opened one eye, to stare into a large black eye looking back. It was a Canada jay standing on the frost-covered outer canvas cover. Close by, Mary was quietly observing. A smile, and "I wondered if he would waken you." The combined sweet aromas of wood smoke and fresh coffee wafted my way. Mary had been up for some time; she says that it is not virtue but love of solitude that gets her up to watch for wildlife.

With the bird eyeing me now from the foot of the sleeping bag, I savored my first cup of the morning. The northern bush is incomplete without its primary resident, the Canada jay, alias gray jay, alias whiskey jack, alias camp robber; friendliest, gentlest and least raucous of the whole jay family. It soars in without a sound, banking, then tilting charcoal wings to drop into a stall and touch down a few feet from you. It cocks its gray and black head quizzically, soft black eyes taking inventory of your camp for possible handouts. Unafraid of man, this friendly aggressor will perch on a skillet handle until it gets too hot, eat food held between fingers or teeth, and rob you blind if you allow it. Seldom seen at less than four thousand feet in the Lower 48, he seems to be at home anywhere in the North Country.

We were bound for a place where the mountains get big, like the 20,320-foot summit of Denali, tallest mountain in North America. Some know it as Mount McKinley, but most who have seen it prefer the Indian name; it translates as "The Great One." Indeed it is. We were in luck, for it was on one of those few gloriously clear days that we gazed upon the full majesty of this monument, shining against a brilliant blue sky, a colossus that had shouldered away every cloud so that we might see the snow-topped Great One in all its magnificence. Long streamers of blowing snow whipped from the summit, a sight worth the whole trip.

In Denali Park wildlife abounded. Moose wandered the bottoms. Ptarmigans, wearing a blend of white and tan feathers in preparation for winter, were flushed from underfoot. We worried about a late moose calf with a bum leg. It was having some difficulty keeping up with its mother, and it seemed doubtful that it could survive through heavy snow. With Bette and Royal we had paused to look over the broad valley, a rich tapestry woven with autumn color, when Royal pointed at what at first looked like two golden-brown boulders about a hundred yards from where we stood. Then one of them moved. It was a bear. Soon we could see three Toklat grizzlies feeding on the open slopes nearby. Not as large as the big brown bears on Kodiak Island or at Katmai National Monument, which have been recorded in weight up to sixteen hundred pounds and in height to ten feet, the Toklats still appeared much larger than the average seven- to eight-hundred-pound grizzly outside Alaska. What was so distinctive was the color, a yellow brown, almost a gold, and dark brown about the shoulders and head. It seemed a contented family scene, the cubs digging for mice while the sow, we guessed at nearly a thousand pounds, sat dozing in the sun, keeping guard, a maternal powerhouse of golden dynamite capable of outrunning a horse or of decking the largest bull with a single blow of a massive paw.

Ever since we first began answering the call of wild places, Mary and I have tended to follow the old trade routes, which were mostly water routes. Having spent nearly all of our marriage on or near the water, we migrate towards waterways, riverfronts, seashores, even dry creek beds. Wandering down the Kenai Peninsula towards the little seaside town of Homer, we headed almost instinctively for the docks. The tall, sandy-haired man walking toward us stepped back in surprise and said flatly, "Tourists!"

Somewhat astonished myself, all I could say was, "Yep."

"But the season's over, the birds all gone, bad weather, fishing's finished. . . ." He seemed to be talking to himself. The three of us were standing on windswept docks above a fleet of boats scarcely moving in the protected harbor: great ocean trawlers, the dark blue of their hulls streaked with rust; large crab traps in neat piles, brilliant with colored floats; interspersed among the big boats, dozens of small fishing boats; and over all, a fluttering of bright flags contrasting with the sodden lead gray of water and jetties.

Clem Tillion introduced himself and immediately invited us for a short cruise, "Got to meet a ship." We stepped aboard a steel trawler, where another tall man, husky, friendly-visaged but cool, said that he was Bob Glud, the pilot. The engine roared, a neighboring fisherman cast off our lines, and Tillion wove his way through the crowded harbor. A seal, frolicking ahead, tried to ignore us, its babylike eyes and spotted yellow-silver fur glittering in the dark, chill waters. It held a small herring in its flippers, contentedly munching the morsel, then rolled its eyes sadly before diving out of sight in the oil-streaked harbor.

A flight of cormorants skimmed by as we cleared the jetties and met a southeast swell. To our port a hundred-odd-foot vessel plodded slowly. "Seismographic, looking for oil," Clem observed. We cruised on, sending murres on either side into diving fits. "'Spect they'll find it; they've already located some." He sounded less than pleased. Glud the pilot spoke up, damning the conservationists, the government, and others. Oil was the key word in Alaska then. Mary and I kept out of the argument. It was the fishermen, the sportsmen, the conservationists, the fur farmers, and the land lovers versus the the promoters and the speculators. A fantastic propaganda battle had been going on, with big money—oil money—launching a campaign beyond belief. Every filling station, Chamber of Commerce, and real estate office was loaded with oil promotion literature. Mottoes like "Let the bastards freeze to death in the dark" and "Sierra Go Home" littered the landscape. Yet a large number of people felt strongly opposed to the oil men taking over the state and the government, though they were nearly overwhelmed and helpless in the face of the big money. Perhaps the Eskimo felt the same way when he was forced from his land, his home, and his ways by the white man after ten thousand years of thinking it would be as it always had been. Clem and Bob continued their exchange above the roar of the engine.

Wind and seas were growing, but the boat *Mary Dele*, solid and stable, rolled easily. Out of Kachemak Bay we could see the opening that is Cook Inlet. Two halibut boats were out for the last of the season, and the superstructure of a larger vessel was emerging over the horizon. "That's her. She's on time." I peered through the salt-smeared windows and the overcast, and they resumed their discussion. "The biggest mistake Alaska made was to become a state," Bob growled. "We should've become independent. They don't have any business telling us what to do. . . ." We'd seen bumper stickers to that effect, too.

On our port were two landing craft converted to pushers, and a small tug lay tied to an enormous mooring buoy. Above them the fangs of a shark-toothed mountain ridge were buried in the clouds, and behind, deep fiords slashed into spruce-shrouded slopes. The sun had not been visible for several days of mists, fogs, and gray to blue-gray clouds hanging low over peaks that already had new snow. A glacier with blue-green crevasses moulded its course through a valley, and whenever fog and mist lifted, across the inlet the Chigmit Mountains loomed like smouldering volcanoes. These are the backbone of the Alaska Peninsula and the tusk-shaped series of islands that separates the Bering Sea from the Pacific.

"Bet they had a rough trip." The black-hulled freighter, bone in her teeth, was closing rapidly. Turning to me, Glud explained, "Those Aleutians are something. Hundred-mile winds and forty-foot seas regular." Tillion added, "Can't do a thing unless you get behind an island. Between 'em the seas funnel through in great squirts. Get the wind behind you and it's like being popped out of a champagne bottle, only worse."

We were in the lee of the peninsula now, but beyond we could see the white-capped rollers. The ten-thousand-ton *Shomei Maru* had sailed from Hokkaidō to to pick up lumber. She was slowing and Tillion swung the trawler to intercept. The crew, somber-faced, looked down on us as *Mary Dele* came alongside the lowered gangway. Glud judged the closing gap carefully and swung aboard. We peeled off and Tillion looked back at the freighter. "The Japanese respect strength. With our declining dollar, our lost war, and what they regard as a weak-kneed people, they don't respect the United States much anymore." We idled towards the mooring, waiting to pick up the pilot. Surf scoters flapped out of our way.

"All we have is what we can export," Glud had said. "But," said Tillion, "there's something people don't understand. Take Kodiak Island and the bear. Experts say that the bears don't need half the timber to survive, so we cut the rest. What they don't understand is that a bear needs territory. It'll kill anything that invades its territory, so cut half the timber and you kill half the bears, without shooting a single one. It's not the hunters who kill the game; it's the subdividers. A two-hundred-house subdivision will nullify a fish hatchery. One oil spill may kill only four thousand ducks, but it will kill a full run of fish."

"I'm a conservationist who looks at political facts," Tillion went on. "That's how I got elected to the Alaska House of Representatives." He was also traveling to Washington monthly as a member of the President's Committee on Oceans and the Atmosphere, representing the Far North and our last frontier, from the North Slope and Prudhoe Bay to the fiords and glaciers of the south; from the pug-faced walrus to the broad-faced Eskimo—equally mute and expressionless before the onslaught of the white man.

In Homer the fishing season was ending. We wandered the docks. The dream of purchasing another boat, maybe a small fishing vessel like the Bristol boat we'd seen, and sailing south, kept coming to mind. It seemed such a good idea, but storm clouds were gathering along the Alaska peninsula now. Every day the promise of coming winter grew closer, and there was still so much of this land to see. Fishermen discouraged us, suggesting that the year was getting late, and the prospect of oncoming gales was verified when Kachemak Bay was grayed in with boiling winds, rolling seas, and white water.

And so we worked our way around the Chugach Mountains, leaving the populated areas and entering the heartland. Here we walked into a primeval forest on duff deep as a featherbed, searching for a lake that was but a blue dot on the map; we bedded down beneath a tall spruce with branches so waterproof that not a drop would touch us in a driving rain. On the lakeshore, it was so quiet, even soundless, that our ears rang with the silence. Breathing, and the rustle of clothing, were all that we heard. The lake, a faintly rippled mirror, reflected a massive mountain, a monument to all mountains, and the lily pads seemed not afloat but in suspension. Just after sundown, battleship-gray clouds lay in easy rolls draped across the western sky. The air was brilliantly clear. Stars, like finely faceted gems, glittered with closeness, but began to fade as clouds slipped across the heavens. The sharp tips of the spruce forest formed a jagged horizon, to be blacked out imperceptibly by stealthy darkness. Now we could hear the popping of the newly lighted fire, the hissing of heated moisture escaping a branch. A fish jumped, and the spreading ripples flattened as they expanded across the placid lake.

What you sense in this northland is the vastness of the land. Rather than feeling insignificant, you and what you sense *are* all that are real. The heat of the fire, the chill of the night air, the scent of smoke—these are real and important, not the platitudes of a pompous politician, nor the chrome-over-rust baubles we have come to esteem. The very reality becomes your security. Here, life can get down to basics.

I'd heard of grayling all my life, or at least since I first took an interest in fishing. My goal had been to catch one. Never mind that I also have had a goal of catching a bigmouth bass larger than my hand. After twenty-odd years I'd concluded that big bass are for other people, and I'd taken up the pursuit of uncommon species like grayling. The grayling is a cold-water fish. I don't know that many live today below the Canadian border, except for some in the mountain fastnesses of Montana and Idaho. They seem to prefer fast, icy water, straight off the ice fields if possible. Such a stream was nearby, and I meandered through the alders, across beds of moose droppings, over rocks and forest duff, until the stream took a right-angle bend. It was fast whitewater about fifty feet wide, undercutting a bank, with a deep pool. There was a long gravel bar where I set down gold pan and shovel. Never go anywhere in the Far North without a gold pan. It's like looking in the gutter for dollar bills—you never know when you'll find one.

A dry fly tied on the leader, a false cast or two, and the fly was floating lightly down to the rippled surface, which, to my considerable surprise, exploded. On that first cast I was out of tune and half dreaming, and my reactions were slow. I hauled back the fly, tried again, and watched it settle in a willow, a species plentiful in the north country. I recovered and made a third cast. As it touched down—I swear it—four fish burst into a battle royal over one dry

fly. I hooked a big one. I can't say that grayling put up quite the fight
of a brook trout or a tarpon, or even that of a bluefish, but for being
as cold as they must be, their performance is not to be sneezed at.

Finally ashore, the flipping fellow, sixteen to eighteen inches
I guessed, indeed proved to be a grayling—sort of cigar shaped,
speckled gray, with a pointed snout and a dorsal fin like a sailfish.
By the time Mary could get the first one cleaned, I had five more, so
I let her try. It was fun watching her catch her first big grayling on
a flyrod: her mouth hung open in shock when it hit; she puffed and
strained, afraid she might lose it. She staggered around on the narrow
gravel bar, surrounded by roaring, rushing rapids, and finally subdued the fish by making a flying leap into the wild water and emerging, fish in hand.

Sitting by the campfire picking my teeth with a fish bone, I
watched my wife cleaning the cooking gear and stowing it for the
night and kept thinking, How could we be so lucky! Only six weeks
before, we'd boarded our escape capsule on the North Carolina coast
to cross this vast North American continent. Wandering west and
north, we'd fished mountain streams and canoed quiet lakes, hiked
rugged slopes and whistled back at marmots sunning on the rocks.
We'd slept under the stars on the prairies and listened to the coyotes
singing their song, taken a pack trip into the Anaconda-Pintlar Wilderness, and now we'd caught and eaten arctic trout. Was there more?
Of course there was.

We had left the Kenai Peninsula, driving towards Valdez, when
we witnessed two huge bull moose pitting their strength against each
other. The moose of this area are twice the size of their relatives to
the south. We had seen one standing beneath a telephone line, so tall,
it seemed, that its antlers would surely become entangled in the wire.
The beast stood at least nine feet at the shoulders. Here, it was the
noise that attracted our attention, a crackling of bushes. At first I saw
only one through the trees and brush, but its action was belligerent:
massive antlers swaying, he pawed the ground. Then a crashing of
brush and another bull came thundering out of the woods. The two
hit head-on with a thud that made both of them pause and shake
their heads before coming at each other again. Soon it developed into
a pushing match, first one yielding, then the other, grunting, trampling the brush. From time to time one would meet with an obstacle

and have to give way, and the other would take advantage and lunge at his opponent's side. All the while, we could hear the antlers clacking.

I did not see him, but Mary said that a third bull was there, too, and he sauntered off with what had been a mildly interested gallery of cows.

Wildlife can be observed throughout Alaska. I'd told Mary years before about seeing rabbits do what as children we called a rabbit dance. Finally, here in Alaska, she was privileged to see such a caper. On several occasions at dusk she was delighted by their gathering, on some signal known only to them. At first just one would dash into a clearing. Soon another would join, and another, and another. They'd frolic in what seemed purely a game of chase, but not for long—a few minutes, maybe ten at the most. We observed their fun not only in camp, but along roadsides whenever we were still traveling at sundown.

A pause in Anchorage had been just a stop in another city with a busy waterfront, but as we drove along a road that clung to the face of a steep mountainside we experienced another thrill. A tidal bore is a phenomenon that occurs in only a few places in the world. We had seen one in the Bay of Fundy, but it was here in Cook Inlet that it took on special significance. Vast mud flats were visible all along the shore and the water was quite calm, with a few wind ripples. Then, out of the distant haze, there came a dark line, like a single wave moving up the inlet. As it came closer the wave became clearer, following up the deep waters, its edges curling back towards the shore as it was slowed by the shoals. From where we watched it seemed impressive though not particularly large, but a fishermen told us that it was an especially fearsome thing if you were on the shoals fishing from a small boat. The bottom friction causes the wave to steepen and a six-foot wall of water will create absolute havoc unless you can get out into deep water. He added, "Of course, that's nothing to some of the tidal waves we get." One fellow claimed that his boat rode a hundred-foot-high tidal wave and landed nearly a mile up in the woods. We had seen the evidence left from 1964, when the most severe earthquake recorded in North America lifted a section of sea bed 275 miles long by about 75 miles wide as high as fifty feet, completely destroying ten villages and severely damaging several more.

The old Valdez was a virtual ghost town when we saw it, washed away by tidal waves up to two hundred feet high.

By now the signs of winter were unmistakable. Snow was falling almost every day, and it seemed a good time to head south again. It had been a successful adventure. Our hearts had soared with golden eagles above icy rivers against mountains already covered with the season's first snow. We'd walked on trembling muskeg and heard glaciers grumble. Rain and sleet had drummed their message on the thin canvas of our tent, we'd washed the sleepiness from our eyes in icy mountain streams, and been nose-to-bill with Arctic ptarmigans. We'd met the great bears and watched the mighty moose fight. And we had seen the light of the awesome, mysterious aurora borealis. Like the gold-plated king whom countless early adventurers sought, many of us have been wallowing in El Dorado for a long time, but have had difficulty reading the label.

A special advantage that we have is that our life-style so far has not required us to dig in for the winter. We have been able to adjust to cold by leaving, somewhat as the snowbirds do. So when the compass swung south it held a certain appeal, for the frost had been nipping at our heels, dusting our sleeping bags every morning now with white icing. The snow line was creeping down and was well below the dripping glaciers, and it seemed time to leave the sour-doughs and muklukkers to look after the brilliance of the aurora borealis, the musk-ox, the unending tundra, the caribou, the white beluga whale, the walrus, and all their ice-filled habitat. It was time for us southern-style mainlanders to meander south, following the migrating birds to wherever they go.

Seldom are distances in the Far North fully appreciated by the average observer, and the fifteen-hundred-odd-mile Alaska Highway from Dawson Creek, B.C., to Fairbanks might not seem long if you say it quickly enough. But recalling what kind of road that highway offers and that Dawson Creek is in northern British Columbia — well, it's a long way before one even gets started. There are, of course, steamship lines south from Alaska as an alternative, but from Anchorage to Seattle is a rather long and expensive cruise, especially when paying passage for your car. There is a shorter route from the village of Haines via the B.C. ferry to Prince Rupert, then more driving to

Prince George and east or south. Even this ferry seemed rather expensive, however, to those who have more time than money.

In Alaska we had heard of a new road, not yet open, from the Yukon border south that ultimately connected with the highway between Prince Rupert and Prince George, some five hundred miles through wild, mountainous country. At that time there were only rumors of available fueling stops or facilities. It was described as a series of logging roads that made passage possible in fair weather. This was just what we were looking for: another adventure, exploring new ground. We took on extra supplies, lashed a couple of tins of fuel atop the van, and sought the new route.

There is a special thrill in trying something different: apprehension, even a fear of the unknown, along with its attraction. We tightened our seat belts, breathed deep, turned off the Alaska Highway near the little mud-spattered Yukon town of Watson Lake, and bounced into a wilderness of sorts. The Cassiar Mountains loomed ahead.

The road wasn't too bad; in fact, for that part of the continent I would rate it as first-class. There was considerable mining in the area, asbestos predominantly. A short bit of pavement led towards the mines, but at this point the main road began to deteriorate. Here and there an occasional decaying log cabin moldered in ruins, perhaps the site of a mining camp. Or there'd be a cluster of Indian shacks. In one lonesome camp the tents sagged in the rain, a campfire smouldered through a veil of smoke, and a caribou carcass dripped from a pole.

Dease Lake was the first major town, nearly 150 miles from our jumping-off place. It consisted of a large log structure housing a combined grocery and general store, post office, service station, and social center. Scattered about were construction equipment and buildings, a windsock complete with an airstrip, and a few dwellings, mostly log.

A side road led seventy-five miles to Telegraph Creek, the end of an early attempt to route a telegraph cable to Europe via Alaska, Siberia, and Russia before the Atlantic cable was successful. General Billy Mitchell, famed for his efforts to prove the superiority of aircraft over battleships, was the Signal Corps lieutenant in charge of this telegraph operation. It is said that he would not allow any of his crew to carry a thermometer. We found that the main road from this junction could scarcely be called open. Our destination was the Yellowhead highway. To the west of us lay Alaska and glacier-infested coastal mountains; to the east rose the Skeena Range. The road, now all mud and gravel, grew narrower and steeper, with washed and crumbling shoulders. Rock slides and mud cascading onto the road didn't offer much promise, yet it continued to be passable. Occasional messages, like "Steve, see you in Terrace, Bill," written on a scrap of board nailed to a tree, told us that we were not entirely alone. Once we passed a van and a car parked alongside the road. Both bore Swiss symbols, though we could not read the license plates through the mud. One vehicle had an exceedingly flat tire. A gang of six or seven people was working on the mud-encrusted mess, up to their knees in muck. They thanked us for offering help and went back to rummaging through the stack of spare tires on top of the car. One man, scraping the mud from his beard, said nothing, but smiled with a certain blank politeness, reminding us that we were the ones speaking a foreign language.

We continued south, only to be assaulted by vistas of astonishing variety and wildness: tumbling waterfalls, interminable forests, great and small lakes speckled with rocky islands crowded with trees, deep valleys hidden in mist and fog, the whole almost totally unoccupied by humans. Then abruptly, the road broadened and leveled to interstate size. The Canadian highway department had simply taken advantage of one of the several emergency airstrips dating back to World War II when hundreds of aircraft were being ferried north for the defense of Alaska and as lend-lease to Russia. It was now part of the road. A windsock near one end billowed briskly; aircraft still had the right-of-way.

Snow on the high peaks covered everything above thirty-five hundred feet with cold whiteness. The woods were ablaze in the golds and reds of autumn, the deep blue-green of spruce contrasting with the 24-karat luster of cottonwoods. Tiny white dots following the rocky ledges were mountain goats clinging to the windswept slopes. Dark brown forms of moose appeared occasionally, then faded, flitting shadows on the wet bottoms. Now and then a bald eagle, white of tail and head, flashed past below tree level, following a stream course that wound among boulders and trees. Squirrels scolded us for invading their domain and small birds followed curiously, chattering at the new folks in their private woods.

Lurching on, we hesitated before each mud hole to evaluate our chances. We were sliding down a steep hill sideways when I chanced to peer over the precipice and noticed the wheels of a truck, far below and upside down. Returning on foot, we could find no occupants. Several miles farther we saw a truck that appeared to be heading towards us, but as we came closer, we realized that it had been abandoned in mid-trail. Its front wheel had fallen off when the axle or some other equally vital part broke.

The gasoline gauge was wavering on "empty" before we found a refueling stop, a log general store operated by a fat, cheerful man, with a half-dozen Indian kids in attendance. The farm-style gasoline storage tank discharged the most expensive gasoline we had ever purchased up to that point, but, considering the alternatives, it was well worth it. It must have been a considerable expense to bring a tanker to his store. I shuddered a bit, topped the tank, and we pushed off into the unknown, with a storm not far behind. It seemed not exactly the very best place to spend the winter.

We still had our reserve fuel, however, and things were looking good now. It would be impossible to get lost on this road. Such had been our thinking when we took this route, for supposedly there were only three turnoffs, one to the asbestos mines, another to Telegraph, the third to Stewart on the Alaskan border. Now, with two-thirds of the mud and rocks behind us, we came to an uncharted fork. Both roads looked equally traveled; it was easier for Robert Frost to choose his path.

By this time we were entering logging country, with an old map that showed none of the alternatives. When in doubt there is little else to do but go—somewhere. I tossed a coin and took the easterly route. We had emptied the final can of reserve fuel into the tank without sighting any signs of humankind and worry was setting in, when we emerged abruptly upon civilization. At first, all we saw was totem poles, with flags flying. Getting closer, we found that we had arrived at the Tlingit Indian village of Kitwankul. The flags were diapers flapping on clotheslines strung between totem poles. We were soon surrounded by children. We were reluctant to leave them and cross the river to a genuine highway, but this was a private road, and the gate would be locked at 6:00 P.M. A few miles farther along, we began to see hunting camps and even occasional traffic.

The trail that we followed is a busy shortcut to the Yukon and Alaska nowadays, but I can state with conviction that when we drove it, it was a tester of confidence, a truck destroyer, an eliminator of cars. We didn't take that route for comfort, but as an affordable challenge. We like to remember it the way it was.

9.

Wilderness Is Where You Find It

Man has no choice of where he is born. I found myself as a child being reared in the Dakotas, a windswept, sunburned, frozen, and tortured land. It was here that I followed the scent of wild plum blossoms into the draws and found the pasqueflower bursting forth from soggy, icy prairie. Waterfowl filled the skies by the tens of thousands, seeking ice-free potholes to dabble away their time while waiting for the isotherms to move northward. I could hear the thundering flush of the pheasant and the singing of the coyote, and could walk across prairies to the music of meadowlarks. Despite having trudged to school through dust storm and blizzard, I am convinced today that I was born under a lucky star to have known this wild land and some of the remnants of its native people while they could still remember where they came from.

One night, seated around a campfire, watching the smoke swirl sparks upward into the night air, we—a rancher, a teacher, Mary, and I—got to discussing how each of us enters life, the guiding forces that cause us to bend towards whatever goal we had seek, and the way that little things can cause us to change. Then we talked of which way might be best for making the exit—in some sort of grand wrap, or just slipping quietly under the covers? It came down to this: if you must die of a heart attack, is it preferable to be seated in a padded office chair watching wild fluctuations on the computer screen spelling out sudden changes in stock prices? Or to reach those final moments standing in a trout stream, with the pump failure occurring just as the scrappiest and biggest cutthroat or brown you've ever seen bends your rod to the breaking point?

There was little disagreement. We figured the mortician might find the office more convenient for him and so would consider that route to be handier, permitting a better show of his professional dignity. Yet think of the adrenalin and excitement that you could provide a rescue squad if it took them all day on the trail, or gave them a chance to go by helicopter into the wilderness. Say what you will, this opportunity could be your final chance to give your fellow man a thrill, a sense of natural worth, with a go at braving something besides street traffic with flashing red lights and screaming sirens.

It was agreed that the guide running the rubber raft on the River of No Return is the fellow having the most fun; the passengers simply pay his way while riding along. They don't get a chance to make mistakes; so why take the safe and sane way when you have a choice? You can always spend your time developing ulcers while being secure and comfortable, but the zest in living comes when you can get a full adrenalin charge, in addition to heart palpitations mixed with a full ration of sweat.

By this, I do not recommend stupidity, such as we met when we were driving the TransCanada Highway in western Ontario and came face-to-face with a very happy inebriate who was trying to stop all automobile and truck traffic from trespassing on the Queen's highway. To accomplish this, he was jumping out from his place of concealment behind roadside bushes to confront every passing vehicle he saw. He, too, was challenging the world, so when the Royal Mounted Police asked help in loading the drunk into the patrol car in order to keep him alive a little longer, the young man felt that we were depriving him of his right to a standoff. I never thought for a moment of depriving him of that right, and I admired his nerve if not his foolhardiness. In hindsight, I appreciate his inadvertently giving me a brief feeling of importance, through enabling him to continue living long enough to issue a few more challenges.

There is a vast difference between living and being alive. I must admit that all those TV blurbs about gusto and beer have a point, though I could never understand anyone's toting an insulated cooler up a mountain so that he could sit on a glacier swigging a cool brew. I have climbed around on glaciers and icefields, and at such times the last thing in the world that interested me was a beer. A cup of hot coffee maybe, but a cold beer?

I'm reminded of a cold November day a few years back, when we were living on our boat on the North Carolina coast. There was a brisk wind out of the north, the air and water temperatures were about forty degrees, and our friend Franc White needed to make repairs on the rudder of his boat. I stood by while he went overboard and immersed himself to the eyeballs without benefit of wet suit, long johns, or anything but trunks and shoes. After a few minutes of working he surfaced to inform me that he was cold and required a good strong shot of bourbon to prevent an immediate seizure of all moving parts. "The bottle is on the bunk," he said through chattering teeth. I measured a quick three-fingers' worth into a glass. Not having anything hot to warm it, I handed the glass of spirits over the stern.

He took a fast swig, paused, looked into the glass with total disbelief, handed the glass back, and reprimanded me, "You forgot the damned ice! There's some in the cooler under the sink."

He was Alabama born and bred. Maybe that was the problem. Still, anyone who will go overboard in such weather and complain only about the lack of ice in his drink, I must admire. He is not afraid of living.

A fundamental purpose of living, I have always thought, is to challenge yourself, boldly facing the elements once in a while. It means experimenting and testing your own resources. Learning not to fear getting cold occasionally or missing a meal now and then. Trying something solo. Being willing to make a mistake and not be afraid to pay the price of learning. Sometimes it calls for throwing caution to the winds and doing what you most desire. It's recognizing life as a one-way trip, with no refunds, no second chances, and making the most of it, but also knowing that it's not over till you greet St. Peter on his turf.

What most thoughtful persons really desire out of life is a sense of accomplishment, along with peace of mind, a dash of privacy, and recognition by a good friend. Each goal by itself is simple, provided that greed is left behind. Important, too, is observing the natural world enough to understand and respect its system and its inhabitants, for we are part of that world.

Often we assume that to explore the natural world it is necessary to go on some grand expedition to far-away places. Yet one of the most stimulating, pump-circulating weekends I have ever enjoyed was spent just a short way from where we maintain our winter home in coastal North Carolina. And it was in about as wild a place as is left on the East Coast. It started one winter day when Joel Arrington suggested that we go deer hunting, using muzzle-loading black powder guns. He knew of just the place.

It may seem surprising that some very wild places still remain on the east coast; regions not only wild, but inhospitable and almost inaccessible. On the coastal plain of North Carolina just south of Norfolk, however, is a projection of land marked on the north by Albemarle Sound, to the east and south by Pamlico Sound. Within the four counties that make up this area, about forty miles deep by sixty miles wide, are some of the most hostile lands along the Atlantic coast. It is fishing, farming, and hunting country, but filled with pocosins—a pocosin was defined by early Algonkian Indians as a "swamp on a hill." Here the land is flat, seldom more than a half-dozen feet above sea level. Drainage, except by the natural blackwater creeks and several canals, is almost nonexistent. There are four good-sized lakes: Phelps, a state park; Pungo; Alligator; and the largest, Mattamuskeet. The last-named became part of the National Wildlife Refuge System after numerous attempts to farm the area had failed. It has long been noted for outstanding concentrations of winter waterfowl.

Just to the north of Mattamuskeet is Alligator Wildlife Refuge, established after conservation groups such as the Wildlife Federation were able to block developers from draining and converting it into more farm land at a time when farms were failing because of excess production and falling prices. The projected drainage would have added further pollution to the already burdened seafood-producing sounds. The owners, Prudential Life (alias Pamlico Properties), then arranged through The Nature Conservancy to donate the tract to the U. S. Fish and Wildife Service, as a tax shelter beneficial both to the landowners and the public.

Shortly before this land became a wildlife refuge, four of us were preparing to test our skills at using hunting devices that normally sensible people had given up a hundred years ago. Joel had made arrangements with Bob Hester, of Fairfield, who lives in a small village on the north shore of Lake Mattamuskeet, long known for waterfowl hunting. Bob had the idea that sportsmen might like to have a wilderness hunting experience and had arranged with Pamlico Properties, then owner of some forty-four thousand acres in northern Hyde County, to improve the wildlife habitat and make the area available for hunting. He had fixed up a little camp on remote Swan Lake.

Reluctantly I had left a comfortable bed to step out into the pre-dawn darkness of this wild Carolina swamp. Pausing and looking about to get my bearings that inky night, almost directly overhead I could see that within the hunter's constellation, the Belt of Orion was shining. It seemed a good omen. After checking our caplock muzzle-loading rifles and stuffing sandwiches and other essential supplies into our pockets, we staggered down the narrow dock that served our wilderness cabin and climbed into a skiff. William Brooks, our guide, was at the helm as we cast off into the blackness of this remote lake. With motor purring smoothly, we slipped into the night.

Everything was dark but for the hazy stars reflecting on black waters that were swallowed by the shadowy shore. A probing flashlight revealed stumps, half awash, all about us. We rounded a point and slid into a narrow, twisting creek, powering onward until the flashlight showed us a stake protruding from the shoreline. Here our guide nosed the skiff against a low bank and, while the rest of us waited, led Fred Bonner into the swamp where a stand had been secreted. A mile or so farther into the creek we repeated the process, dropping Gerry Almy, a visitor from Virginia, at his stand. Joel was next.

By the time we reached my stand, a faint grayness was just appearing in the eastern sky. I was expected to remain seated on a couple of two-by-fours that had been nailed to a cypress tree to form what hunters call a tree stand. The purpose was to ambush a deer. Dawn was beginning to dissolve the shadows as I climbed the six long steps that placed me twelve to fifteen feet above the swamp. Sitting with my back to the tree, the rifle across my lap, I waited for the light. And the deer.

Being cursed with a trace of acrophobia, a big word for being rather nervous in high places, made the waiting no easier, but at least it kept me from dozing off. Dozing off is an occupational hazard in a tree stand. Our friend Lois White was in a tree stand in Uwharrie National Forest one time, and the nearest hunter was on a stand just out of Lois's sight. After a long period there was the blast of a shotgun and a noisy crash. Lois scrambled out of her tree and rushed to the man, fearful that he had somehow shot himself. It turned out that the hunter had dozed off and discharged the gun, which caused him to fall off the stand. As I said, tree stands represent hazardous duty.

To the northwest I could hear the lap of waves washing ashore, and as the sky lightened, I could see the edge of the broad Alligator River, maybe a hundred yards away. A loon was laughing its weird, maniacal call. Mosquitoes buzzed happily at the fresh food supply I was making available to them.

There was movement in the brush to the east. A raccoon, followed by two half-grown young, wandered across the muddy cypress bottoms, stopping, sniffing, inspecting every object they came to. Raccoons seem never to lose the curiosity of their youth. They looked in my direction, but appeared unaware of my presence until they hit the trail I'd walked from boat to tree. There they stopped, looked about, and retreated, circling behind my stand and disappearing into the thick vegetation.

Now and then a yellowed leaf floated down and landed on the forest floor. All was still. A "kee-uck!" and the flash of wings as a wood duck hen splashed onto the stream nearby. Cruising back and forth, she gave a plaintive cry until a drake, resplendent in dressy blacks and whites, joined her. Together they paddled downstream. An east wind was soughing among the trees, gathering strength. The chill cut through my clothes. Longing for a down vest or jacket, I watched a squirrel run in short, jerky motions as it carried a cypress ball down a tree. It was burying its treasure in the muddy ground when the cracking of reeds caught my attention.

Behind me, two—no, three—black forms emerged from the shadows. A black bear and two cubs were approaching. They wandered along until they were only a few feet away from me, the cubs playing with each other as the sow inspected each bush, log, or stump. They continued on to the river, then they turned and came back to the place where they'd first appeared.

I kept wishing that I'd brought a camera. A long time ago the idea of combining hunting or fishing with photography had seemed an ideal way of life for working in the outdoor writing field. But after several years and numerous unsuccessful efforts to do all at the same time, I learned that it was impossible to do justice to either that way. It had to be one or the other.

Several minutes later I heard the bears returning. Slowly the sow approached, pausing occasionally to stand and sniff the air, remonstrating with the cubs for some prank as they drew closer. Now she was almost directly beneath my tree. I was watching the cubs, too, when I became aware that the sow was no longer just standing at the base of the tree, but was climbing it!

Thousands of square miles of trees at her disposal—why did she chose this of all trees? She acted as if she didn't know I was there, but damned if I wanted her sitting in my lap! She was getting mighty big and close, so close that I could easily have kicked her in the snout. But something told me that this might not be a smart move—if she objected and grabbed my boot with one of those meat hooks she could easily pull me out of the tree.

The bear was now only a foot or two from me. Her brown muzzle and black body were close enough that I could smell her steamy breath, see her beady little piglike eyes glittering. Instead, I slid the rifle across my lap, pointed it at her head and gave a hard shove.

Startled, bewildered, she peered at me, let out a loud "Woof!" and fell with a resounding crash. The cubs fairly flew up trees on either side of me, hitting twenty feet up or more in a few leaps, it seemed. The sow careened and ricocheted into a thicket. I didn't move. Soon the cubs slid backwards down the trees and disappeared.

All was silence again, except for my own giggling and laughing. I couldn't believe it. Without a picture, no one else would believe it, either. Again I cussed myself for not having brought a camera.

William and Joel showed up in the boat an hour or two later. I pointed out the tracks and the imprint the bear had made when she fell. Joel had seen her and the cubs early in the morning, and William confirmed that those were truly bear tracks beneath the tree. While Bob Hester's wilderness camp showed potential, right then I was wondering whether it might be just too wild for the average hunter.

Like the Indian of old who never got lost but did admit to misplacing his camp and tepee a time or two, so far I have never been what I could call so completely lost that the problem hasn't been solved with some calculations. That's not to say, of course, that there have not been times when I've been confused and worried enough to appreciate the feelings of those who have misplaced camp and were mighty glad to have someone, anyone, show them the way home.

Coastal swamps are often called "dismals," the once-great Dismal Swamp of North Carolina and Virginia not having exclusive claim on the word. Such country is the easiest place in the world to become "confuddled," as an old seafaring friend used to say. I had come in the next day before first light to take up my position in the same tree stand, again hoping to ambush a deer. The weather now was overcast, windy, with an occasional spattering of rain, and it seemed unlikely that I would see any wildlife whatever. Soon, however, with the gray of dawn creeping into the sky, an owl swooped in silently and landed in a tree about fifty feet away. Scarcely a blur at first, the bird seemed to materialize with the growing light and take form out of thin air. It sat on its tree stand as I sat on mine, silent and motionless. We watched each other and the forest floor. Both of us waited, hunters under the skin.

The owl gave up first, flying directly at me as if to observe me more closely, then veering off and fading into the woods, soundlessly. Hours passed with no sounds but those of wind and dripping rain.

Suddenly something crashed with a heavy thump on my head, amid a shower of cypress needles, so startling me that it was all I could do to stay on the stand. Immediately a severe scolding was laid on me by a squirrel, so engrossed in its own owl-watching that it hadn't noticed me until after it landed on the convenient platform that was my hat.

The quiet settled in again. I strained to peer through the foglike mist, which lent a steamy dimness to the already dusky swamp. Raindrops sent out rippling circles that merged in the black pools knobbed with cypress-knee islands. The rain splattered on sodden leaves, and gusty winds shook water from the treetops. Water coursed off my hat brim, and my heavy rain gear seemed to be as wet inside as out. I was resigned to the depths of misery and boredom, when I saw a movement on the edge of a thicket.

It was a deer, ivory antlers dripping as he eased through the tangle of cane, trees, and vines. Heart palpitating, I raised the sights to align with his vitals. A shaft of flame and white smoke mingled with the steam and fog, nearly obliterating the animal as it flipped over backwards. The thunder of the shot echoed through the wet woods. Through smoke slowly drifting away I could see the form of the deer, lying on its back. It kicked a couple of times, then made no further motion.

Dumping a fresh load of powder down the barrel, I rammed at another ball to get it started. Meanwhile, I was trying to avoid losing the cap I had in my hand and to keep the increasing rain from dampening the charge. Accomplishing all this, I shifted around, turning my back to the deer so as to get my feet on the steps, and started climbing down from the tree stand. Stepping off the ladder into ankle-deep water, I faced about and started towards the brush where the deer, now concealed from me, had fallen.

I'd taken only a few steps when there was a thud against my leg, then another and another. I looked down, and a dozen cold chills exploded up and down my spine. I was standing on a big snake, a giant copperhead, that was slamming its fangs repeatedly against my leg, trying its best to puncture my rubber trousers and boots.

All thoughts of deer were wiped clean; there was nothing in the swamp but me and the biggest snake I'd ever seen, attaching its fangs to me. Totally unnerved, I executed the fanciest of high-stepping before I finally collected my senses enough to pick up a stick the size of a small tree and express my feelings properly toward this monster serpent. As I struck at its head, from the corner of my eye I caught the movement of an animal fading into the brush at stream's edge.

The descendant of Eden disposed of, I began looking for my deer. It was gone, any traces of blood or footprints now obliterated by the rain. I searched all around, covering every hummock and thick stand of brush without any luck, all the time being very much aware that if one serpent were in the neighborhood, it wouldn't be alone. The only thing to do was to wait for assistance. I knew how easily I could get really lost wandering about in these woods, for the visibility through rain and fog was by now less than fifty feet.

In an hour or so I heard my companions coming down the river to pick me up. William and Billy Brooks and Joel came ashore, and together we looked diligently for any sign, scouring the woods through the streaming rain. It was possible that the deer had swum the river, so we crossed by boat and continued a thorough search of both banks and surrounding forest. William did observe some water-filled tracks that could have been made recently by a deer. They led off into the deepest swamp, so I began to make a wide search; my plan was to start working to the north, then circle back away from the river and return to camp.

Rain was pouring down my rain gear, sweat fogging my already water-splattered glasses. I stumbled through jungles of brush and vine, at times sinking in muck and mud over the tops of my knee boots. So intent was I on the search that the futility of it was slow to reach my benumbed brain. I then realized that I should have sighted the river some time ago, for I had turned back long before. Could I be off course? It was getting dusky dark, with the gloom from heavy rain and deep woods cutting off any chance of determining direction from the sky.

I paused to get my bearings. The wind was out of the southeast, the direction, I knew, of the tree stand and where my friends were waiting at the boat; but from where I stood on the forest floor, the tossing treetops seemed to go in every direction. It began to dawn on me that this was the way one could get into serious trouble.

A long-gone friend, Cap Wiese, had told me of once having become lost in a similar swamp. We had been discussing woods navigation, and he was convinced that regular methods didn't work in Carolina's pocosin country. Thereafter, he said, whenever he went hunting he bought a large commercial spool of nylon thread and put it into his backpack, after tying one end to the handle of his car door or to a tent stake. At the finish of the hunt he could rewind himself safely back to camp. With another hunting companion, Turner Battle, I once discussed the same problem. He had bought a book on how to use a compass. The first instructions were to locate two objects, such as church steeple and mountain top, then take bearings on each. Where the bearings crossed would be his location. His response was, "Hell, if I could see a church steeple or mountain top to take a bearing on, I wouldn't need the compass, because I wouldn't be lost. There aren't any of those things in a swamp." I'd laughed then.

Well, better safe than stupid. You can let your ego get in the way of common sense by refusing to admit the facts. I yelled several times, but heard no response, so I fired the gun into the air and waited. The silence of rain and wind, of dripping and sloshing, seemed ominous.

Belatedly, there was the muffled sound of an answering shot that seemed far away. I had been on the right course; it was simply that I had gone farther than I had realized. Maybe I wasn't really lost this time, either, but the idea of spending the night in a swamp, soaked to the skin, knee-deep in mud, and swatting hungry mosquitoes while seated on a pointed cypress knee and worrying about snakes, didn't appeal to me.

The rain continued strumming on the roof of the shack that night as I skinned out the copperhead, all three and a half feet of it. It really had seemed much larger earlier in the day. I cut out fillets of serpent loin, to be deep-fried. Most of our crew agreed that copperhead is probably better eating than rattlesnake any day, though none had tasted rattlesnake. Only two dissenters claimed they'd rather eat venison.

Our natural resources are being consumed at a rapid pace. Our national parks show the built-in paradox: their justification depends upon tourism, yet the preservation of their values depends upon their contents not being molested. One finds the public campgrounds at places such as Yosemite Valley and Yellowstone so popular during the summer season that they become ghettos of tents and trailers, with people enjoying the relative seclusion of intertwining tent ropes. By Labor Day even the Steller's jays look shopworn.

If Americans were asked to vote for retaining these parks in as natural a state as possible, there is little question that they would vote overwhelmingly in favor. Why? Only a small percentage of the some 240 million people living in the United States actually visit any one of these preserved areas. Those who do seldom spend more than a day or two there. So why does the public place so high a value on such natural areas? The answer might lie in the response given by our friend Eleanor Robinson, who had visited a national park fewer than a half-dozen times in her whole life: "I need to know that they are there. I don't expect ever to visit the Grand Canyon, but I must know that such wild and beautiful places do exist, and that I can go to them, if only in my thoughts, when I need reassurance."

National parks and wildernesses are public preserves, while most other public lands—national forests, lands under the control of the Bureau of Land Management, and the National Wildlife Refuge system—generally receive mixed uses. It is not out of context to allow hunting, fishing, timbering, grazing, and water use on these lands, so long as such uses do not adversely affect the land and its future value. Yet it is of growing importance that we remember who are the owners: not the rangers, not the various titled agents, nor their employees, for they are only the servants of the owners, that is, of all of us who make their employment possible. They are not employed by some selfish interest that sees public lands as an opportunity to create a profit, but by those elected to represent the people as a whole.

The whole concept of management of our forests came late, begun, perhaps surprisingly, by a captain of industry, a robber baron, a despot turned benevolent after amassing his fortunes through the control of railroads and shipping lines. To realize better profits from a portion of his vast estates located in western North Carolina, George W. Vanderbilt hired two men: a German forester named Schenck to set up timber management programs, and Gifford Pinchot to improve the woodlands. Observing the results, President William McKinley offered Pinchot a post as chief of the U.S. Bureau of Forestry. Pinchot accepted the job and later, as head of the Yale School of Forestry, wrote a good many books on the subject and promoted the conservation movement.

Pinchot continued to serve under both presidents Theodore Roosevelt and William Howard Taft, and from his good works the U.S. Forest Service grew. He understood the need for forest reserves, for protection of public lands. It was during the time of his influence that President McKinley, in order to thwart the greed of some timber interests, established Yellowstone National Park, the keystone of our park system, envied and copied today throughout the world.

Many private corporations still practice conservation, usually as a way to increase their profits, in much the way Vanderbilt had in mind when he reorganized the forestry practices at his Biltmore Estate. Problems arise when, lacking foresight, we destroy the natural, complex ecosystems in favor of accepted monocultures. For example, in draining a swamp or pocosin to enhance the growth of slash pine used in the pulp industry, we very often lose not only the cypress, tupelo, and cedars of the swamp, but those creatures dependent upon them as well. We also fail to reckon with the added runoff of water into streams and estuarine systems—the siltation, the pollution by fresh water, and its effect on the shellfish and finfish that fishermen are dependent on. In North Carolina, somewhere between 60 and 70 percent of the coastal pocosins and swamps have been drained within the last quarter century, so that fewer than a million acres remain today. These areas are generally the same as those where the coastal black bear lives, and as a result fewer than one-tenth of their numbers still survive of an earlier population that exceeded ten thousand. In the same period, nitrogen levels were 50 percent higher and other nutrient levels four to ten times higher in the waters draining farmlands than in the pocosins. Epidemics of red-sore disease began to appear in the surrounding fisheries.

It is much the same with agriculture in general. Traces of herbicides and pesticides, added siltation from poor land practices, and lack of understanding of the natural system as an entity contribute to further deterioration. As with the proverbial horse, somehow we never seem to get around to preserving the habitat until the resource is gone.

With endless pressures to make more and more efficient use of the land, whether by forester, farmer, or land developer, the pressure on public lands is also increased. Meanwhile, man becomes ever more efficient in his ability to affect land and water. Gerry Talbot, a former National Oceanographic and Atmospheric Administration official, tells of his early work in a salmon fishery. He would take his equipment by canoe and work his way up a stream; it often required several days to get to his work sites, and it took three days just to reach one of his camps. Then he was issued a motor boat. What had been a three-day river passage shrank to a few hours. Now crews go in by helicopter in a matter of minutes; thus the river has shrunk ever smaller.

A thousand-acre lake that can comfortably handle several dozen canoes without problem of collision or confrontation is overcrowded and overwhelmed when only two or three boats with 100 horsepower use the same lake. They ruin the swimming, contemplative fishing, and the sort of privacy that most of us desire. The same might be said of off-the-road vehicles on remote trails, for they eat up the distances and destroy the very concept of isolation, wilderness experience, or escape from civilization. Horses, a traditional mode of wilderness travel, can seldom work on the same trail as off-the-road vehicles. Backpackers also resent the noise and smell of gasoline engines, for one of the reasons that they seek the wilds is to escape from these very sources of irritation.

The ultimate need for a wilderness is as a place where we have the opportunity to go freely in order to make our own mistakes, to profit and learn from them. In a true wilderness we cannot summon help; we are unprotected by civil servants. If we err, it is we who pay the price and learn the depth of our courage. It is the last word in freedom, one of the few opportunities ever offered for us to solo. If we keep company with another in the wilderness, we learn the full meaning of interdependence. Wilderness rewards intelligence and punishes foolishness. Nature does not care that we get wet, cold, or hungry, but provides the basics and offers a chance to learn self-worth, to release tensions, to cleanse the mind. Here neither monetary wealth nor station in life, place of birth nor ancestry will feed, warm, or protect us. It is basic, comprising fundamental elements that lawyers, judges, and courts cannot change.

There are many who cannot conceive of the need for such an opportunity, and some who would deny others the right to err on their own, in the mistaken notion that man must at all times be protected from himself. They would deny the right of self-determination under the guise of protection; that is, seeking security for one person at any price to others. Along with the ancients who recognized the need for a desert place to meditate, modern men, too, tend to seek out the restorative values of wilderness in times of stress. In the American West few trappers or mountain men ever elected to return to civilization, and those who understood the wilderness most often chose it over the alternatives. European man, having little experience with unpopulated areas, feared the woods, the wild. These were the bases for his horror stories, where evil and dragons lurked. During the early years of English monarchy it was the custom to send a detail of workers ahead of any royal carriage in order to clear the road and prepare a large meadowlike opening in the wilds, so that the monarch could stop without feeling threatened by the wildness.

Is it any surprise, then, that wilderness is a vanishing commodity? Most wilderness areas that have been so designated came from public lands under the jurisdiction of the U.S. Forest Service. The

Forest Service was set up during the "age of extermination," when public lands were being carved up and despoiled by loggers, mine operators, and other exploiters. The first alleged "lockout" of the land rapists began when presidents Grover Cleveland and Benjamin Harrison established the Forest Reserves. Complaints of lockout continue today from the same sources, even though approximately 25 percent of all plywood and building timbers come from public land. The land rapists are joined by those who seek a paved road to the head of every stream and the top of every mountain, public access to every lakeside and across every swamp and point of beauty. John Muir remarked that God cannot save anything from fools and, in an obvious reference to wilderness, "only Uncle Sam can do that."

Today we rely on the Forest Service, the Park Service, the Fish and Wildlife Service, and the Bureau of Land Management, and all too often they judge their success largely by the numbers of people that they can crowd onto their lands, on the assumption that popularity is the prime index of need. An average of ten thousand miles of new roads are being constructed each year through National Forest lands, mostly in de facto wilderness. This constant tightening of the noose diminishes any potential for the future.

The wild beauty of America is a national possession. The preservation of this heritage is everybody's affair, not just for a select few who choose to profit from the public's land. No nation on earth has been more blessed with more bountiful and varied forms of natural beauty and resources. Whatever erodes, mars, or destroys it robs the future as well as the present. Whatever the proprietors of wild places choose to do, even if it seems to affect only some faroff corner of the land, is of more than personal, more than local, concern; it is the concern of all.

It was 1922 before the first suggestion of wilderness preserves was carried to fruition, when forester Aldo Leopold offered, "with the object of preserving at least one place in the Southwest where packtrips should be the dominant play—a national hunting ground, one form of recreation which has not been provided for or recognized by the Federal Government." In 1924 the Gila Primitive Area was decreed. But it was to be forty years before Congress passed and President Lyndon Johnson signed the Wilderness Act of 1964, proclaiming fifty-four tracts as wild.

The concept was and still is bitterly opposed, and not only by the entrepreneurs who see public land as theirs for personal gain. Even such august groups as the Department of Agriculture's own Forest Service and the Department of the Interior's National Park and Fish and Wildlife services have objected, saying that extension of the wilderness concept interferes with their management of the lands. Once trees have been cut, roads or buildings built, the land is considered "trammeled" and can no longer be regarded as eligible for wilderness designation. Some suspect this to be one reason for the Forest Service's recent undertaking of one of the most ambitious and expensive road-building programs in its history. There is another clause in the land agreements, too, that all to few of the citizens know exists: "established practices may be continued . . ." So, if you see sheep or cattle grazing on wilderness lands, that's why.

Man is a manipulator of nature, but he is still far from understanding all of the processes in his manipulations. In his eagerness for "improving," he often alters or destroys the ecosystem itself, and with it the genetic diversity that has taken nature eons to devise. We have virtually destroyed the prairie system that supported untold millions of buffalo, that fed Indians and pioneers, prevented erosion, and left room for prairie chicken, antelope, wolf, billions of passenger pigeons, whooping crane and uncountable waterfowl, and the grizzly bear. A good number of our native American animal species are now extinct, and worldwide we lose more every year.

We are suffering from extensive soil erosion, water shortages, and overproduction—all conditions we've created ourselves. It is a natural error of man. Even the great sage, Solomon, decreed the cutting of vast cedar forests in order to expand his realm. Little did this wisest of men realize that it would contribute to the erosion that caused the once-Fertile Crescent to become barren and rocky desert, plaguing and limiting this biblical land for thirty centuries.

When the very agencies on which we rely to conserve our natural resources fail, where can we turn? *Ipsos custodies, quis custodiet?* the Romans used to say. We teach management when we should be teaching leadership, says Admiral Grace Hopper. Realizing that this earth is a closed system, and that at present interstellar help is beyond anything but a wild dream, we should hoard our dwindling wilderness as a nonrenewable resource. The odds are that any intelligent life on other planets envies our abundance.

Man is hooked on progress, as dependent upon it as any addict. A modern sports fisherman may have the illusion that he is out facing the wilderness on an eye-to-eye basis, when most likely he is using the latest sum of science and technology: his rod of Tonkin bamboo was brought by diesel-powered ship from China and impregnated with resins made in Pennsylvania; a Hardy reel manufactured in England was flown to a Vermont warehouse, ordered by telephone, shipped by truck, paid for by credit card. Even in the wildest of today's wilderness, he is absolutely dependent on today's society and addicted to its form. At such a time, man is confronted by a paradox: it is foolish of him to pretend that he is a natural man, free of civilization. To consider it so is absurd. The real question we must ask ourselves is, *Do we use civilization, or does it use us?*

We want the hunt to go on forever, but it cannot. Many of us are faced with the choice described by Keats in his "Ode on a Grecian Urn": to preserve timelessness in the living world of change, perfection is to be found in art alone, not in life. The desires must remain unattainable, the unravished bride whom he can never possess and never cease desiring—"forever wilt thou love and she be fair." Faulkner in *Go Down, Moses* speaks of the bear, driven back into the last remaining space by the clearing of the land until finally it has no further wilderness retreat. The desire of the old man is not to kill the bear, yet the hunt must end. The wilderness and the woods ended with the arrival of civilization. If you go back now to where the logging yard was, very likely the road where Ben was buried will now be the site of a power plant.

Once man has been introduced to a new toy or convenience he is extremely reluctant to abandon it. I heard a story—I do not know the full truth, but the message is clear and honest—about a hydroelectric company wishing to erect a very large dam in Canada. The location was to be partially on Indian lands and their resistance was being felt, enough so that for a while the project seemed to be in jeopardy. So the company hired an anthropologist, perhaps a sociologist—no matter. His solution was simple: string some power lines to the Indian village and provide TV sets and electric stoves to the leaders of the community, free for a year. At the end of the year offer a choice: the dam and jobs building it, or removal of the power.

In essence, it requires a very unusual and strong-willed individual to abandon "progress" once he has bitten into the apple. What would it take for the average modern family to forsake its water heater, its dishwasher? There would be almost as much smoke and fire raised as if somehow we tried to abandon television, stereo, automobiles and air conditioning; it would be about as easy as quitting smoking, or persuading Congress to get serious about the national debt.

There is no way to go back, even if we should want to. Captives of all the modern conveniences provided by mass production and the industrial revolution, we now consider what our fathers regarded as luxuries to be absolute essentials. Our children will wonder how we could have survived without the things we consider today as indulgences. This will continue as long as we think of it as progress, even though we become slaves to the system.

But wilderness provides a place of relief, an escape valve. While we shall never escape from our system, wilderness in any form gives us a chance to pause, if but for a moment, and think about where we are bound, and why; to sort out what is vital from the constant bombardment of our civilized industrial world, the truth from the ballyhoo of hucksters and fast shufflers who keep our minds so filled with trivia that we cannot rein up long enough to consider what we are really seeking. Wilderness is where that can happen.

So how does man keep his balance in this industrialized society? It is fair to ask, Why should we continue to hunt and fish as times change? Hunting and fishing are an almost sacred part of human life. Unless wildness is preserved, man becomes a mechanical being. This is the basic American paradox, for, historically, the United States has been on one big, prolonged real-estate promotion binge. In Cooper's *Leatherstocking Tales*, a man who cannot cope with civilization goes to live with the aborigines in order to escape, but ends up as a guide to those who would destroy that which he values most.

If we could but realize that the best way to preserve is not to possess. This is the key to conservation of our wilderness. Examples abound. A beach that once was public domain becomes an endless row of condominiums and because it is possessed it is no longer available to people. Those beaches that are as yet unpossessed become more scarce and therefore more valuable, and the cycle begins again.

Mountain goats, Alaska

Stagline at the rabbit dance, Alaska

Bouquet of mountain flowers

Mountain trout caught in Pintlar Wilderness

Snow geese in central flyway in the Dakotas

Successful hunters packing out, Sapphire Mountains

Author, left, and Royal Brunson with bear, Cabinet Wilderness

Gene Tingle at campfire

The rifle measures five feet, ten and one-half inches long; the taxidermist charged for six feet, four inches of bear

Bighorn rams, near Continental Divide

Returning from riding drag at the Hunter Ranch: Gene Tingle, in red cap, and author

Monarch of the harem, a bull elk

Author with buck mule deer, Missouri River

* * *

About the time the tourists move down to the Carolina coast hoping to escape the heat upstate, my wife gets the notion in her head that it will be cooler in the higher reaches of the Rockies. What she means is that she misses the horses and trout streams, the glaciers and cool nights where you have to wear a jacket every evening when the sun goes down, and the sound of a coyote along about moonrise. She reminds me that there are places with few mosquitoes and no red bugs, where some lonesome trails up forgotten passes still need exploring.

When she mentioned hearing the first cicadas I knew it was coming. She associates their shrilling with the open road. Spending too much time in the hot sun affects her that way. Before long, my thoughts were of loon laugh or wild goose talk, or the howl of a wolf in the Canadian bush, and I, too, had that itchy feeling. Though I am wise to her, I allow myself to fall for her blandishments: I began loading the blue van.

In a final flurry we threw the last gear into our escape capsule, handed the house keys to my brother, and headed west, fully infected with wanderlust. Ahead lay romantic vistas, new adventures, and distant unexplored horizons—not to mention shucking imagined responsibilities and trudging on to experience the unknown.

Not having checked the weather map, how were we to know that a heat wave was descending over the entire nation? The sun was a searing violet through the haze as we left the cool coast. All day we drove; the dense, humid haze had turned to darkness and the heat had eased a bit when the engine began to miss, just a little at first. We tried to pretend the miss wasn't there, but it developed into a severe case of hiccups.

A little cove that we'd discovered on a fishing trip offered a campsite where we could lay out bedrolls and spend the night. Next morning everything would be better. The mechanic agreed that it was a shorted solenoid, and sure enough, he soon had the car running great. Great, that is, until twenty-five miles later, when we noticed the back window fogging with oil, spewed from deep within the bowels of the engine.

Well, what could be expected from a twelve-year-old car with one hundred eighty thousand miles on its odometer and dust from Alaska, Mexico, and the Gaspé Peninsula mixed with Mount Saint Helens grit and Carolina sand? We mushed on, adding quantities of fresh oil at intervals until the next available auto doctor found the needed seals and treated its ailments.

We were now noticeably poorer, and the heat was rising as we reentered the raceways. Leaves hung limp. Swirls of dust danced by the roadside with every smoking eighteen-wheeled behemoth that thundered past, leaving the sunbaked road even hotter. That yellow ball hanging in the smog-filled air sent thermometers shooting skyward. Tires sang and asphalt sizzled. The sun was full in our eyes, the state of Illinois baked.

Ordinarily, we don't spend much time in motels, but thoughts of air-conditioned rooms began to tantalize. We checked into a motel in Bloomington, Illinois.

By chance that same day, the American Legion–sponsored baseball team from Bradley had trounced their opponents at the local ball park. They retired joyously to a motel nearby to celebrate. Conveniently near the swimming pool was a trail-weary blue van topped by a blue canoe.

Very quickly the canoe and all its contents ended up in the pool. The motel clerk obligingly kept the pool full, and the celebration was still going on at 4:00 A.M., when the owner of the canoe came out of his room and started looking for his belongings. Some of his now completely waterlogged gear was bobbing about in the pool; a duffel bag sitting sodden in a puddle, dripping from the back end of a pickup. Maybe it was the wet boots, or the drenched down sleeping bags, or the early hour, but the full humor of the situation escaped the traveler.

The Bradley coach, red-eyed and belligerent, set an example of responsible conduct for his young charges by denying all to a pair of disbelieving policemen, by now sweltering in their bulletproof flak vests. The team "sports" huddled like a covey of quail behind their mentor and spokesman, who believed in fronting for sixteen-year-olds. *Gaudeamus igitur*, as the song says.

As we drove away, we hoped that by the time a tow truck driver had responded to a certain cryptic message about the team's bus needing a tow, the victors would have reached the hangover stage.

The sun rose higher and hotter over America's heartland, the meadowlarks were singing, the prairies were endless rows of undulating green. The drawn-out dullness of common life had been interrupted, and we were one giant step closer to that Big Rock Candy Mountain waiting somewhere over the horizon.

It was still hot, the sun simmering down on a steaming, sweltering land, as we drove along tortuous, twisting back roads of Iowa, heading north and looking for relief, spelled s-h-a-d-e. We sought out the Great River Road, an historic path that follows the Father of Waters, the mighty Mississippi River, a trail opened by Indians and expanded by explorers, including adventurers from every nation, still a main artery in American history and industry.

It was also research for a dream, for I still want, someday, to point the bow of *Sylvia II* (our thirty-six-foot Core Sound sink-netter that we restored in the book *When The Water Smokes*) down this river's muddy course and show the descendants of Mark Twain and all those other steamboat pilots and captains a real saltwater boat. It seemed fitting to get a little more acquainted with this ancient waterway from close up.

We paused atop a high bluff—the sign said that we were 485 feet above the river—to look down on myriad backwaters, algae-green bayous, side channels, and sloughs. From our vantage point the channel was clear to the eye, but, looking mile after mile into the blue summer haze blanketing the maze below, it was easy to see how one might readily get lost in this contortion of waterways.

Barges that seemed the size of dominos clustered here and there. Scooting about like water bugs, the pleasure boats were leaving rooster tail wakes that widened and merged in crossing patterns. Without the use of binoculars their occupants were indistinguishable. The river was the color of a ripe olive, with a blue-green cast that undulated in the heat.

Wherever the waters permitted, a dark hardwood forest had covered the islands and banks with its green. Yet the power of the river couldn't be masked, for clumps and clusters of uprooted trees lay piled like sweepings along the edges, marking the flood lines. Tucked along the sides, up where the high water allowed, clung the river towns, old and sleepy, with turrets and towers, gingerbread facades, grillwork, and red brick–walled warehouses along the lumpy streets, where floodgates and dikes and levees spoke of the ever-waiting river.

A small sign, half-hidden in the dusty weeds, pointed to a trail, Bulger Hollow Public Area. We were public, and thoughts of shade and cool breezes were dancing through our heads as we shifted to a lower gear and began to wind down a steep gravel road, leaving a towering cloud of dust to mark our descent. A tunnel of green leaves, dulled by layers of gray-brown dust, led us across a railroad track into a shaded meadow where a half-dozen small boats lay unmoving on a placid backwater. Massive hardwoods made a cool shade over grassy flats merging with former mudbanks and present shallows. The air was cool and dank, and aquatic plants tied the green water with shorebound grasses.

This is the home of turtle and mud puppy, of catfish and carp, where the fishing shanties that perch slightly above the river edge are semi-expendable, the bluff tops being reserved for more permanent structures. We set up our camp on Corps of Engineers land that had been returned to public use after the Corps had finished with its dams, locks, levees, and gates.

We shared our camp with robins and goldfinches. As evening fell, the fishermen returned to the landing with an unspectacular accumulation of fish, mostly catfish. A veritable blanket of fireflies floated above the grass, illuminating the shadows with a flashing of fire-green phosphorescence that almost overwhelmed the growing glow of the campfire. Gradually they yielded the field to the mosquitoes that dominated the next watch. Only the croaking frogs and the silently flitting bats were undaunted by the mosquitoes' blood-thirsty presence.

Navigational lights blinked through the mist and a tugboat pushing a raft of barges moved irresistably downstream, six barges long, four wide. Grain bound for New Orleans now; returning upstream, the barges would be loaded with coal. High on the ridge, trucks rumbled by. Every few hours, on either side of the broad river, a long line of railroad boxcars clattered past, each boxcar carrying the contents of several trucks, while in the river each barge carried the equivalent of fifty to a hundred rail carloads.

Morning came. Mist had blanketed the river in a ghostly haze. Overhead in the fog-shrouded cottonwoods the noisy flicking of warblers busily gathering their breakfast competed with the distant sounds of waterfowl rafted somewhere in the river. A growing sun picked up strength, glinting off a far-distant sandbar as if rising out of the water. We gathered our gear and started the engine, moving back up the dusty road to the top of the bluff. There we paused, looking back to see the river's history written in the land, its strength, its unending force.

De Smet traced the Mississippi from the north, de Soto explored it from the south. Engineers dammed it and put it in straitjackets, but from where we watched, the river just seemed to smile and push on, an irresistible force that will win with time, no matter what man does. We hoped to get better acquainted, but the heat of the summer was not the time for that and time is what this river has plenty of.

10.

The Breath of Winter

Winter was sliding south from the Arctic Barrens, and the fox of the northland had put on his white coat, as had snowshoe hare and ptarmigan. The same mantle was settling on the higher mountains of Montana and gradually working its way towards the valleys. Almost every morning the sparkle of hoarfrost on river bottoms reflected the gold of fallen leaves. Even before the Moon of the Drunken Bear, when frostbitten huckleberries begin to ferment and bears revel in blue-stained stupor, the steam-whistle bugle of the bull elk had begun reverberating through the mountains, and knowing ranchers had already stacked cord upon cord of firewood neatly in yards and on porches.

Mary and I were again on our way to the E Lazy H, where faint plumes of white smoke drifted upward from the chimneys of the log ranch house that sat on a little bench near the Burnt Fork drainage of the Bitterroot River. We opened and closed familiar gates and drove past fat Angus cattle that watched us with expressions of seeming solemnity. The horses down by the creek stopped their middle-aged frolicking to stare at us, ears alert. The rocky washes and gumbo ruts of the ranch road were the same, and we remembered Gene Tingle's saying often that some day he was going fix that road. The ranch house, too, looked the same, with the enormous elk antlers over the front door and the pole fence around the yard.

Gene and Marion had invited us to help in their annual roundup. Our reward was to be a pack trip for hunting in the Sapphire Mountains that loomed dark and majestic east of their ranch. With old-fashioned western roundups going out of style, this was a rare oppor-

tunity. Today the cattleman often uses pickup, trail bike, even helicopter, to drive cattle. Neither Gene nor Marion cottons to that sort
of ranching. They prefer the old ways, with cow ponies, riders in
chaps, pole corrals, sleeping bags, Dutch ovens over open fires.

There are certain preliminaries to playing cowboy: first, there are
saddles and gear to be lined up, and hay, grain, and other provisions
made for the stock. Next, you must catch your horse. A horse that
knows what's up, as most seem to, is not easy to con into swapping
freedom for long hours of hard work. It usually takes a patient and
devious approach with a bag of grain, and the halter hidden behind
your back. Eventually, when the horse has you near exhaustion and
out of patience, it will deign to let itself be caught.

Some years earlier I had discovered that the E Lazy H was short
of saddles, so I found it desirable to obtain one. Rummaging around
in the barn, I had come across a relic left over from the Texas cattle
drives of the 1870s. Buried under the hay was a worn-out mass of
deteriorating leather, with broken rawhide tree. It was missing some
parts, and vestiges of manure still clung to it. By anyone's standards it
was a discard. But even a mediocre used saddle starts at a minimum
of around $150. Good ones run higher.

I had much help back in North Carolina rebuilding the old
museum piece. Blackie, who ran a shoe repair shop, had a machine
capable of duplicating the original stitching. The men at Taylor Boat
Works reinforced the tree with fiberglass. With sheepskin for a new
lining, new leather for straps and replacement parts, many hours of
trimming, and the finish stitching done with the aid of an old sailor's
palm, the final result was a saddle that not only passed the most
rigorous test of the roundup but proved unusually comfortable for
long hours on the trail.

We would be going into the foothills and beyond to run the stock
down from the extensive summer pastures that lie on the western
slopes of the Sapphires. Then we'd corral them and separate the
calves for branding before feeding out and marketing. The cows were
to be subjected to spraying, vaccination, and other indignities before
being turned onto winter range.

On roundup day fog filled the valley like a soggy mat. Trees and
stock were indistinct shapes fading in and out of the predawn mist
when Gene backed the big stock truck to the loading chute. I secured

the horses in the truck with short leads and climbed into the cab
with Gene. We lurched and groaned down the rough ranch road.
The fog grew more dense. Headlights were reflected in all directions,
confusingly, as we crept along. We were bound for the Hunter Ranch,
an eleven-thousand-acre spread stretching from the Sapphires to the
upper elevations of the valley, where Gene and a few other ranchers
shared the range, as well as some adjoining grazing land in Bitterroot
National Forest. The truck lugged up a gravel trail, higher and higher,
until we reached a log barn.

The first bunch of riders was already disappearing up the fog-
shrouded hillside when we pulled alongside the corrals. An open fire
glowed in the pre-sunrise gloom. An oversized, blackened coffee pot
sat in the coals, spouting a small column of steam. Horses nickered
greetings as we backed to the loading ramp. Sam, a horse of several
seasons' riding and hunting acquaintance, was my mount.

After throwing on blanket, pad, and saddle, I double-checked the
rig. Having been mule-trampled in the past because of a loose cinch
was enough to make me remember the lesson well. Rolling up slicker
and down vest and tying them securely behind the saddle, I swung
aboard, with Sam dancing around, eager to hit the trail. Four of us
were assigned to an area described vaguely as "coal pit to Brown's
Creek." Fire, corrals, trucks, and cars disappeared behind us.
Squeaking leather, the clop of hooves, and the heavy breathing of
horses still stiff from inactivity were the only sounds. The air was
damp and chilly, the sky lightening through fog and a layer of low
clouds. Abruptly, we emerged from the dense fog, though it still lay
below us, from the foot of the Sapphires across the broad valley to
the distant Bitterroot Range where Montana and Idaho meet.

Soft from easy living, the horses soon began to sweat. We paused
frequently to let them blow as we followed the faint trails leading to
higher elevations. The odor of horses permeated the cool crispness
of pine-filtered air. Skirting washes and draws, we pushed steadily
higher. Above us the mountain tops were backlit by a sunrise that
rimmed the crests in gold and white. We were about three miles
above the corrals when we split up: the other two riders to the right,
Gene and I to the left. We were to sweep a big loop and meet later
on the ridge. We plodded up and on. The draws were still in deep
shadow, the snow fields of the Bitterroots only now catching the first

rays of the sun. Ours was a vast, unspoiled world that seemed to glow under the vaulted blue heavens.

It was late morning before we found fresh signs of cattle. Then I heard a cow bellowing. Gene kicked his horse into a run and immediately broke a band of cows out of a little draw. Sam and I dropped over a ledge and found ourselves in the midst of a couple of dozen cows and calves in assorted colors. They exploded like a covey of quail. It's a bit hard to surround that many cattle with only one horse. Hopefully, I took the far side, intending to drive them towards Gene's little group. Some cooperated. Those that headed the right way I ignored, and Sam and I took off after the rest. Having known a few real ones, I've never claimed to be any great shakes as a horseman, so right then I had a crash course in how to stay aboard a horse that is running full throttle through pine forest on a steep, rocky hillside. Mostly I just hung on, praying a bit, crossing fingers whenever there was time between ducking the larger branches. Sam, sure-footed as a cat, leaped logs and draws, plunged into valleys, and charged up hills. Any good cow horse knows what he's doing, so I left most major decisions up to him—he'd done this work far more often than I.

Whenever we stopped to let the horses blow there were a few moments to appreciate the scenery. The valley below unfolded against a backdrop of sheer, craggy mountains reaching into clean, clear air. The growing warmth of the sun enhanced the scent of sage, the fresh aroma of pine. A shadow passed, and we glanced up to see a golden eagle, wings braced for easy gliding. It circled overhead, so close that I could see talons tucked into feathers as golden eyes searched the brush for a stray gopher or rabbit that might make a meal.

Such interludes were short-lived, though, and it was a long time before we were finally breaking the stock out of a deep draw. I was shaken and shook up and sweating, Sam merely winded and sweating. The cattle surged ahead, apparently going in the right direction. Another horse and rider cut in front of us at a dead run. I pulled up, and a second rider—in heavy leather chaps, dirty, battered Stetson, and shirt of electric blue—wheeled up, motioning me to take a new tack over a hill. I did, and ran right into another string headed the other way. It was confusion supreme, with me trying to deduce the logic and the pattern. Anywhere, as long as it was down and to the west, seemed right. Sam and I pushed on.

Gene reappeared ahead of us with a small band of cattle. Sam and I urged on the stock we were moving until they caught up with Gene's. Finally, it all made sense. The herd was growing larger. Long columns of cattle, stretched out a mile or so, were winding their way across broad foothills, leaving columns of rising dust wherever they passed. Riders, scattered alongside, guided and pushed strays back in line. Next thing I knew I was riding drag, whooping, yelling, and waving with the rest, Sam and I wheeling and racing back after a breakaway of one or a dozen, herding them into line again.

To the south, a handful of black dots began to appear on the cougar-colored foothills. They were cattle being pushed by another black dot that was horse and rider. Soon other riders began to converge from the far corners of the ranch, distant specks growing larger, each pushing a few head of cattle. The herd grew as new stock joined. The dust rose. Hooves pounded the hard earth harder. There were strong smells of sage and cattle, horse sweat and dust, the clatter of steel shoes on rocks. The herd now numbered some thirteen hundred head, leading a column of dust. I was still riding drag, picking up strays, keeping the blinding cloud of dust moving. On the bench below was the sprawl of corrals, gates open to receive the herd.

Of growing importance to me was the thin wisp of wood smoke marking the place where tables stood heaped with grub, to be washed down with boiling hot coffee. There were no timid appetites. Talk was sparse, though one cowboy told of sighting a bull elk with a regal head. He had mapped his strategy, then tried to throw a loop over the antlers. Unfortunately for himself he connected, and had a few wild moments before letting go his end of the rope.

Some open land is left, a few large cattle ranches. There are people still riding the range the way I did as a kid. The rest do it vicariously, via the tube. It's a great life, but it won't last. Slowly, inexorably, development is breaking up ranches into smaller and smaller units. And who can hold out, when $50-an-acre range land can be subdivided to the tune of $5,000 an acre?

"Enjoyment of anything," a philosophical young mountain-goat-type friend once said as he skipped over the crags, "is in direct proportion to the amount of effort expended." If this were true, I was going to have a hell of a good time collecting my reward for working in the roundup. A pack trip in the West is in no way related to the popular sport of backpacking. Here it is a way of life, perhaps left over from our grandfathers. It involves great preparations. The usual excuse is hunting, sometimes fishing, other times, just to go. Because the prime mover is horse, this requires extra gear.

The roundup of those thirteen hundred head of cattle had been the biggest obstacle in the way of getting into the hills for pleasure. As soon as the calves were sold, and this might take a week or so, we'd be free to get under way. So we began getting our gear assembled. To take a horse into the back country surely has to be a labor of love. First, you must accept the fact that it takes about 40 pounds of horsefood for every pound of food it takes for a man. The safe and accepted load capacity for a horse is 175 to 225 pounds; one horse can carry enough food for itself for about a week. This can cause logistical problems if you plan to be gone for two weeks, especially since man, his food, and gear are going along. Sometimes several trips are needed to build up food caches for winter trips when the weather might cause problems.

Time became of the essence. The hunting season had already opened. Horses travel faster than man, trucks faster than horses, so the beasts must be hauled as far as possible by truck. All this to transport four people—our hosts Marion and Gene, Mary and me, and our mountains of gear: tents and tarps, boots and sleeping bags, camp stove, panniers of food, boxes of food, bags of food, horse feed, saddles, blankets, and nose bags. It is very important to keep a horse happy, for you and your horse are interdependent. The horse may recognize this sooner than you do, for once removed from the ranch pasture it seems to change in personality, accepting its responsibility and letting you know that it's depending on you.

At last everything was in a ready mess, the gear piled high and mantied. Mantying consists of throwing everything into a big pile, wrapping it tightly in canvas and tying it securely, then untying it and resorting it to rewrap and tie again. The bundles are in pairs and should weigh within a few ounces of each other, the breakables secured against the horse falling or getting kicked by another. Prescrambled eggs in the sleeping bags are something you suffer but once before you learn. The horses must be rounded up from the range, stuffed with food, and locked in the barn the night before, the trucks must be fueled and the last toothbrush packed.

While all these preparations were taking place, a cold wet rain had been creeping up the valley, and the mountains were being plastered white with snow. The dirt roads became slick. A sweet-faced girl on TV was making dire weather predictions. The phone rang and a neighbor asked if any of our horses was sick. Two of his had the flu, and ours had been exposed. A call to the vet, and horse vaccines and emergency medicines were added to the first-aid kit. Was all in readiness? You never know.

A magpie, feathers dripping from the rain, sat in morose contemplation on the meat bag, inspecting it for holes. As we loaded gear, Sitting Bull, the romantic Angus hero of the ranch, settled his massive bulk on huge haunches in front of the bunkhouse and watched us pack. I'm always nervous working with a thousand-odd-pound bull observing me from ten feet away, even when he's sitting. His harem gathered. There were Lunch Meat and Dual Wheel; one was good only for lunch meat, and the other had been so skinny as a calf that it was claimed she could squeeze between a pair of dual truck tires. Then Squawk Box, obviously the bellowing type, and Octopus Plug, so named by an electrician because she had too many faucets. And Exotica, whose mother had got into a neighbor's pasture and met her true love, a European import. These were ranch cattle, either family favorites or too valuable to be left with the range cattle that dwelt on the mountainsides in summer and were rounded up a couple of times a year.

The truck was loaded. The passenger side lacked handles for either door or window. Getting out required stamping hard with the right foot—no, not the left. We couldn't drive after dark, either, because the calves had eaten off the wiring on the lights. I looked at four calves measuring our car, one nibbling at the spare tire, another examining the side mirror. At the second gate I told Gene to wait while I ran back to get my rifle.

The elk had been leaving the high country for some days. Tracks and occasional sightings confirmed our theory that they were on the move, yet the weather was still pleasant. A few flurries had left a foot or more of snow on the higher peaks, freezing at night and usually thawing by afternoon. Two elk already hung in the camp below us, but we weren't interested in cows and calves. Instead, we were seeking one of those stately bulls with racks to scrape the clouds.

We set up camp on a small wooded bench just above where

Skalkaho Creek tumbles down the steep slopes towards the Bitterroot Valley. After relieving the horses of their burdens, we erected a white wall tent, typical in mountain camps, and pulled a sheet of clear plastic over it to shed the snow and give a little additional insulation. Then we set about building a simple corral, using downed lodgepoles. Baled hay was stacked nearby and covered. The bags of oats and range pellets—those concentrated mixtures of highly compressed hay, held together with molasses, that serve horses so well in the back country—were stored in the tent. Riding and pack saddles were racked on poles, high enough to discourage salt-hungry porcupines and inquisitive chipmunks. We installed a small sheepherder's stove in the tent. Even with the pile of firewood, crude wooden table, log chairs, bed rolls, and pack boxes of grub, we still had enough room to navigate without collisions.

An idyllic scene it was, all snug among the limber pines, spruce, and lodgepoles, below the sharp ridges that reach down from Fox Peak, a wind-scoured nine-thousand-foot monument in the company of Signal Rock, Kent and Condon Peaks. The creek murmured through a grassy bog with seeming cheer before plummeting towards civilization miles to the westward. A golden eagle silhouetted against a bright blue sky soared on the updrafts with an ease to cause envy in the hearts of hang gliders. A weasel, fleet of foot and already half dressed in winter white, dodged in and out among the fallen trees along the creek bank.

Our meat bag was slung by rope and pulley high in a tree beside camp. By the next morning a bear had left a scuffling of fresh prints beneath it and, frustrated, had shuffled on its way. Whiskey jacks and Steller's jays competed with chipmunks and chickadees for camp food, stealing pancakes and grain from a plate of food scraps set on a stump near the tent door.

We spent several days riding the ridges and slopes, tracking and exploring, and saw signs aplenty. One morning we were riding when we saw a seemingly awkward cow moose, proud of manner, leading her calf up the trail ahead of our horses, pausing occasionally to eye us. We kept our distance, for the powerful beast, while not seeking trouble, was not to be pressed.

Then one day we sighted a small band of elk gathered across a valley, resting on an extension of a ridge. Immediately we planned our strategy: stay downwind and circle up a deep draw towards a saddle that would give us cover as we closed in. Expecting to find game any second, we left our horses tied conspicuously in a large opening. We hoped that blanketing them with blaze orange and placing flags on four sides would help wandering hunters to distinguish them from wild four-legged critters.

I was beginning to feel that I could actually smell and hear game concealed in thicket. Slowly, quietly, we crawled over and through a tangle of downed lodgepoles, and eased up a rocky slope.

We were just slipping over the lip of the next draw when— BLAM! BLAM-BLAM-BLAM-BLAM! The fusillade sent us diving behind a log as bullets whistled past, cracking through the brush. Silence. Then a final BLAM! We stayed low for a few moments before creeping cautiously over the ridge to see a sallow-faced man standing over an elk. His rifle was leaning against a log, but we still approached with a great deal of caution. He soon saw us, but paid no attention, just looked at the elk without moving. I was curious as to what kind of rifle held so much ammunition. Gene wanted to know what kind of man had to use six or seven rounds on an animal. The man neither spoke nor acknowledged us in any way, but just stood there looking at the animal. Still wondering, we went back to where we had left the horses.

Another day dawned, windy and overcast. A gray haze filled the sky, the sun a glow behind high cirrus clouds. Gene and I rode out, but without any great expectations. Marion and Mary stayed in camp to console the remaining horses and, after finishing the camp chores, went for a hike along the trail that follows the creek. They communicated with a curious marten for a while, found the last mushrooms of the season, and returned to camp to sit on a flat rock and eat their sandwiches.

Suddenly Marion spotted movement at the foot of a ridge less than forty yards away. She said not a word for a few moments. Then, in a stage whisper, "My God! What a bear! I've never seen such a big bear!"

"Where? Where?"

Mary finally saw it as it was about to disappear behind the ridge: a big, brownish fellow, but gaunt, with large patches of fur missing, proceeding steadily but in no hurry. They wondered if the bear would live through the winter.

The elk weren't moving, so we returned to camp early. The wind lowed through the trees, building up from the valley below, gradually increasing from a moan to a howl, then a scream, as treetops bowed and swayed. The entire forest was a continuous groan of trees, sawing, squeaking, grunting, complaining. The horses fretted nervously in the corral. We piled up additional firewood. Inside the tent the tin stove was glowing, the fire rumbling and popping. Darkness came early. The Coleman lantern, shedding its bright white light, hissed reassuringly from the ridgepole, accompanied by the sounds of the coffee pot, bubbling and gurgling its fragrance. We spent the evening telling tales and recounting how big the bear was that had passed by camp earlier. Marion said yes indeed, it was a grizzly.

The snow began, pelletlike "hominy snow," striking the canvas like sleet, lightly at first. All night it snowed. We turned in, listening to snow and wind and the rattling of trees. Gene was at the far end, where he could lift the sod cloth and spit, for he loved his snuff. Marion took the next space and Mary followed, leaving me nearest the door. Gradually, we settled down.

Marion spoke up. "Gene, your glasses are in my boot."

Already half asleep, Gene mumbled, "That's fine, Marion, my teeth are in mine."

All was quiet for a few minutes. Then, "My! That was a big bear!"

At some time in the wee hours there was a crash outside, the scream of a horse and the stamping of hooves, whinnying and raising hell. All I could think of was that the grizzly had returned. I ripped open the sleeping bag. Grasping for the flashlight, I leaped to my feet. The rifles were unloaded, of course, so I grabbed the .45 as I searched for my boots. Another scream from a terrified horse and I still hadn't found my boots. Another crash—forget the boots. I snatched at snugly tied tent flaps, then plunged barefoot through the opening, ripping the canvas. I wasn't going to let any damned grizzly get those horses.

Floundering around in hip-deep snow to the corral, shining the light through the storm, I surveyed the scene. All the horses were there, eyeing me, bewildered. No sign of a bear. I searched all about, throwing the light at the snow-covered meat sack that hung high in a tree. Slowly it dawned on me what had happened. A large branch had dropped its overload of snow on the sleeping horses in the corral. They had responded instinctively.

I tramped back to the tent, cursing, patched the tent flap with a couple of clothespins, and tried to shake and scrape off the snow before returning to my warm sleeping bag. I went back to sleep, convinced of another universal truth: that a man can get out of a warm bed, run around in his skivvies in the midst of a snowstorm, stand barefoot in hip-deep snow, and never notice the cold, if he is sufficiently excited or scared.

A pop, then the sulphurous smell of a match penetrated my sleep. Next, the rumble of wood shavings roaring into flame, and the acrid, metallic smell of hot steel as the stove shuddered in expansion. The hissing lantern abruptly bathed the tent in a white glare. Sleeping bags rustled, zippers scratched, the coffee pot clanked above the grunts and groans of reluctant awakening. Outside, the world was still dark, but white with steady, silent snow that heaped brush and tree, piling glistening white over everything, deep and deeper. No game would be moving in this weather, so we would spend most of the morning lazing around the tent, gathering more firewood, and tending to the horses and other chores.

A column of white smoke from the stovepipe drifted straight up into the brittle air. Ice-filled now was the boggy meadow where we'd met a senior bull moose the previous year on a summer fishing trip up the south slope. The little Skalkaho that meandered between camp and the trail was frozen over except where we had chopped a hole for water. It gurgled and bubbled beneath thick ice. The mare named Star pawed at the frozen ground, her muscles stiff with the cold and the effects of yesterday's long, uphill trek.

In years past we had made our hunting camp here in the heart of the Skalkaho watershed. This time we were not entirely alone. Another camp was somewhere above us, most likely on the ridge three or four miles away. Down the trail Hank Falk and Del Reynolds had come from Hamilton to set up an elk camp, mostly as a base for Hank's kids.

The sky was brightening, and we had a final hasty gulp of coffee that would have to last the rest of the day. The horses had been fed before we sat down to our breakfast — code of the West — the night blankets removed and the saddles applied, lightly cinched. The hardware was prewarmed before being placed in reluctant mouths, the

horses were bridled, the cinches given a final tightening. With sandwiches and candy bars in the saddle bags and small bags of oats and
range pellets slung from the horns, we swung aboard. The crunch of
snow and the clatter of shod hooves on rock echoed across the
narrow canyon as we headed up the trail.

Elk hunting is done in various ways: sneak up on the elk, wait
for them to come to you, or road hunt. Road hunting is the most
common. It consists of riding along in a vehicle on back roads, logging trails, or wherever you think an elk might be seen. If one ambles
out, you pop it. Not exactly the most sporting, but satisfactory for
those who are either invalided or extremely lazy. The next most common method is to hide in bushes where, theoretically, elk will pass.
During the breeding season your efforts are helped considerably by
sounding like a bull trying to assemble a harem. When the neighborhood bull comes looking for the intruder—bang! The least common
method is the stalk. This requires figuring out where they sleep,
feed, or travel. Then you get on their trail, follow, and intercept.

The problem with the last is that the elk has long legs, which it
can use with great skill. It thinks nothing of traveling straight up one
mountain, down the other side, and on to the next peak. Man, weak
and clumsy, follows over the massive obstacles of fallen trees and
climbs rocky slopes of mountains that reach to eight thousand feet
and more. The elk strides along at about four feet to a step. Man does
well if he can average a foot and a half. The elk clears a four-foot log
by stepping over it and can jump an eight-foot obstacle easily—that's
a standing high jump. The elk has been cruising these mountains all
its life. Man seldom ventures out of sight of a road and is lucky to
be able to stay on a marked, well-used trail. To find his way out of a
dark and mysterious valley is almost beyond his conception. The elk
has good eyesight, can spot a leaf wiggling at fifty yards, hear a fly
spit at a hundred, and smell a man for a mile. To most men, an elk's
legs look like lodgepoles, its antlers like branches. In its preferred
hiding place, a thicket of spruce, its dark coat blends in perfect
camouflage.

If the run-of-the-mill hunter would accept these realities, he
probably would never even make the attempt, but he believes the
stuff he reads in the sporting journals and keeps on trying. On an
average, one man out of seventy-five will eventually stumble across

a dumb elk, the one that stands on the roadside, in the wide open meadow, or, more likely, comes to see what that funny-looking two-legged critter is doing beside the white tent down by the creek. Hunters have high hopes. Some are fulfilled.

I am reminded of another hunting trip with Gene. We had started early in the morning and hunted all day in the snow without seeing a track or hearing a sound till we returned to the pickup. Just as we approached and were starting to unload the rifles, we saw a big five-point elk less than twenty-five yards away, feeding on some hay in the back of the truck. The elk saw us first and left as we were fumbling with our rifles and watching him bound up and over a slight knoll, to disappear immediately into the woods.

On this hunt, though, we had been ranging all through good elk habitat, following fresh tracks and other signs, hiking, riding, and sneaking about. There were plenty of recent signs, but no elk had been taken since the first day. Yet every time I had passed a saddle just to the north of Signal Rock I noted fresh tracks where the elk had moved from their bedding area to cross the ridge where I now stood. It always seemed that they had crossed just ahead of me.

I vowed that this time I would fool them. Gene, with much more experience than I, decided to stay in camp, preferring the security of the heated tent to my proposition of waiting in cold ambush all night. Besides, someone had to look after the horses and the women. I thought that the women did a pretty good job of looking after the horses and themselves, but I wasn't about to argue. I packed my sleeping bag and some food aboard Sam, and Gene and I rode up the trail. It was late afternoon by the time we reached the saddle and could look down on the forest we'd left. This mountain, though seventy-five hundred feet above sea level, is just another knob on the ridge of stone, earth, and forest that constitutes the backbone of the Sapphire Mountains. And the Sapphires are a part of the Rockies as they extend through western Montana, running almost due north and south. Our vantage point was high above and to the east of small towns named Darby, Hamilton, Corvallis, Victor, and Stevensville, all nestled on the floor of the Bitterroot Valley. Off to the west loomed the towering snow-clad peaks of the Bitterroots, some higher than ten thousand feet, blue in the haze of a wintry evening.

The wind was northwest, soughing through the black forest

below, swaying the dwarfed trees on the ridge, where our horses plodded through crusted, knee-deep snow, already losing its wet crunch and beginning to make the powder-dry squeak that tells of deep cold. A thick spruce with snow-laden branches that swept the ground offered the best shelter. I unloaded my gear from Sam, handed his reins to Gene, and he rode back to camp. Trampling out a sort of trench beneath the thickest growth, I lifted up and rearranged a few frozen branches, spread my poncho, shook the bag to loosen the down and carefully laid it out in my snowy crevice. I sat down to wait. I was ready for any passing elk.

Gradually, as the sky darkened and the cold began to find its way into the cracks and thin spots of my clothing, I realized that no game would be passing this evening. Pulling off my boots, I stuffed them far under the tree where the snow couldn't reach them and slid into the down bag. Then I took off my hat, emptied into it the lumpiest objects from my pockets and carefully stowed it beside my boots. Next, digging out a cold ham sandwich, I slid a little deeper into the bag and munched my supper while watching the stars appear. A good sandwich is a delightful luxury. I remembered a time fighting a forest fire in southern California, and how we had worked in stifling smoke and heat from early morning through the entire day without any sustenance but a canteen of water. And, how cold the mountains got at night! I was huddling, shivering and exhausted, in the burnt-out hollow of a tree to get out of the cold wind, when headlights, then the sound of a jeep coming up the side of the mountain, aroused me. How grateful I was then for the thick bologna sandwich and cup of boiling coffee served from a Marine Corps jeep sent to look for us. Now in the security of my sleeping bag, I savored my ham sandwich.

I could use some of that coffee right now, I thought, but I had to keep a cold camp. In the woods, if I could smell a campfire a half-mile away, so could any game at twice the distance. I settled for a handful of snow for a drink. Thinking how few people ever have the chance to live as I was doing, I suspected that few would want to, but I wouldn't swap such a night in the hills for all the plush, overheated hotels in the world. And you have to pay for them!

In the west a different star appeared. Paying no heed to the natural orderly movement of other celestial bodies, it moved past the established constellations and planets, hastening on towards the eastern slopes, where it soon disappeared behind a mountain. I speculated on what kind of satellite it could be, if there was anyone aboard, or if some magic eye was watching me, and wondered what the ancients would have thought. Sleepiness crept in. I was tired. My final thoughts before skidding off into a deep sleep were: if my boots, complete with overshoes, weigh five pounds, a conservative estimate, that adds up to lifting 17,500 pounds a mile. But snow makes a soft bed that accommodates itself so well to the body's shape that I was beyond further thinking.

A rustling noise penetrated the blankness of sleep. I started awake and alert. There it was again. My first thought was that something was gnawing at my boots. My gosh, I had just greased them, too— with bacon grease! Snatching at the zipper, I sat up and groped for a stick. It must be a porcupine eating my boots! Just as quickly the gnawing stopped. I couldn't see anything but motionless shadows. I felt the boots. They seemed all right, but I hung them overhead from a limb. In so doing, I dumped a load of snow into the sleeping bag. Carefully I scooped and brushed it out and settled down again, doz- ing off at once.

The distant sound of barking that roused me was geese that seemed to be milling about high above. By the light of a feeble moon I could see them in great vees, uncountable numbers of minute black spots. I remembered Magnus Nyman, Finnish trapper and our guide in Ontario, who had told how the first blow of the season causes the waters of Hudson's Bay to flood the western shores of James Bay, covering the food supply and thus starting millions of geese on their autumn migration, high above prairie, mountain, lake, and city, stopping only long enough to refuel until they reach their wintering grounds. I could hear the song of wind on feather, the eager, insistent barking. Then they were gone, the sky silent and the stars dimmer. I drifted off again and dreamed of falling goose feathers tickling my nose, and how a friend long gone claimed that the highest honor a man can have is to be chosen by the gods to be knighted by a falling goose feather.

Waking up to a bitterly cold, gray dawn, I found that the goose feathers had been snowflakes that had sifted through the sheltering spruce, now nearly covering the sleeping bag. My hat, too, was filled with snow, except where a mouse had spent the night eating my breakfast candy bars. I emptied the snow from my boots. They were cold and stiff. My fingers were soon numbed from tying boot laces; I rewarmed them, pulled on shooting mittens and checked the rifle, clearing the snow from the scope. There were no fresh tracks in the new snow, but I waited.

Time slipped by and I was thinking of camp and coffee when I became aware of the crunch of snow behind me. Four-legged. Rifle in hand, I turned stealthily and peered through the snow-covered spruce boughs. He was big, whatever he was. I could feel my heart speeding up, senses alert, then a flash of orange. Orange on an elk? Riding a handsome buckskin was Lloyd Rennaker, an outfitter from Hamilton. He was as surprised as I. He was looking for signs for his hunting party. We agreed that the elk must have moved on to new country. We talked a while before Rennaker rode on. I gathered up the sleeping bag, shook off the snow, rolled it and the poncho into a stuff bag, hitched it onto my back, and headed down the long trail. In camp my wife and a hot cup of coffee would be waiting. It had been a very good night.

It snowed steadily for nearly five days. The first three days brought high winds whistling through the lodgepoles, setting them to scraping and groaning. Gusts kicked up blinding clouds of powdery snow, and spruce trees frequently dumped their accumulated overloads of the stuff. But now it was calm. Mary and I had even made a tentative stab at climbing to the ridge, giving up after the second mile. It was snowshoe weather at best, but she viewed the effort as worthy—for the first time, I was able to show her snow spiders, the only other living creatures that we saw. Steady, silent snow day and night had obliterated the trail. Bushes were white lumps. The tent was sagging under its load of snow, half buried in the drifts. The sheet of plastic kept it from going out of sight. Knee-deep to hip-deep, we floundered about, uncovering the hay and the woodpile, and burrowing for the lantern fuel.

The blackened, soot-smeared stovepipe poked out through the canvas, emitting a faint cloud of smoke. Our horses, their frozen blankets heaped with snow, stood in quiet submission, occasionally stamping a foot. Their ice-festooned ears sagged, bellies dripped long icicles, eyelashes and nostrils were thick with hoarfrost. Still they were well sheltered and fed and were as much bored as uncomfortable.

Limber pines, each black-green branch overloaded with heaping snow, drooped under their burden. The waterholes in the frozen creek were small patches of black in a whitened valley. Delicate green fronds of aquatic plants that only a few days before had undulated in the current were hidden for the winter under the fast-forming sponge ice reaching out from the banks. The tips of branches and underbrush, heavy laden, were frozen fast in the stream. Listening closely when I went for water, I could hear the little Skalkaho still murmuring beneath its winter coat. I wondered how the trout were faring.

The earlier snowbound hours had passed quickly. In the snug tent we drank coffee, embellished our tales of other hunts, other adventures. We spoke of great horses, discoursed on game and land management, people and politicians, and how much money and effort we'd saved by not shooting an elk. We even discussed how much lead to take on a running elk at three hundred yards, finally agreeing that one should aim ahead of the chin whiskers. Then Hank Falk came up from his camp to confer on the weather: we could stay and chance it, with still enough horse feed for a few days, but our own chow was beginning to thin out after the past weeks of living high on delicacies such as elk liver from Hank's camp, Marion's stews, and Mary's sourdough hotcakes. Hank was running out of horse feed. We agreed to leave together the next morning.

To break camp at minus fifteen degrees is no easy task. Sleeping bags, camping gear, and supplies had to be packed or mantied inside the tent. While the horses ate, we removed their blankets and thawed them enough to fold. We threw on saddle blankets and pads, pack and riding saddles. We tried to beat the ice out of cinches, latigos, and ropes; it was too cold for more than a few seconds barehanded, too clumsy with gloves. Finally, we had to give up the hoarded warmth of the tent, pulling out the stove and dumping ashes and burning wood onto the snow. Striking the tent, we beat off the snow and ice as best we could and folded it for a top pack. Even in mild weather, loading packs and panniers is a critical operation, the more so when fingers turn to numb thumbs or ache to the bone. With the footing on ice or in deep snow, the sixty- to eighty-pound bundles must be balanced, lifted to a horse full of hay and eager to go, and tied securely with frozen ropes. Never in snow camp is there enough room inside the tents to protect everything from freezing.

To spare the horses and avoid making a second trip, Mary, Hank, and I had decided to walk out and pack our horses. Actually, I had no choice. Someone had to break trail, and I had the biggest feet and the biggest horse. Mary had a different excuse for walking, with some comment like, "Tall in the saddle is fine, but cold in the saddle—no thanks."

Hip-deep—why did it always have to be hip-deep?—I plunged through the snow, leading Sam along the steep slope. The trail had to be felt out, for we couldn't afford a downed horse. Each step was a major effort. Despite the cold, a rivulet of sweat was soon running down my back, while frost was building up on my whiskers. I puffed on. Sam nudged me from the rear. He was eager to get back to the ranch, so I had to keep staggering. Mary had fallen behind, literally. She had slipped off the side of the trail and disappeared into a snow-bank. Her horse stood still as she pulled herself back onto firmer ground, using the horse as an anchor. I waited, grateful for a break, while she climbed out, caught her breath, and cleared herself of snow.

Onward and down—thank God, it's mostly down—legs aching. We had gone scarcely a mile, each step a quest for solid footing against the soft resistance of snow over uneven rocks and a twisting trail hidden somewhere several feet below. Despite the extreme cold, sweat was streaming now. I pulled off gloves, removed the down jacket, and the icy air felt good. It seemed that whenever I looked back I saw Mary picking herself up again. Her legs just weren't long enough. She was walking drag, following behind the whole string. Here the plowing was easier but the footing slicker, for she would step in the horses' tracks and find that every rock and log was now slick with the packed snow left by the horses. I noticed that the sweat was dripping off my face onto my rifle and freezing.

After the first few miles the trail became easier, the snow less deep. We had dropped considerably from the camp elevation of about seventy-five hundred feet, and the snow was only up to my knees. By now my legs scarcely noticed the difference. We were off the steep and treacherous slopes, and the horses could safely break the way. Gene, riding Star, took Sam's lead rope and pressed on. I stepped back to lean against a tree and let the eager horses pass. In doing so, my rifle stock struck the tree, and by conservative estimate several hundred pounds of snow cascaded down, virtually burying me. Sam snorted—I think it was more of a laugh—and plodded ahead.

Our packing had begun in the early morning. We were under way before noon. Then, the sun was dropping behind the mountains and the sky showed clear above gold-burnished snow. It was night by the time we finally crossed the main branch of the ice-filled creek and reached the pickup.

Gene was already there and cussing. Snowmobile and other tracks were all around, the gas cap was missing, and the fuel gauge said dead empty. It was another twenty miles to the nearest gas station through more deep snow, then slick roads and icy pavement. I don't mind a man's helping himself to something if he really needs it in an emergency, but how could anyone justify the need for an entire tankful?

Remembering that we had a full can of Coleman fuel, plus a little bit in the lantern, I dug them out of a pack. If the pickup would start on what was left in the fuel lines, perhaps Gene could at least get to the highway, maybe even to the first ranch.

Gene and Marion would make the run. The rest of us would stay with the horses while Gene attempted to get a stock truck big enough for all the animals. The pickup started easily, the trail was downhill all the way, and we settled down to feeding the horses and getting a fire started. Mary and I pulled out sleeping bags, an axe, and some leftover pancakes. Hank found a jar of instant coffee and a big ring of bologna.

The sun was gone, disappearing with a bright flash of red indicating that the storm was breaking. But the cold was intensifying, a deep chill that seemed to penetrate to the bone by the time the smoky coffeepot was boiling. Coffee drunk in the shelter of a big spruce cheered us. The evening star appeared, diamond bright in a deep violet sky over mountains now fully shrouded in white. The fire popped and crackled, casting orange-red light into the darkness. The snow squeaked underfoot. It looked like a long night. Our sleeping bags would be warmest when partially buried in the snow, so we began preparations. Finding a deep drift, I borrowed some of the horses' hay to line it, banked the fire, and piled up enough wood to last most of the night. Hank would bed down under his small pickup.

It was late when the flash of headlights probing across the snow pierced the darkness. Gene and Marion were followed by another larger truck driven by their reliable friend Ted Coller, who had left his warm fireside to help. It was reassuring to know that there was an outside world after all. We learned that one set of snowmobile tracks had been made by a search party that was planning another attempt in the morning, having been stymied by an unfrozen creek crossing. We took time for coffee, loaded the horses, and headed for the ranch.

Thawing before the great fireplace in the ranch house, we heard that three people had been lost and that several were still missing. I remember thinking that someday, sitting in front of another fireplace, I would recall the great blizzard that swept the Rockies early that year, but right then I thought I'd just as soon forget it.

Hunting big game summons a mixture of emotions: great release, freedom to roam hills and fields, communion with earth and sky, savoring clean air and the sweet smells of sage and dry grasses, thrilling to the wild goose's barking aloft. It is the expectations that mean so much, like anticipating a noble bull hiding in the next clump of brush. There is also the discouraged feeling of leaving without game, the twinge of envy at seeing the successful hunter who bags a trophy the first hour of the hunt. You may have spent the better part of three weeks hunting hard, riding and hiking in the mountains, sunup to sundown, without seeing a sign. But then you remind yourself that you are the one who has had the fun of hunting—that poor scoundrel's hunting was over after the first hour.

Comes a time when you finally have to accept that the hunt really is over and you must pick up another trail—no more moose meadows this year. At the ranch, gear stowed for another season, the farewells were bittersweet. It was time to say good-bye to all the companions of the expedition, down to the last horse and dog, ears scratched, heads patted, tidbits offered to the faithful beasts that carried you or guarded camp in the back country. Sam and Star nickered softly as I gave each a range pellet and rubbed their noses good-bye.

The big road led easterly, and the Rockies, now half-buried in snow, were fading in the rearview mirror. The weather had moderated. It was hard to give up what was probably the one last chance for the season. So I argued. Mary, my guide, cook, gun bearer, pathfinder, wife, and bunk warmer, authorized one more try, a twenty-four-hour redemption hunt.

Under gray skies we swung north. I knew a secret hole that had never failed. Eastern Montana is a vastness of plains, grasslands and buttes, the monotony broken by deep-scoured valleys where over the years a mighty river system has cut its way. It was again the great and wide Missouri that had carved fantastic canyons, leaving minarets and temples and castles towering over the scruffy gouges that are filled with ponderosas, sagebrush, and mule deer. On the river bottoms are cottonwoods and willows and whitetails. There are no real roads, only scattered dirt trails that turn into slick and sticky gumbo with the miracle of rain. Hiking is also rough. There is no stretch of level land more than a few hundred yards long, and it is all cluttered with trees and rocks.

Beside the Missouri we made a late camp that cold and windy evening. The river glittered dully under a lead-gray sky. Long fingers of ice reached out over still pools. The current tugged at partially submerged, frost-laden logs and the wind cut deep. I gathered wood for the supper fire while Mary laid out camp, sheltering the sleeping bags behind a fallen tree. It hadn't warmed up any by the next morning when we began to look for game. Frosted cottonwood leaves crunched wherever we walked along the river bank, on the edge of sprawling Charles Russell National Wildlife Refuge. Named for the great Western artist, it teems with game. From where we stood we could see the sign: NO HUNTING BEYOND THIS POINT. As we looked, an outsized whitetail with enormous antlers burst out of the willows, crossed an open field and paused about thirty feet from us and safely within the refuge. He eyed us calmly and pranced away, taking care to stay inside the no-hunting zone.

An hour later, on a ridge some distance from the posted area, we saw a mule deer, a big doe, behind some scrub ponderosas. At first glance she looked like another clump of brush, but few bushes have such noteworthy ears. After three weeks of unsuccessful hunting for a winter's meat supply, I was tempted—does are legal in Montana; in fact, some areas specify antlerless deer only. But I had hopes of something bigger and better and let her go. Another four hours passed, with Mary reminding me that there wasn't much time left for me to be fussy. I kept remembering the bird-in-hand theory. It isn't that I must have venison to tide me over for winter food. There is always a grocery store with plenty of fresh meat, but I like venison above all other meats, and Mary feels much the same. Or it may be that I just hate to give up. I have several friends who frown upon my hunting trips, suggesting that I do not care about life and wild things. Yet most of them will accept with relish one of Mary's meals of venison Burgundy and sourdough bread without qualms, while claiming that they can't stand the taste of deer.

It was getting cold near the end of a full day of searching, wandering through sage and cactus, scanning draws and ridges. By now the sun was hovering over the western horizon, and the land was kaleidoscopic with golds and blacks, blues and grays and reds. A pair of sun dogs hung in silver and gold just above the far western hills. It would be well after dark before we could get back to camp. Then a flash of white caught my eye: the rear end of a deer disappearing into a draw.

Keeping behind a ridge, I took off at a run, slowing down when I reached the protection of a clump of brush, where I could search the darkening valley. Two does stood feeding. Then they appeared to have caught some movement and bounded away, in the coil-spring bounce characteristic of mule deer. Up a steep canyon, they paused now and then to look back. I lifted the rifle.

To shoot or not. It wasn't a matter of hitting, but even in the last moment of a long trip, I still did not care to kill a doe. Oh, yes, I know about the biological studies and that good game management includes—often strongly recommends—keeping the doe population in balance. I lowered the rifle. Mixed emotions were boiling. I could see Mary on the distant hillside watching me with binoculars, hoping, I knew, for success. Over the many years that I have hunted, more than one guide has turned to me—accusingly, it seems—to say, "First time I've been skunked in twelve years (or seventeen or twenty)." Once again, I knew that I must be jinxed.

Perhaps fate stepped in then, or the gods sympathized, for, as the does disappeared, a big mule buck came sneaking out of the bushes. It was he, not I, that the does were dancing away from.

Late that night by the light of the campfire I looked up at the carcass hanging between two cottonwoods, all trussed up in a bundle for transporting. It would be frozen solid by morning. Smothered in onions, the liver was sizzling in the pan. The coffee was bubbling. It's luck when the other man gets his game, I told myself, but pure skill when I do it.

Except for a storm at sea, there is little to equal the fury of a western blizzard. I have been scared half out of my wits when storm-mad ocean waves have swept my boat from stem to stern with smothering, surging green water. On such an occasion you do not have time to think. You just react to the elements, anticipate the next blow, and try to soften it the best you can. In a western blizzard, by contrast, time hangs still. Blinding, spinning snow and intense cold, like an angry sea, are waiting for you to make an error. If you make a slip, it may be your last.

Impatient for better weather and anxious to get back to the Carolina coast, Mary and I set out from the Russell Refuge in temperatures already subzero, with a little blowing snow. We hoped to escape the early winter that already had much of the land locked in a remorseless grip, for, having been raised in the Dakotas, I had learned at a tender age what winter on the plains can produce.

We were prepared about as well as one can prepare. The van heater had just been overhauled, cleaned inside and out. We had a new thermostat set at 195°, a cardboard windscreen fastened over the radiator, and fresh antifreeze added for −50°. Inside we had doubled winter sleeping bags, with insulating pads. A pressure kerosene lantern would provide heat and extra light, and the Coleman stove had spare fuel. These, with enough food and water for several days, an axe, and a shovel, were only part of the preparation.

The wind had started blowing from the east and now was increasing. The road conditions were reasonable as long as we minded the glaze of packed snow and remembered that the use of brakes would only produce skidding, with virtually no slowing of speed. The only way to slow down was to touch the brakes just slightly and immediately release them.

Glittering shards of ice filled the air and whirled out of a gray-white sky onto a gray-white landscape. Soon there was no horizon. Hills had blended into sky. We rolled on, along an ice-coated highway that gradually disappeared from view into a land leveled by snow.

Once away from the eastern slopes of the Rockies onto the vast plains and prairies that stretch from eastern Montana to the Mississippi River, there is nothing to interrupt the wind's sweep from the arctic to the plains of Texas, the flatness broken only by sagebrush and an occasional barbed-wire fence.

The wind increased, the snow thickened, the temperature kept falling. The lowest that the thermometer within the van would read was zero. For three mornings in a row the indicating needle hovered about the same distance below the zero mark as the twenty-degree mark stood above. All we could do was guess. Local radio stations were reporting down to thirty below. The high for the day would be minus nine degrees, with a wind chill factor that varied from forty to eighty below. The wind, now veering to the north, was increasing to forty and forty-five miles per hour, with snow drifting rapidly. We toiled on, pausing only for fuel, never letting the tank get below half full, hoping to get out of reach of the storm.

A blizzard, according to the dictionary, requires violent winds and snow, usually accompanied by subzero temperatures. That is a conservative definition. Actually, a good blizzard could be described as having winds that shriek like banshees undergoing the tortures of hell. The visibility drops until the roads, the very ground beneath you, vanish under seething veils of snow, a whiteout where there is no up or down. Fine snow penetrates every crack, the earth shivers under the pressure, and there is a shrillness to the cold seeping in from every corner while the bitterest of winds sucks away any residual heat.

By now it was impossible to do more than creep along. The interior temperature of the car hovered at forty degrees with the heater full on and the kerosene pressure lamp putting out about 3,000 Btus, a trifling token of heat. Stalled trucks and cars dotted the roadsides. Several times we paused at abandoned vehicles to check for stranded passengers.

The heroes of the West today are the highway patrol and the road crews that plunge on through the worst, seeking to aid the unfortunate. Trucks were lying on their sides, drifts growing at every bridge and overpass. Such times bring out the best of the human race.

It takes a special vehicle to keep the highways open. Large trucks, laden with about ten tons of sand and equipped with ten-foot blades of curved steel, race down the interstate, hitting the three- and four-foot drifts at forty to forty-five miles per hour, with a resultant explosion of snow. The trucks usually win, but if they fail, next comes the rotary plow emitting great wind-blown plumes of white that erupt like an oversized version of Old Faithful geyser. Even so, though they never failed in the end, there were long waits. Nearly all side roads were blocked. To leave the main highway could mean being stranded.

Sometime after midnight, when the winds began to diminish, a visibility of sorts returned. By dawn the land was covered with drifts, carved by the winds, glazed with ice, gleaming in the coming light. It was the ultimate in grotesque sculpture. Two or three scrawny blades of grass were sufficient to start a monument of drifts that loomed like ocean combers. Rivers, frozen in motion, were tumbled masses of ice, with any open waters smoking in the subzero air.

The storm was over. Flocks of snow buntings rose in swirling flight, exultant in the dawn. Cattle, backs hunched and encrusted with snow, stood numbly in feed lots or in the lee of haystacks. The road crews, red-faced and bleary-eyed, were still at work. Gradually the traffic returned to normal. We could not claim that we had defeated the weather, for no one can; but we had survived it. Many did not. Like the storm at sea, the middle of a blizzard is where you do the best you can.

11.

The Denali
of Black Bears

To most of us, bears are synonymous with the wild, and, generally, a great deal of respect is given this dark prowler of the woods, for its strength is legendary, particularly that of the grizzly. One Montana hunting party tells of an elk season up a canyon in northern Montana near the Idaho line. One night, the wrangler heard telltale sounds of horses going astray. Knowing that most likely they were heading down the trail towards home pastures, he went hustling after them, armed with pistol and feeble flashlight. He took a short cut, with the idea of heading them off. When he judged that he was ahead of them, he cut over to the trail to intercept them.

Suddenly he was interrupted by a warning growl coming out of the inky blackness. He backed off. His flashlight revealed nothing, but he heard the clatter of hooves approaching, then a thud, a sickening scream, and silence. Reasoning that he was too late, his flashlight too feeble, and life too precious, he postponed an in-depth investigation till morning. Daylight told the story: the bear had killed a twelve-hundred-pound horse with a single blow to the head, breaking its neck. Much as he hated to lose a valuable horse, he was relieved that the bear had warned him not to get in the way.

The strength of a bear, especially a grizzly, would be difficult to exaggerate. The average grizzly is equivalent in size and strength to, say, four black bears; two Montana grizzlies might total the size of the grizzly of the Alaskan coast. It is not uncommon for such a beast to kill a bull elk or a moose—we are talking of an animal of more than a thousand pounds—and then pick it up and carry it for long distances before burying it. Fortunately bears are not usually aggressive. If they were, there would be many more human casualties than extensive press coverage leads us to believe whenever a kill does occur.

I had an itch to hunt bears. Not grizzlies, for in my opinion they are too close to the threshold of extermination in the Lower 48 for me to contribute further to their demise in a land that can produce an animal of such magnitude. For as long as we can keep uncollared bears and wolves and eagles that can stalk or soar free, ours is a healthy and robust land, with these great creatures as symbols of its greatness.

Royal Brunson and I had done quite a bit of successful hunting together previously, for deer, antelope, and bear. Along the way another friend, Al Robinson of Roseburg, Oregon, had got me interested in the use of muzzle-loading firearms. Al, a master gunsmith, in helping me make a flintlock of my own, had taught me much about guns and gunning, which had led me into doing a fair amount of competitive shooting. Perhaps I had been praising their accuracy too enthusiastically and frequently, for one day I was admiring the two large black bear skins hanging in Royal's den when I heard him ask if I would like to get a bear rug for myself. He suggested that I take along "that old smoke pole" and show him just how good it really was.

So, with our wives and my flintlock, we headed into back country where relatively few venture, a remote area of northwestern Montana that brushes Idaho, in the fringes of the Cabinet Wilderness. Here I found myself sitting on a high ridge, binoculars in hand, scanning the depths of a vast, deep basin before us. It was completely surrounded by rugged mountains that stretched off into the distance as far as the clear air would reveal. The only sign of man was in the ragged remnants of clearcutting, several ridges beyond us, where loggers had skinned an entire mountainside. Nothing remained but scars where machinery had ripped open the land, leaving a devastation of stumps, bare rocks, and eroding soil.

Just below us, perhaps five or six hundred feet down, was a draw with the telltale green of springs and trickles that had gathered in a tiny pond and wrapped it with boggy land. It was laced with game trails, while about halfway up the draw were thickets of huckleberries interspersed with beargrass and an occasional clump of dwarfed spruce. To our immediate left the slopes were slightly less steep, with a scattering of small trees among the rocks. Somewhere in the midst of this scenery there must be game, for the signs were recent.

It's an art to spot game. Royal has that phenomenal ability. Almost anyone can see game if he stumbles over it, but to see a bear, elk, or deer half hidden in a thicket of matching colors and patterns at several hundred yards takes very sharp eyes and a knowledge obtained only through experience. At times, hiking a back country trail, he has said, offhand, "See the goats up there? Looks like ten of 'em." I've peered through binoculars all over the mountain only to be told to look "just to the right of that clump of green near the top," for example. Maddeningly, he always seems to be right. He has an incredible nose for game, as well. He'll sniff, "Bear," or "Elk," and I'll think he is pulling my leg, but pretty soon—fresh signs.

Royal nudged me and pointed down the slope. Hastily, I focused binoculars on the black dot that he indicated on the opposite mountainside. Among the clumps of grass, a dead tree, a few bushes, and scattered boulders, a charred stump stood up and sniffed the afternoon air. Its shining coat was reddish-brown in the dappled light.

"And how far will that smoke pole shoot?"

"It could hit him at two, three hundred yards, but I wouldn't want to try it any farther than at most a hundred."

It wasn't a matter of accuracy, but of the velocity of the ball falling off rapidly after that distance. The bear, unconcerned, was sitting a half- to three-quarters of a mile away, feeding among the reds and greens of a frost-struck huckleberry slope. The ridge we were on was littered with rocks and trees, the steep slide below us extending almost to the bottom of a deep valley dotted with scrub pine. Rocky outcroppings poked their way above the brush in rough confusion.

"He's a big one," whispered Royal. "See how small his head seems in comparison to the rest of his body." The wind drifting up the valley precluded any possible approach from below, and our slope was too steep, besides being without cover. The bear would spot any movement in an instant. The ridge where we were led to a peak on our left, but careful scrutiny showed another ridge extending to join the slope directly above the bear. It was our only chance. "Is that thing ready to shoot?" Royal asked.

My long-barreled flintlock, of a type used before the Civil War, again contained a hunting load. Although the caliber was minimum for bear, I was confident that a well-placed ball would do the job as long as I stayed well within the hundred-yard range. Before firing a flintlock, you first measure the correct amount of gunpowder for the caliber and results you want. In this case about 120 grains would be plenty. You pour the powder down the barrel, insert the patch-wrapped ball into the muzzle—again the type of ball or slug chosen can vary—and with a ramrod drive it down the barrel until it is securely forced all the way to the bottom. Bottoming it is very important. Then you draw back the cock that holds a shaped piece of flint and pour a small amount of very fine priming powder into the ignition pan. You close the frizzen, a specially hardened plate that covers the pan, and the gun is ready to fire as soon as the flint strikes the frizzen and knocks it forward. The burning sparks drop into the pan and ignite the main charge.

I had taken care of all the preliminaries, so now I checked the prime, making doubly sure that the pan was full and the gun on half-cock, its only form of a safety. I wiped the blade of the front sight with my thumb to brighten the brass for contrast against a dark background. We took our bearings and headed into the timber. Our plans were to make a long arc so that we could come on the bear from above. Now, during the heat of the day, the warming air would be rising and so would not carry our odor downhill to the bear.

It was at least a mile by this, the only practical route, and the bear wouldn't be there forever. With the animal a half-mile or more to the west, and perhaps two hundred yards below us, we would have to keep to the south, the back side of the ridge, until we could drop over on the other side and come up a draw to the west of him.

There was little worry about the bear's being aware of us after we had started a retreat over the ridge behind. Keeping up a fast pace for about a half-mile, we circled behind the mountain before making a slow and cautious approach, following a small copse till we got back to the ridge top where we hoped to be in line with the draw. We were. Staying on the back side of the ridge until we figured that we were just above the bear, we slipped slowly over the top, keeping below the skyline and in the shade of any brush. The bear was nowhere in sight.

Hadn't we judged our location closely enough? We eased down

the ridge a bit farther, carefully eyeballing every inch. Keeping a
fallen tree in front, I peered around the trunk, scanning, searching
the vicinity for any sign, while Royal did the same. It seemed to be
clear of any game, so we followed the draw, moving very slowly,
trying to recall our bearings as we crept from one bush or rock to
another. The wind had become variable, and this concerned us, for
while the eyesight of a bear is not the best, neither is it anything to
sneeze at, and its nose and ears are an unbeatable combination. For
perhaps a hundred yards we pussyfooted on, watching each step
beneath our feet and ahead. There was no sign of him. We scanned
the empty draw. I was sure that we had guessed right, but there was
no sign whatever. We waited in almost complete silence: nothing but
the faraway sound of wind sighing in the trees, a distant mountain
jay scolding.

A jay scolding? We turned to look for the source. Abruptly, Royal
dropped and motioned to me. I joined him. He pointed. The bear,
perhaps two hundred yards away, was ambling up the slope. Royal
whispered, "Let's work back up to that rock pile. Darned wind's
shifting." Then, "I'll keep you covered," as he snicked a cartridge into
the chamber of his .30-'06. "He's a helluva big one." We dropped
into a little draw and moved up to the rocky outcropping, then
paused. Royal hissed and pointed slightly uphill at a spot about a
hundred yards away: I saw nothing at first, then a slight movement.
Rising gingerly, I saw the bear, too, stand up to look around.

Keeping a ridge between the bear and ourselves, we hurried to
a blowdown of ponderosas, weathered silver after a splintering storm
long past. Carefully we crept to another rock pile and looked down.
The bear wasn't in sight. I straightened up slowly, searching.

There, about seventy-five yards away, an enormous black mass
also rose and looked at me. I can't say that I remember the details,
but the brass blade of the sight was gleaming against the black neck
of the biggest bear I'd ever seen. I pulled back to full cock as I raised
the long barrel. The shine of brass of the front sight was wavering at
the base of his throat. Then a click, and a sheet of flame before a
great cloud of white smoke obscured the black form.

I was only vaguely aware of Royal's presence behind me as the
sound of the shot reverberated through the mountains, crossed
valleys, and echoed back. I stepped to one side, trying to see around

the smoke, while shakily measuring out a charge of powder. Patches
—where are they? After dropping one ball, I was reaching for another
and trying futilely to get it started down the bore while assessing the
scene. A gargantuan black ball was rolling end over end down the
slope, bouncing off rocks and trees. "You got him!" yelled Royal.

Immediately my feet went out from under me. I had stepped on
a clump of beargrass and was now sliding down the mountainside on
my rear. The slope was steep, and slick with grass. Frantically, I was
trying to grasp onto something, to hold the rifle so that it wouldn't
get broken and, most of all, to find where the bear was. I could feel
the seat ripping from my new jeans as I slid over rock and brush.
Faintly, there came the voice of Royal yelling some warning at me just
as my right boot caught and slowed my forward momentum. The
powder horn was banging in my face as I grabbed a clump of grass,
hoping to stop. I ground to a halt and struggled to sit up enough to
get my bearings. Just below me, perhaps fifteen to twenty feet, the
bear lay on its belly, looking at me. My God, it was big!

I froze, trying to assess the situation. The gun was still unloaded,
with an unrammed ball and lacking prime; it could be used only as a
club or fencing foil. When I started downhill I had a folding hunting
knife with a four-inch blade. It might be my only available weapon,
but did I still have it? Wrestling an angry bear, even with a knife, was
not an inviting prospect. Digging in with my left heel, I started to
pull the ramrod, when I remembered that I had been wearing a .45
automatic when I started down. It was still there. Shucking a shell
into the chamber while holding the rifle pointed at the bear, I began
to feel a little safer.

When I realized that the bear hadn't yet made a move towards
me, I pondered my next action. High above, Royal was still shouting.
I could hardly hear his yelling, "Watch him! He may be playing
'possum!"

If I put down the .45 that I held aimed at the bear's head in order
to load the rifle, and the animal charged, I wouldn't be able to move
fast enough. I also might start slipping again; if so, I'd land on the
bear, for I was now using the rifle butt as an anchor.

Keeping the pistol sights on the bear, I started digging my boot
heels harder into the rocky soil. As soon as I was slightly more secure
I worked my way to a better vantage point to my left, at no time

letting the barrel of the pistol waver from the bear. The critter still hadn't moved, so I worked out of its view. Then it occurred to me that if I simply dropped the ramrod down the bore it would subsitute for a ball—maybe. It was still without priming powder, though.

The complete inactivity on the part of the bear was beginning to encourage me. There was no sign of life, no movement of its rib cage, no blinking. I could hear Royal sliding down the mountainside but still didn't dare take my eyes off the monster. Circling slowly, the pistol braced against the rifle, the ramrod extending out of the barrel, I moved in close enough to touch the eye with the ramrod. It didn't blink. The bear was dead. A beautiful red-brown boar, old and tooth-worn, but big, he looked to be about six feet and I guessed at least four hundred pounds, by far the largest black bear I'd ever set eyes on.

Just then Royal arrived, .30-'06 in hand. "I didn't dare shoot—you were always in line and I figured it was just wounded," he scolded. Then, "Well, you might as well get started dressing it. I'll go back and get the pack frames so we can pack it out. Maybe I'd better take your rifle, too—we'll have a big enough load to tote getting out of here. I'll bring back a camera, too. He's a big one; he'll weigh in at well over four hundred pounds." As he was disappearing up the slope, I was scarcely listening when he paused long enough to give a warning, "This is grizzly country—if one happens along and catches the scent of either the bear or the blood, he's liable to come after it." By now I was starting to skin the animal.

Time went on. The bear was a big one and progress was slow. Then gradually the hairs on the back of my neck began to rise, and I realized that I was no longer alone. Royal's warning came back. I still had that Browning knife with the four-inch blade. My rifle was gone, and chills were racing up and down my spine. Very slowly I switched the knife to the left hand, slid the right to the butt of the .45, and drew it, throwing off the safety as I looked up. There was a sudden "Woof!" and a grunt.

There, on a slight shelf maybe fifty feet above me, was the massive bulk of a bull elk, deep brown except for the ivory of its antlers and its creamy rump that glinted in the fast-setting sun. A loud snort, a clatter of hooves, and the great animal was off. With a peculiar running lope and without regard for steepness, he bounded up the nearly vertical slope and into thick forest cover. I was left shaking, sweating, and giggling with relief.

Only a few minutes of sunlight remained by the time Royal was able to return with pack frames and ropes and accompanied by Mary and Bette, who had come to see the trophy. They had been watching the whole operation from the ridge where we had started the stalk, but had lost sight of us when I slid down the hill. They had concluded where I was only after they spotted the elk watching me. The trip back was steep, so they took the heart and liver and disappeared up the hillside towards camp while they still had light.

Bears being surely the hardest of critters to skin out, I'd thus far managed to remove the cape and two shoulders. Royal helped me finish the butchering. After lifting one of the pack frames, loaded with the shoulder meat, onto Royal's back, I took the other frame with the hide. Now, a bear skin doesn't sound like much, but green, and thick with unscraped fat, plus a foot-long skull, it was easily seventy-five pounds, I estimated. It was about fifty degrees, and our course five hundred yards virtually straight up and at least a half-mile as the crow might fly.

We'd make fifteen to twenty yards of pulling ourselves along before pausing to blow, then struggle some more. Royal ahead, grunting and puffing, we climbed the steep, craggy slope. An experienced mountain man fresh from a summer of hiking daily ten to fifteen miles at high elevations, Royal was in good shape. When he stopped to get his breath, I was desperately sucking in and wheezing at the thin air. Heart pumping, eyes bulging, I was dragging myself along. It took four flat liedowns, more leaning than lying at that slope, and innumerable minor stops. After each liedown one had to pull the other upright before we could start again. The sun was just disappearing, the depths of the valleys were already dark, and distant ranges had turned blue in the haze as we staggered into camp.

I needed no inducement to sleep that night. The Belt of Orion was high in the southern heavens before we turned in. The next day, as the sun rose, we'd have to descend into that bottomless canyon to bring out the rest, the heaviest parts, before raven, coyote, or something else discovered our cache. The thought set my bones to aching afresh.

It took two more trips the next morning to finish bringing out the rest of the meat. The taxidermist charged for six feet four inches of hide. Today, what may well be the largest black bear taken by flintlock rifle in recent history adorns the office of our winter home in North Carolina. My conscience always bothers me when I kill game, but not for hunting it. Like the Native Americans, I feel compelled to apologize to whatever game I deprive of its life. Royal reminded me that the old boar had been king of the mountain for a long time and had probably killed far more cubs than the bears I would shoot in my lifetime. We like bear meat—in bear Burgundy and corned bear, and bear grease pie: there was sufficient fat from the bruin to please all our pie-baking friends, more than fifteen one-pound coffee cans of prime lard. It makes the finest pie crust in the world. Even so, I doubt that I'll ever hunt another bear, because I've already had the Denali of black bears.

It seems a long time ago that I was standing on the mountainside overlooking a wide valley in southwestern Montana. Snow covered the ground almost knee-deep. Scattered clumps of ponderosa pine, almost black in contrast with the white land, looked cold and lonely. It was only right that I should be hunting again with Val Loesch, wrangler, cowman, ditch rider, and good friend who had escorted me on my first big game hunt years earlier. We'd been hunting since sunrise without sighting sign or track.

Val had circled up the ridge above me while I followed a lower crest. I'd spotted him standing by an open meadow waiting for me. A draw below me was the last place to check before rejoining him. Advancing slowly from tree to rock, I was eyeballing every lump and shadow.

Then it happened: a herd of elk burst over the ridge, single file in a fast lope across the broken hills. All these years I'd been hunting, and here they came! The sight will remain burned indelibly in memory, and I expect to be able to recollect the moment until I die. They were maybe a half-mile away, heading in my direction. I stood behind a pile of boulders staring in disbelief. They trotted down the hill almost directly towards me, then, about two hundred yards away, turned to follow the valley towards where Val was waiting.

The time had come. Now, or forget it. I dropped to my belly in the crusted snow, and watched the tapered crosshairs come to bear first on one animal then another. There were no giant bulls of my dreams, only spikes and cows and calves. This is not what I had come for, but all were legal game. I recalled that I had spent more than a thousand dollars over the years for the privilege of hunting these great beasts and had yet to fire a shot at one.

The new scope settled to select a spike bull just before he would top the ridge and disappear forever. I have known buck fever, that ailment that sends sights wavering and causes uncontrollable shaking, when hunting deer and smaller game. But there was no sense of unsteadiness now, just a careful alignment and mental adjustment for lead. The jarring recoil of the .300 magnum went almost unnoticed but for the blank whiteness of snow exploding before the muzzle blast. The sound of the shot echoed repeatedly through the silence of the mountains, and the elk lay unmoving, like a brown log sprawled on the snow.

I worked the bolt, reloading, slipped the safety on and hurried down the rocky hillside, sliding and falling in the snow and ice, until I arrived at the scene, slightly winded. A head shot, as I had aimed. The bull hadn't known what hit him.

Now the fever and excitement began to take effect. Shaking, I unloaded the rifle carefully, laid it against a stump and opened the Browning knife that Mary had given me years before in anticipation of this moment. It must have been an hour later that I struggled up the mountainside, fastening a bright ribbon high in a dominant tree and, exhausted, headed to where I hoped Val was still waiting.

He was smiling, "Finally broke the jinx? It's about time. Mark it good so we can find it?" I nodded assent.

It took four men to get the elk up the hill and the nearest logging road to where we could load it later into a four-wheel drive. With lugged snow tires spinning and the truck snorting and lurching, we were still getting the game out the easy way. We even made it back to the ranch before dark to hang the animal in the tack room to cool, away from coyotes, ranch dogs, cats, magpies, ravens, and whatever else might be waiting for fresh meat.

Fresh elk liver is traditional for the victory dinner, and all hands rejoiced. But alone, as I stepped out into the cold, crisp night to pick up more firewood for the big stone fireplace, I pondered the day. The snow-capped Bitterroots glittered blue-white across the valley. To the east Orion the Hunter gleamed cold and clear.

Somehow the very achievement of my long-cherished goal was a letdown. Hunting the legendary, mysterious elk had dominated the back of my mind most of my hunting years, and now I had gone and done it. But in so doing I had achieved a goal I wasn't exactly sure I wanted to reach. I tried to console myself that meat and hide would be utilized, as usual, but that didn't erase the realization that I had caught the dream. Perhaps I'd feel differently tomorrow. By the time I remembered to pick up an armload of wood and return to the fireside, I was shivering.

12.

Postscript

Driving east across torn earth that marked the remnants of a road being restored to the standards of whatever engineers dream, we were in Indian country, where Crow and Cheyenne reservations lie side by side. We had left the interstate to drive along a less-traveled road leading towards a fast-darkening eastern horizon. It follows hilltops and ridges barren of trees or brush except for those in myriad draws and washes. Here the true high-prairie grasslands have nodded and bowed over the centuries in obedience to the west winds. Just beneath this tawny blanket of wild grasses are the beds of the almost unlimited coal reserves that stretch across Montana, Wyoming, and the Dakotas. Intermittent outcroppings of this mineral wealth rise in low buttes or black lumps.

It was just after sundown, and to the south a lonely monument stood silhouetted against the depths of a darkening sky. It is a monument to the arrogant stupidity of a surplus Civil War general who disobeyed orders and went Indian hunting in order to add a little glory to his golden locks. All history buffs know the story well, how he led the cavalry charge down the hillside through an unprepared and undefended Indian village, only to find that he had kicked a hornets' nest. Pursued by irate Indians, he had retreated to the top of this very hill, where the monument marks the abrupt end of the careers of the Seventh Cavalry and General George Armstrong Custer on the high prairie grass.

Final and futile, too, was this last stand of the original America, where the Indian and the buffalo, the wide openness of a wild way, will never be again. It was a shift in the tides of history.

The woman was unmistakably Cheyenne. Her dark hair, large eyes, and smooth face combined in a unique beauty that marked her as one of the "handsome ones." She was standing in the middle of the road that skirts the valley of the Little Big Horn, holding a big red flag aloft and wearing orange vest and hard hat. She waved us down and passed her message on, "Road work ahead, keep to the shoulder." I'd thought before how these Indian girls make me think somehow of a wild thing, like a doe deer, vital, graceful, with enormous brown eyes that seem to see beyond you into the essence of early America.

A jackrabbit, long and lean, raced ahead of us to careen off into prairie grasses still doing the bidding of the west wind—wild and free as the original inhabitants once were, a proud people who wanted only to be left alone to roam their land in freedom. One wonders just what are rights, and for whom. Does that jackrabbit have the right to exist? The right to evolve, improve, adapt, or fall by the wayside in order to make room for the coyote, the cow? Or was he placed on this earth only for the immediate convenience of man? If a jackrabbit has the right of survival, what about a tree?

Hunting pheasant earlier, I had come upon a thicket and a small stream meandering within it. Searching for a place where the ice was thick enough to cross, I saw signs indicating that something had been dragged across it, forming a path to an open hole in the ice. Nearby were some freshly cut willows and around the bend was the start of a beaver dam. The presence of beaver lent another meaning to this creek; I knew that it was there, a numen: one of those manifestations that cannot be explained physically or scientifically—a presiding spirit.

If things such as trees were put on this planet by some still-mysterious force, then I find it difficult to believe that they were put here only for man's temporal desires. Could there be a higher reason, such as to supply shade and oxygen, prevent soil erosion, and provide places for birds to nest? Could there be a plan for trees to evolve? If we are not to believe in evolution, the alternative must be to think of each and every thing as a clone, an identical copy, of perfection achieved with no future for improvement.

We spent the night camped on a hillside in Custer National Forest, where a stand of pines broke the worst of the icy wind. It was mule deer country, and I still had another deer tag that I was prepared to use before we changed states. In a deep ravine nearby, the mule deer were thick. I knew the trail they followed, so there seemed to be no problem. When a wan sun broke free of the horizon, we were waiting. Sure enough, within the hour three deer poked their heads above the brush and were looking about, scarcely forty yards away.

It must have been old age, or sentimentalism, but when I looked through the telescopic sights of the rifle, all I saw were big brown eyes, and all I could think of was that Indian woman, the Cheyenne and her brown eyes, who had set me to musing about the America that was. There are still deer in that last remnant of wild America, and if the Lord wills it and man permits, there always will be.